"I can't walk."

The ambulance crew and the police gathered in a group, trying to decide what to do. Suddenly, the ambulance's EMT driver whispered, "I've seen this guy before and I've got an idea." He walked over to the man, still seated in the middle of Main Street, followed by the rest of the crew. "Do you believe in the power?" he intoned.

"Don't give me that," the man said, "I can't walk."

"He's a healer," the crew chief said, catching on quickly. "He works with us sometimes."

Several police and the crew of the fire engine surrounded the seated man. "Amen," they chanted, joining hands.

"Do you *believe*?"

"Amen." Over and over they chanted.

Finally, the patient was chanting "Amen" along with the rest of the group. When the group had reached the proper degree of fervor, the driver placed his hand on the patient's head. "Then arise and *walk*. . . ."

By Joan E. Lloyd and Edwin B. Herman:

RESCUE ALERT
DIAL 911*
LIGHTS AND SIREN*

**Published by Ivy Books*

LIGHTS AND SIREN

Joan E. Lloyd
and
Edwin B. Herman

IVY BOOKS • NEW YORK

Ivy Books
Published by Ballantine Books

http://www.randomhouse.com

Library of Congress Catalog Card Number: 95-95315

ISBN 0-8041-1404-8

Printed in Canada

First Edition: August 1996

10 9 8 7 6 5 4 3

Acknowledgments

We would like to acknowledge the wonderful people across the country who've taken the time to share their stories with us: Barry, Helena, Luis, Kitty, Sam, Barbara, and many, many more.

And our special thanks to Larry Eidelman for his assistance in helping us to understand the workings of the Fairfax Fire Department.

Chapter 1

Phil Cassidy was in love with Belinda Morrison. Both sixteen, they were working together for the summer at McDonald's and the moment that Belinda first walked into the back room Phil knew it was true love. Tall and slender, Belinda had a headful of golden curls that he longed to slide his fingers through. When she said hi with a soft southern lilt, he thought he'd faint.

Two weeks and several aborted attempts later, Phil finally asked Belinda to go swimming with him at the quarry, an old gravel pit several hundred feet deep and now partly filled with water.

"Sure, Phil," Belinda said, her smile dazzling, her blue eyes gazing into his. "I'd love to go with you. Sunday? That's great. It's supposed to be real hot."

"Yeah," Phil said, tangling and retangling his fingers, "that's really great." He would wear his new Speedo suit that made his body look pretty darn good if he did say so himself. Holy shit, he thought, I wonder what she looks like in a bathing suit? Trying to control his overactive libido, Phil said, "I'll pick you up at about noon." He wrote down Belinda's address and phone number and began to count the minutes till Sunday.

At eleven-thirty Sunday morning, Phil parked down the block from Belinda's split-level house and waited, tapping the dashboard of his five-year-old Nissan in time to the radio. At exactly noon, he walked up Belinda's front walk and rang the bell. The girl he'd been dreaming about all week greeted him wearing a hot pink two-piece bathing suit and a lacy white cover-up that covered very little. He couldn't keep his eyes off the two tiny cups that covered . . . Rubbing his palms on the thighs of his jeans he said, "Let's get going."

As they drove down Route 10 toward the long-abandoned gravel pit, Belinda said, "You know, I've never been swimming at the quarry but I've heard about it, that it's off limits and all. I asked one of my friends and she says it's very deep with steep rocks. It makes me a little nervous. Are you sure it's safe?"

"Don't worry about anything," Phil said, puffing out his chest a bit. "I've been there lots of times. There'll be a zillion kids there and no one that I know has ever had a problem." Other kids. Damn. Maybe later . . .

"But what about the cops? Isn't it illegal to be there?"

"Yeah, officially. But don't sweat it."

Phil parked his Nissan beside half a dozen other cars, at the beginning of the circuitous path to the edge of the pit. He handed Belinda two large sodas and an old olive-green army blanket, took Belinda's beach bag in one hand and the bucket of KFC he had picked up in the other. With a large towel tied around his waist, he led the way through thick scrub to the flat picnic area above the water. "Wow," Belinda said as she deftly flipped the blanket onto the flattened grass. "It's much bigger and deeper than I expected."

"It's been deserted for about twenty-five years. They say that there are still trucks and even a railroad car at the bottom."

Belinda walked to the edge and peered down. The water was about fifty feet from the top of the sheer sides. "How do we get down there?" she asked, seeing about a dozen people paddling and splashing in the clear water.

"There's a path," Phil said, pointing to the narrow track that wound down through the rocks. "Or you can jump. That's what a lot of us do. We jump down and then climb back up."

"Wow. I don't know about jumping though."

Settling all the stuff on the blanket, Phil stripped down to his Speedo, watching Belinda's eyes roam appreciatively over his body. She dropped her cover-up as well and started to remove her sneakers. "Leave them on. We'll climb down to the baby spot, swim, then climb back up."

"Baby spot?"

Phil pointed to an area visible just above the water level. "It's that flat place down there. Someone named it that because it's where people go who won't jump in, I guess."

"I'm for the baby spot first, if you don't mind."

"I don't mind," Phil said, taking Belinda's hand. Together they slowly made their way down to the small level area beside the water.

After they splashed each other they climbed into the icy water, laughing and joining other teens in water play. Later, they climbed back up the path and had lunch.

"Diving lessons, only ten bucks," someone shouted at about two-thirty.

"Diving lessons. Yeah, right," another said. "You never did a decent dive in your life."

"Everyone off the edge." Several teenagers gathered at a spot where the cliff overhung the water and, one by one, they plummeted into the water below. Over and over they clambered up the trail, then jumped back into the water. Some did spectacular somersaults and swan dives, others wrapped their arms around their knees and cannonballed into the deep water.

"Wanna jump in?" Phil asked.

"Sure. But I can't dive."

"I don't really dive either. We just jump. And the water's hundreds of feet deep so there's nothing to hit anywhere."

Belinda stood up, put another layer of sunscreen on her arms and face, and said, "I'm game. Let's try it."

Phil went first and after a few jumps, each was trying to outdo the other with the silliness of his positions. From the water Phil watched Belinda go off the cliff in an L landing bottom first, her legs straight in front of her. She disappeared under the water and, a few moments later, when she hadn't surfaced Phil yelled, "Hey, Belinda. Where are you?"

Suddenly Belinda surfaced about twenty feet away sputtering and gasping for air. Phil swam over. "Are you okay?" Belinda just moaned. "What's wrong?" Phil yelled. "Are you okay?"

"Back," Belinda puffed. "Hurts." She puffed again. "Can't breathe . . . Can't feel . . ."

"Oh shit. Help! You guys help us!"

I was on duty that hot summer Sunday afternoon when the call came in. "Fairfax Police to the ambulance."

"Fairfax Ambulance is on," Nick Abrams, crew chief for the afternoon answered.

"The ambulance is needed at the quarry for a diving accident. Unknown type of injury."

"10–4," Nick said. "45–01 is responding to the old quarry for a diving accident." I climbed into the back of the ambulance beside Stephanie DiMartino. Nick drove out through the wide garage door and, as it began to close, Dave Hancock climbed into the shotgun seat.

"Have any of you ever been to the quarry?" Dave yelled from the passenger seat through the window to where Stephanie and I sat. "Neither Nick nor I have."

"Me neither," I said. "Remember I'm the couch potato in the group."

"I have," Stephanie said, pointing to her left knee, "before this." She had just returned to riding after ligament reconstruction. "And if there's someone in the water, it'll be a bitch to get him out. The path to the bottom where the kids swim is a disaster."

"Should we get the fire department?" Nick asked, deftly steering around a line of Sunday traffic that was pulling over to make way for us.

"That might be a good idea," Stephanie said. "We could use the manpower, and they can rig up ropes if we need to carry someone up from the bottom." We knew we didn't have enough available ambulance members to handle a tough carry and the fire department frequently urged us to ask them for help when we needed it.

Dave picked up the mike. "45–01 to Fairfax Police."

"Police on."

"Tone out for the fire department and have them respond some men to the scene at the quarry." He released the key. "Should I ask for the stokes?"

The stokes is a rigid body-length, basket-style stretcher made of heavy metal mesh. Our patient could be secured in it, then rope-lifted up from the quarry if necessary. "That wouldn't hurt," I said. We don't carry a stokes since it takes up a lot of room and is seldom used. The fire department, however, had one on their rescue truck, in addition to ropes and whatever other extrication and immobilization equipment we might need.

Dave rekeyed the mike. "Fairfax Police?"

"Proceed, 45–01."

"Better have the fire department respond with the rescue."

"Already on the way, 45–01."

"You know," Dave said, replacing the mike in its holder, "I don't think I'm going to like this one at all." We all nodded in agreement.

Nick pulled the rig into the quarry's unofficial parking area and turned off the lights and siren. "This is as far as we go," Stephanie said. We piled out and she motioned toward the opening in the scrub. "The path's over there, but it's about five hundred yards to the quarry itself."

"Okay," I said, already anticipating the walk with dread. "What do we bring?"

"I'm afraid we'll need everything," Nick said. "I'll grab the megaduffel; someone get the collar bag and head blocks." I opened the side compartment and pulled out the light blue bag filled with cervical collars, straps, and tape. I unzipped it and stuffed in the soft, bright yellow, plastic-covered cubes we would use to stabilize the patient's head.

"Defibrillator?" I knew that if the patient was in cardiac arrest and we needed to jump start his heart, there wouldn't be much hope. However . . .

"Yup," Nick said, and I pulled the heavy instrument from its cabinet.

"Longboard?" Dave asked Nick. "Reeves?"

"Longboard, I guess," Nick said, rejecting the slatted, rollable Reeves stretcher. "We'll probably need the board and we can get the Reeves if we need it later. Whatever we want to bring will be a bitch to carry."

"Stephanie and I will take the board," Dave said, pulling the six-foot-long wooden board from its compartment, "if you can manage the megaduffel."

"Sure thing," Nick said, hefting the bright red bag containing trauma supplies and an oxygen cylinder onto his shoulder. "Joan, you've got the collar bag and the defibrillator."

Single file, the four of us made our way toward the picnic area at the top of the quarry. About halfway up the trail, we were met by two girls in wet bathing suits. "She jumped in and hurt her back," one said, leading the way to the picnic area.

"Is she still in the water?" Nick asked.

"We pulled her onto the baby spot, and she's lying there."

"With her back injury, I wish you'd left her in the water," Nick muttered.

"We know. We wanted to, but Rick—he's a lifeguard at one of the town pools—said we had no choice. She was too cold. She'd been in the water more than fifteen minutes and she was turning blue."

"Sounds like you did the best thing," Nick said. "Let's see what we have to deal with."

We arrived at the picnic area, dropped our equipment, and I looked over the edge. On the flat baby spot I could see a group of youngsters gathered around the supine body of a girl in a pink bikini.

Although I'm not afraid of heights, I truly am a semiprofessional couch potato. I am an avid sports fan and root for my local teams in baseball, football, basketball, and hockey—all from the comfort of my sofa. I do, however, do aerobics to try to control my sky-high cholesterol. Although I dearly wanted to stay behind and wait for the firemen, I realized that I was in better shape to climb down than Stephanie with her recent surgery. "Steph, you stay here and wait for the fire department. We'll go down and see what we've got."

We piled all the equipment we had brought beside the top of the trail, and I patted the radio clipped to the waistband of my jeans. "We'll leave the stuff here and stay in touch." Stephanie nodded, the portable radio in her hand.

Nick jammed a BP cuff and stethoscope in his pocket, and I pulled a few more things from the duffel and filled my pockets as well.

Following Nick and Dave at an increasing distance, I made my way slowly down the narrow, winding path. By the time I reached the bottom, I was panting and sweat was trickling down my face and body. As I looked around, I realized that this was going to be hard work.

A young man in plaid trunks was holding head stabilization while Nick checked for responses in the girl's extremities. "Belinda," he said, "can you squeeze my hands?"

After a moment, he said, "That's great." He turned. "Anyone got a penlight?" I took a slender flashlight from my pocket and handed it to him. "Thanks." He shined the light in Belinda's eyes. "Pupils equal and reactive. Neuros good in all four extremities." That was good news. There was no paralysis. Yet. But that didn't mean that her spine wasn't damaged. Hundreds of people are paralyzed in diving accidents each year. In many cases, the damage is complicated by the way the patient is handled by bystanders after the accident. We had the difficult job of transporting Belinda to the ambulance without causing any additional damage.

I saw Belinda's bluish lips and said, "Anyone got a blanket we could use to cover her until we can lift her up the cliff?"

"I'll get something," one young man said, and he scampered back up the path.

"Portable 01 to EMT Abrams," Stephanie's voice said from the radio. I handed my portable to Nick.

"Yeah?"

"The rescue truck is at the head of the path and I've got five firemen and Chief Bradley here with me now."

"10–4, Steph," Nick said, not worrying about correct radio procedure. "I'll be right up." Nick turned to me. "Joan," he continued, "stay with her while Dave and I talk to the firemen and decide how we're going to get her out of here. Find out as much as you can." They started back up the rocky trail.

"Will do," I said, glad I wasn't going to have to make the long trip more often than necessary. I knelt beside the shivering girl. "Hi, my name's Joan. I gather you're Belinda."

"Yeah."

"Well, you just hold very still. I see we have someone already holding your head to keep you safe." I looked at the young man with his palms against her ears. "What's your name?"

"My name's Rick."

"Oh, you're the one who got Belinda out of the water."

"I got her out as carefully as I could. I'm a lifeguard at the town pool and I thought this was the best thing I could do till you guys arrived. She was so cold. We couldn't get her into the sun, though. I didn't want to carry her that far."

"You were absolutely right about everything." I looked into Belinda's wide eyes. "You're very lucky that you had Rick here to help you. Where does it hurt?"

"My whole back. A lot at about my waist."

I slid my hand into the hollow at her waist and touched her lumbar spine. "Here?" I asked, touching lightly.

"Yeah. Right there. But really all over."

I was distressed to see Belinda wince when I touched one area in the small of her back. "How did you do this?"

"It was my fault," a young man who had been crouched at her side said. "I told her we could jump off the edge. Everyone does. We did a few jumps then she went in . . ." He hesitated, then tapped his rear end. ". . . behind first. That's when it happened."

"It's not your fault, Phil," Belinda said. "I was the dumb one. I shouldn't have jumped that way." She reached out and took the boy's hand. "It's really not your fault."

A skinny boy in navy swimming trunks ran up with a red-and-black blanket draped over his arm. I took it from him and tucked it gently around Belinda's body. "This should help to warm you up."

The boy handed me three plastic pouches. "The lady at the top, she gave me these."

Great idea, Steph, I thought. I smashed the inner container on one chemical heat pack and placed it under one of Belinda's arms. I placed a second under the other arm and a third on her abdomen, then retucked the blanket. "That should warm you up pretty quickly."

"Thanks," she said, smiling for the first time, "that's really great."

We chatted for a few minutes, then we saw Dave and Nick, accompanied by several firemen, struggling down the path. They carried the collar bag, a huge coil of rope, the stokes basket, and the scoop stretcher. "This is the best we can think of for getting the girl up the slope," Nick said. "We'll scoop her into the basket, then the fire department will help us carry her up to the top."

"Okay, Belinda," I explained. "Here's what we're going to do. This"—I indicated the six-foot-long, metallic device that Nick was unfastening—"is a scoop. It's kind of like a giant pair of scissors. Don't worry; it's not sharp though. We'll slide one piece under your left side and one under your right. Then we connect the two pieces and we can lift you without moving your back. Okay?"

"Okay," she said, dubious.

While the others got the scoop ready, I fastened a cervical collar around Belinda's neck. "Let's give you one last check out." I placed two of my fingers in each of her hands, glad her skin was now warm. "Squeeze." She did. "Wiggle your feet." She did that, too. "Great. Everything's working fine."

"That's good," she said softly.

"If you're warm enough, I'll take these." I removed the heat packs.

She looked from me to Phil and back. "I'm scared," she said, her voice tiny. "Will you both stay with me?"

"Try to get me away," Phil said.

"We'll be with you wherever we can. Ready?"

Belinda smiled. "Do I have a choice?"

"Not really," I answered, winking at her.

She grinned. "Let's go."

With Rick holding head stabilization, Nick, Dave, and two firemen slowly wedged the sides of the scoop stretcher under Belinda's body. As she started to wiggle to allow the edges of the scoop under her rear, I said, "Don't help. I don't want you to move. Let the guys do all the work." When the tops of the two pieces met, Nick snapped them together. Then they slowly scissored the sides closer until the bottom pieces snapped into place. "Okay, we've got you now," I said.

"What we," Nick quipped.

"Well," I said, grinning at Belinda, "I supervise and you do the work. That's what women do best—supervise. Right, Belinda?"

"Definitely right," she said.

The four men lifted Belinda, scoop and all, onto the stokes basket. Usually the patient rests in the basket, but we didn't want to move her back in any way. "Can we strap the scoop on top? Then we can lift her out more easily later."

"Good idea, Joan." Using straps, head blocks, and duct tape, the firemen quickly secured Belinda to the stokes basket. As I looked up at the trail, I saw that other firemen had strung heavy ropes along the path to use as handrails. Someone tied a rope to the basket. With six firemen alternating positions, they managed to carry Belinda more smoothly and efficiently than I could have imagined, up the path and then down the trail to the parking area and the waiting ambulance.

We used the scoop to lift Belinda off the stokes basket and onto a long backboard. Then we unfastened all the tape and straps, released the clips on the scoop, and pulled it clear. We secured her to the board with more straps, replaced yellow plastic cubes beside her ears, and taped her head securely. "You certainly are on there good," I said. "Still, don't move."

Finally, we placed the board on the stretcher and lifted her into the rig. I checked Belinda's neuros again and found them still good. Nick and Steph joined us in the back of the rig.

Phil climbed in, sat down on the crew bench, and, as

Dave drove, code 3, lights and siren, toward St. Luke's Trauma Center, took Belinda's hand. I smiled at the young couple. "You know for all that's happened to you," I told them, "you were very lucky."

"I guess," Phil said.

"You had Rick around with the lifeguard training needed to get you out of the water safely. He held your head and kept your neck safe. You had the resources of the fire department and, of course"—I bowed in my seat and winked—"you had us."

"I guess I *was* lucky," Belinda said.

A week later I read about the "Dramatic Rescue at the Quarry" in the local paper. The article said that, although Belinda Morrison was, fortunately, going to be all right, the police were warning everyone to stay away from the quarry. "It's dangerous and it's illegal," the police chief said.

"Fat lot of good that warning will do," I muttered.

My name is Joan Lloyd, and I'm an EMT, an emergency medical technician. So is Ed Herman, my partner. Being an EMT means that we've taken a course that consists of between one hundred ten and one hundred forty hours of class time and twelve hours of service in the emergency room at our local hospital. We have classroom lessons, homework, and practical skills sessions in which we learn how to assess the extent of a patient's injuries, splint, bandage, use oxygen, and all of the other skills needed to help the sick and injured. We learn how to safely extricate a victim from an automobile, a situation we encounter more often than any of us would like. Since Ed and I also have the designation EMT-D, we have had to master the defibrillator, a machine that can restart a stopped heart. The EMT course includes skills exams—practical tests to assure that, when someone's life is on the line, we'll be able to successfully treat our patient. And there are written exams testing everything from our knowledge of the capacity of the circulatory system to reporting properly the degree and extent of burns. We study and are tested on our ability to adjust our techniques to children, the elderly, the inebriated, the abused, and the just plain nasty.

Once we pass all these exams and obtain state certification, we can act as crew chief with our ambulance corps or rescue squad. We have to recertify every three years, at which time we're tested again, both on our physical skills and our factual knowledge.

We are not, however, paramedics. Paramedic training in our state consists of anywhere from six hundred to twelve hundred hours of instruction, depending on the level of certification. In addition to learning to diagnose thousands of possible problems and to utilize hundreds of drug protocols, standard dosages, and administration techniques for every age and weight, the paramedic learns how to start intravenous (IV) lines and how to intubate—pass a tube down the patient's windpipe to assist breathing.

In addition to being an EMT-D, I am a CPR instructor for both the American Heart Association and the American Red Cross and I teach Red Cross First Aid. Ed and I are both state certified EMT instructor coordinators (chief cooks and bottle washers) which means we administer and teach all aspects of EMT courses.

I have been riding with my local ambulance corps for more than ten years and Ed has been riding for more than twenty. Ed now also rides with the Prescott Rescue Squad, a neighboring agency that utilizes the services of paramedics. We are both volunteers and, aside from the teaching, we get no money for any of our work. We like to think of ourselves as unpaid professionals.

At the request of a local teacher, I recently put on my uniform and took the ambulance over to my local elementary school to show it to two hundred first graders on Career Day. In addition to the ambulance, there was a snow plow, a cable-TV truck, a fire engine, a vehicle from the local power company, and a police car. As each small group of children gathered around me, I said, "You know, unlike all these other folks, I don't get paid for what I do." Then I asked, "Why do you think I do this if I don't get any money?"

I was amazed at the blank stares I got. Finally, in each group, one or two hands slowly appeared. "Yes?" I asked.

Some six- or seven-year-old would say, "Because you like to help people?"

"Absolutely," I answered. "It is very important that whatever you choose to do with your life makes you feel good about yourself."

And that's the basic reason I do what I do.

This book is filled with stories about ambulance calls. All of them are based on true experiences, ours and those of our friends and fellow EMTs and paramedics. But in writing this book we must protect the privacy of all our patients and of the rescuers involved. In order to do this, we've invented the fictional towns of Fairfax and Prescott, and all their uniformed services and medical facilities. We've taken the true stories and fictionalized them so that all the people involved are disguised. Although emergency procedures change more rapidly than you might imagine, the medical procedures used are accurate as of the time of the particular call.

We, of course, have our jargon, and the names of some of our pieces of apparatus and techniques will be unfamiliar to you. We've tried to define every term and describe each piece of equipment the first time we use it. If you need your memory refreshed at any point, however, we've also put a glossary at the end of this book, as well as a list of our ten-codes.

So sit back and ride with Ed and me and the members of the Fairfax Volunteer Ambulance Corps and the Prescott Rescue Squad.

Chapter 2

Jeanette Hirsch was in a hurry to do her shopping and get back home. Her twelve-year-old, Jim, was home with six-month-old Taylor, but the baby had been colicky for the past few days and Jim was not the most responsible adolescent. He meant well, but he was likely to get involved with something on TV and ignore the baby's crying.

The engine of her car had been making a funny kind of whine all day, then there was a pop, and the whine stopped. Jeanette was relieved. With a colicky baby, she had neither the time nor the energy to get someone to repair her car, and she couldn't afford to be stuck at home all day. She didn't notice that as soon as the whining sound stopped, the temperature indicator started to go up.

As she pulled into the Three-Square mini-mall parking lot and stopped in front of the convenience market, clouds of white steam, accompanied by a high-pitched whistle, began to pour from under the hood. Damn, she thought, my husband warned me about that worn fan belt. I should have realized that the whining sound meant it was about to go. Well, I'll do my shopping, then get some cold water to pour into the radiator. Once the engine cools off, I should be able to get home before it overheats again. It's just a short drive.

Jeanette finished her shopping in about ten minutes, stuffed her groceries into the backseat, and looked at the hood. "Good," she muttered. "It stopped steaming." She went back to the store and asked the manager for some water to pour into her radiator. She carried a half-full bucket out to the car, popped the hood, leaned over the engine, and began to unscrew the radiator cap.

I was working in my garden when the Prescott pager on my belt began its insistent beep. "GVK–861 Prescott to the Rescue Squad. Be advised the rescue is responding with a full crew to the Three-Square mini-mall for a female with facial burns. A second medic is requested."

I'm glad it's a weekend and they have a second full crew, I thought. I had heard the first ambulance go out with the medic about fifteen minutes earlier. I certainly didn't want to respond. Dealing with facial burns was about the last thing I wanted to do. There's something about facial injuries and burns in general that's particularly hard for me to deal with. And they can be particularly dangerous to the patient because the victim is likely to have inhaled hot air, injuring the respiratory tract and making it difficult or impossible to breathe.

I continued my gardening while listening to the communications between the ambulance and the fire department dispatcher.

"Rescue 1 on location."

"10–4, Rescue 1. Your time is 14:32. No second medic has responded."

Then, about a minute later: "Rescue 1 to GVK–861 Prescott."

"Go ahead, Rescue 1."

"Dispatch the helicopter to this location."

"10–4, Rescue 1."

"Medic 1 to Rescue 1. Be advised I'm clear from this call and I'll respond. But it will be a while. I'm on the other side of the district."

"10–4, Medic 1."

It must be a bad one, I thought, wondering whether I should go over to the mall in case they needed extra help. But they had a full crew and there was only one patient. And the medic was responding. I decided not to go.

"Prescott Headquarters to Rescue 1."

"Go ahead."

"The helicopter has been notified. The bird will be lifting off in about five minutes."

"10–4. We need some more sterile saline at this location. Is there someone at the firehouse who can bring some down to us?"

"Negative. Do you want me to tone out for someone?"

"Affirmative. We need that saline stat."

The firehouse is about a two-minute drive from my house and the mall is about one minute further. I could get it to them within three to four minutes. I dashed for the house as my pager started to beep.

"Prescott GVK–861 to the Rescue Squad. A member is needed to make a pickup at the firehouse and bring supplies to the ambulance in front of the market at the Three-Square mini-mall."

I hit the speed-dial button on my phone.

"Prescott Fire Department, McCann speaking."

"Hi, Ted. It's Ed Herman. I'm on my way. I'll be at the firehouse in two minutes. Have the saline ready."

"10–4, Ed. I'll be in front of the firehouse."

I raced to my car, switched on my blue emergency light, and headed toward the firehouse, hoping that other cars on the road would respect the flashing light and allow me to pass. As I approached the firehouse I could see Ted standing in front with three bottles of saline in his hands. I stopped momentarily as he threw the plastic bottles through the open passenger-side window onto the seat of my car, then pressed down on the accelerator and headed toward the mall.

As I pulled up behind the ambulance, which was parked next to a car with its hood up, I could see a ring of firefighters that had already cordoned off part of the parking lot as a landing zone for the chopper. I grabbed the saline bottles and opened the rear doors of the ambulance. The patient was on her back on the stretcher. Sterile dressings had been placed so that they covered her face except for her nose and mouth, which were covered by an oxygen mask. Only her eyes were exposed. She was moaning and writhing with pain while Sally Walsh poured the last of a bottle of sterile saline over the dressings on her face. Sally grabbed one of the bottles I was carrying, unscrewed the top, and trickled more water onto the dressings.

"Would you get a set of vitals, Ed?" she asked as I handed her the additional bottles of saline. I looked around and saw that Sally was alone in the rig. "Brenda's outside, catching her breath."

I nodded. Sometimes even the best EMT gets into a situation that's too much to handle. Catching her breath meant that Brenda was having trouble dealing with this call. I understood.

As I took Jeanette's blood pressure, Sally told me, "I requested the chopper because she has first- and second-degree burns on her face. I'm concerned about respiratory tract damage."

"Prescott to Rescue 1."

"Go ahead," said Max Taylor, the driver, who was up front monitoring radio communications.

"Be advised the chopper has just lifted off. ETA about four minutes."

"10–4," Max responded.

I had to talk to Jeanette continuously to calm her enough to get a set of vitals. She was in extreme pain and couldn't stop writhing. About a minute later, the paramedic fly-car arrived with Hugh Washington aboard. "Our call turned out to be indigestion and once she vomited and the pain disappeared, she refused treatment. Need help?"

"Are we glad to see you," Sally and I said in unison.

I continued to talk to Jeanette and hold her hand while Hugh started an IV line in her arm.

We soon heard the pulsing sound of the helicopter making its descent to the parking lot landing zone, about one hundred feet away from us. Within seconds, the rear doors of the ambulance opened and I saw one of the helicopter's flight nurses.

"They'll have you at the trauma center in less than ten minutes," I told Jeanette, when she was ready to be moved to the helicopter. But she wouldn't release my hand.

"Would you come with me?" she asked.

If there were room in the helicopter, the crew chief would be allowed to accompany the patient. I looked at Sally.

"Go ahead, Ed," she replied to my unspoken question. "I think it will be better if you go. You seem to have established a relationship with her. And, besides," she added a bit sheepishly, "I'm scared to death of helicopters."

After transferring Jeanette to the helicopter's stretcher, six firefighters carried the stretcher to the chopper. I continued to hold Jeanette's hand and talk to her as the helicopter crew guided us so that we avoided the dangerous, invisible blades of the chopper's rear rotors.

"I won't be able to talk to you once we're in the helicopter because it's pretty noisy," I told her, "but I'll hold your hand during the flight. Okay?"

Jeanette nodded silently.

Once our patient had been loaded aboard, I sat on the crew seat next to Jeanette, put on and tightened the safety shoulder harness, and put the headset over my ears. Because of the noise level, the headset would be my only means of communicating with the crew. One of the flight nurses sat next to me and the other sat in the crew seat at the patient's head. Jeanette gripped my hand hard as the aircraft vibrated and began to rise. Glancing out the window, I saw the ground drop away as the helicopter rose straight up. Then it tilted as it turned and began speeding toward the trauma center. It was my first trip in a helicopter and I was surprised at how smooth the ride was.

As we headed toward the trauma center, I heard the pilot call in to his base that we were en route with one female patient. He proceeded to name each of the crew members aboard and concluded "and an EMT named Ed." I wondered why he had to radio the names of each person who was aboard the aircraft, then suddenly realized that, in case we went down, searchers would have to know how many people to look for. This made me a bit uncomfortable.

About one minute into the flight our flight crew received a call from the trauma center. "We have another request for an air rescue—PIAA with entrapment on Interstate 27."

"10–4," our pilot replied. "Do you have another flight crew available?"

"Affirmative."

"OK. Have them meet us at the pad. We'll do a hot offload."

Normally, for safety, the helicopter would shut down its engines before we would remove our patient. But since the aircraft was needed for another call, we would be doing a "hot offload": removing our patient rapidly, with the rotors still moving. These flight nurses would take the patient to the ER and another crew would board and respond to the second call.

A few minutes later the noise and vibration of the helicopter increased as we began our descent to the landing pad at the trauma center. The landing was so gentle that I did not realize that we were on the ground. Guided around the rear rotor by the pilot, we rapidly removed Jeanette from the aircraft. Within seconds, the second flight crew had climbed in and the chopper lifted off, on its way to the second call. Shortly after, Jeanette was under the expert care of a trauma team.

* * *

I learned a few days later that Jeanette's burns had been mostly first degree, probably lessened by the cooling saline that had been applied to her face soon after the accident. Luckily, she had instinctively closed her eyes when the radiator steam had exploded into her face, so her eyes weren't injured, and she had not inhaled any steam. She was kept overnight at the trauma center and released the following day.

My name is Ed Herman and, like Joan, I am an EMT-D. If you ask an EMT why he chooses to do emergency medical work, he will usually say, "I like helping people." Sometimes he will add that he enjoys the excitement and the feeling of importance that he gets from the work. Rarely will an EMT talk about the feeling of power, the almost total deference to him at the scene of a medical emergency, or the fact that everyone must get out of his way when he drives down the road with his emergency lights flashing and the siren screaming. Although most EMTs will readily admit to the socially acceptable motives, I have long accepted that my motives don't have to be noble. It's what I do that counts. I have learned a great deal about myself through my EMT experiences, including my motivation for doing emergency medical work.

I recently went through a period of depression, during which I lost interest in almost everything in my life. I had just learned that one of my closest friends had been diagnosed as having lung cancer. It made me very aware of my own mortality and triggered one of my greatest fears: that of being a patient—helpless and dependent on other people. Strangely, during this period, my involvement in EMT work increased dramatically. I found myself more "addicted" to responding to ambulance calls than I had ever been. Whenever the pager went off, I would drop whatever I was doing and respond, whether the call was serious or not, and whether other EMTs were available or not. But I wasn't acting out of selflessness or caring. I felt compelled to play the role of EMT as much as possible.

My intense feeling of depression ended after a few weeks, when I suddenly began to again feel involved with the people and activities of my normal life. I felt very much alive, and very glad to be alive. I felt exhilarated, and I knew why. Part of my personal resurrection was due to the fact that my friend's condition seemed to be curable and, after surgery, he was doing well.

But I had also passed a psychological milestone in my life that had been terrifying me. I had been very much aware that I was approaching the age at which my father had died of a massive heart attack. Some quick calculations made me realize that on the day my depression lifted, I was one day older than my father had been on the day he died. It would all be gravy from then on. Apparently, although I was unaware of it, part of my mind had been keeping a very close eye on the calendar. Learning of my friend's illness had greatly intensified all my feelings of dread that had been building up for years.

I also understood why I had been immersing myself in emergency rescue work and why, in part, I do EMT work. When I am with a patient, I am defined as the healthy one, and sometimes even the alive one. Somewhere in my gut I feel that, as long as I am playing the role of EMT, I am immune from illness or death. It's a kind of immortality. The patient is always someone else. Never me.

I wonder how many other health professionals feel as I do. I guess I'll never know. Oh well, it's what we do that counts, not why we do it.

Chapter 3

"Fairfax Police to the ambulance corps. An ambulance is needed for a man hit with a baseball at the ball field behind the high school."

"10–4. The ambulance is responding. We need one more member to meet us at the scene." I recognized Steve Nesbitt's voice.

What the hell, I said to myself, I'm almost done anyway. I swallowed my mouthful of coleslaw, grabbed a gulp of Diet Pepsi, and signaled to the waitress. "Got a call," I said. In my local Friendly's, as well as other lunch spots around town, they're used to my jumping up and rushing out the door. "I'll pay you when I get back." I raised the radio to my mouth and keyed the mike. "45–24 to FPD. I'm responding to the scene."

"10–4, Joan."

I jumped into my car, flipped on my green light, and drove toward the high school through the cool, overcast early May air. I pulled into the parking lot nearest the ball field just ahead of the rig. As I climbed out of my car I saw Steve wave at me to go to the patient while he got the megaduffel. I ran partway around the cinder track that surrounds the field and toward the small crowd that had gathered around second base. The group parted to let me at the patient. "What happened?" I asked as I knelt beside the supine man.

"He's our shortstop," someone said. "He got a line drive right on the forehead."

"I couldn't help it," another man said. "I just hit the ball, it hit him, and he went down."

"Like a sack of shit," a third said.

As I placed one palm against each ear to keep the patient from moving his head, I looked at the man. He seemed to be in his thirties, and he wore a bright orange sweatshirt and black sweatpants, an outfit that matched that of many of the other men standing around him. Lying beside his head was an orange-and-black baseball cap. Someone was pulling a large fielding glove from his right hand. "Don't move him," I said, fearing neck injury. Anything that hit his head hard enough to cause the large, bright red egg that was forming on his forehead, could have caused injury to the man's neck. "What's his name?" I asked.

"Darrian," someone said. "Darrian Bradley."

I held his head and leaned toward his ear. "Darrian, can you hear me? Darrian?"

He didn't respond, but I could see his chest rise and fall evenly. He was breathing and obviously had a pulse. "Steve," I yelled as Steve Nesbitt and Tim Babbett ran up, "we'll need a collar, head blocks, straps, and a longboard."

Steve relayed our needs to Tim, a probationary member, who sprinted back toward the rig. "Tim, bring the stretcher, too," Steve yelled at Tim's back.

"Okay," Tim shouted back.

"Steve," I said, "see whether you can get any reaction in his extremities." We needed to know whether there had been any neurological damage.

Steve tapped Darrian's right hand, then pinched the web of skin between his left thumb and palm. I saw the man jerk his hand away, then suddenly struggle and try to sit up, eyes glazed. "No!" the man screamed. He reached his right hand under the small of his back and pulled out a gun. "Never!"

"Get away," I yelled. As the crowd scattered I flattened myself beside Darrian's head, still trying to restrain him and keep him on the ground. "Darrian," I said loudly, "it's all right. You got hit with a baseball."

"You can't do this!" he shrieked. "Get back in your cells!"

Someone from the crowd yelled, "He's a corrections officer."

"Someone hit the alarm," Darrian screamed.

As Darrian continued to wave the gun I said again, "Darrian, it's all right. It's all right. We're friends. We're on your side. Everyone's safe." I was just barely able to keep him from getting to a sitting position.

Panting, he calmed a bit. "What's happening?" he said.

"You got hit with a baseball. You don't need the gun. You're here in the park with your friends."

"Can't let them . . ." he said, moving the gun back and forth.

"It's okay," I said softly. "They're all taken care of. It's all right."

I saw Detective Irv Greenberg standing about fifty feet away. "There's an officer here who can take care of your gun, Darrian. Can we give it to him?"

"Officer?" His eyes were open, but he wasn't focusing on anything.

"Officer Greenberg is here to help us," I said softly. "Can we give him your gun?"

"Can't let them . . ."

"It's all right. The police are here. Can you see him over there?" He was now propped up on one elbow so I used my hands against his head to guide his gaze toward the uniformed officer. "Can you see him?"

"Officer," he said.

"Yes. He's a police officer. I'll give the officer your gun."

As the man seemed to relax, I caught Steve's eye from where he lay flat on the ground beside Darrian. "My partner is going to take your gun, Darrian, and give it to the officer. Everything's under control now."

I nodded and Steve gently took the gun from Darrian's hand. I heaved a large sigh as Steve handed the gun to Irv Greenberg. "That's good, Darrian. Very good. Let us take care of you. Lie back down and let us help you." The man lowered himself to the ground.

"When he's more alert, tell him that I'll secure his weapon," Irv said. "He can pick it up at police headquarters."

"Will do," I said.

"My head hurts," Darrian moaned, focusing on my face.

"It's good that your head hurts. You're back with us now. Can you wiggle your fingers?"

I saw his fingers move. "That's great, Darrian. Now your toes." His feet moved. "Can you tell me where it hurts worst?"

"My head." He gingerly reached up and touched his forehead. "God, it hurts."

"I'll bet it does. How about your neck? Does that hurt?"

"Neck." He concentrated. "No. Only my head."

"Do you know where you are?" I asked as Tim arrived with the stretcher and immobilization gear.

His eyes swiveled. "Outside."

"That's right. Do you know why you're outside?"

"Not really."

"You were playing baseball, but you don't have to think about that right now. While we talk, Steve—that's my partner—is going to put a collar on your neck to protect it. Will you lie still for us?"

"Why? What happened?"

As Steve slipped the plastic under Darrian's neck, I continued, "My name's Joan, by the way. Do you know what your name is?"

"I'm Darrian. I'm outside. What happened?"

"You were playing baseball and you got hit with a line drive. It knocked you out and scrambled your brain pretty good."

Steve fastened the collar, then took a penlight and checked Darrian's pupils. "PERL," Steve said.

"That means your pupils are equal and responsive to light. That's good." As Tim and Steve positioned the backboard so we could logroll our patient onto it, I asked, "Do you know what day it is?"

"I don't think so," he answered.

"Okay. It will all come back to you. We're going to roll you onto this board so we can protect your neck and spine," I told him. "Just let us do all the work and relax. Okay?"

As Darrian closed his eyes Steve showed two of the ballplayers how to help us. "Okay, guys," I said, controlling the logroll since I had the patient's head. "On my count. One, two three." We rolled Darrian's body as a unit, slipped the board beneath him and rolled him back, sliding him into the center of the six-foot wooden board. We used a multitailed spider strap to fasten his body down and head blocks and tape to secure his head. Suddenly Darrian reached under his back and yelled, "My gun! Where's my gun! They took it!"

"Officer Greenberg has it," I said as we lifted the longboard onto the stretcher. "It's with the policeman. It's all right."

"Policeman?"

"We gave your gun to Officer Greenberg. He'll take it to the police station and you can pick it up when you leave the hospital."

"Hospital?"

On the way to the hospital, I had to keep reassuring Darrian that his gun was safe. When we arrived at the ER I explained the situation to the staff. As he was wheeled to X-ray, I could hear him asking again about his gun.

A few days later I saw Irv again. "Did that corrections officer get his gun back all right?" I asked.

"Yeah. He picked it up the next day. And boy did he

have a lump on his head. It was every shade I can imagine. Two black eyes, too."

"He'll enjoy a few days off."

As Irv walked away, he said, "I would love some time off, too, but I don't want to get slammed in the head to get it."

Josh Rieber had had a dreadful day. A successful plumber, he had had three jobs, each of which should have taken an hour and had actually taken closer to three. The last one, a leaky bathroom faucet in an older house on Deerfield Street, had been the final straw. Every pipe or fixture he had touched had crumbled, and eventually he had replaced what seemed to be every piece of pipe and gasket in the entire bathroom. Finally, at nearly six-thirty, he had called his wife. "I'll be home in half an hour," he growled into the phone.

"Of course, dear," Mrs. Rieber said, careful not to upset her husband. "The kids are all out, and we're having steak like you wanted. I'll have the grill all ready."

"You mean I have to cook?"

Mrs. Rieber took a deep breath. "I'll have everything all organized."

"Shit," he hissed.

"Dear, you said that was what you wanted to eat tonight. I made hot German potato salad. The kind you like."

"All right," he said, quickly calculating. "I'll be home in an hour."

"I thought you said half an hour."

Not if I stop at The Red Foxx for a beer first, he thought. "It'll take me a little while to clean up here." He looked at his watch. Six-forty five. "Make it eight."

Knowing exactly where her husband would spend the hour, Mrs. Rieber took another deep breath. It would be better if he worked off his mood at The Red Foxx. Already hungry, she quickly decided to grab a piece of fruit to hold her until dinner. "That's fine, dear," she said. "I'll be ready when you get here."

Josh carefully stowed all his tools in the back of his dark blue van with RIEBER PLUMBING neatly lettered on the side and drove to The Red Foxx. Some of the regular gang was there, and a Scotch and three beers later he climbed back into the van for the short drive home. He drove down Route 161 and turned onto Hunter's Hill Road. With his reflexes slowed by the alcohol in his system, and distracted by a teenage girl in a pair of tight black leggings pedaling her bike up the winding road, he underestimated the van's speed into the turn about halfway up the hill.

"Shit, shit, shit," he yelled as the van swerved and several of his tools sprang loose and bounced around the inside of the van. The van rolled onto its side, then onto the roof, flipped and righted itself just before it struck a large outcropping of rock.

"Fairfax Police to Fairfax Ambulance. We have a report of a personal-injury auto accident about halfway up Hunter's Hill Road."

"10–4. 45–01 is responding to Hunter's Hill for a PIAA." Jack McCaffrey, crew chief that evening, put down the mike and, with Sam Middleton and me right behind him, headed for the rig.

"If you need any more help," Pam Kovacs said, opening the big garage doors, "just call." Although she wasn't on duty, Pam had been doing some paperwork at headquarters and would bring another ambulance if we needed one. Pam closed the door behind us, and we sped down Route 10 toward the parkway.

We turned onto Hunter's Hill and soon saw the van. "There's just the driver," Merve Berkowitz, the cop directing traffic, yelled.

The van was a mess. Although the windshield was intact, the front end was crushed against the rocks and there was a lot of damage to the roof and sides.

Jack trotted to the driver's window and looked at the driver. "Joan," he said over his shoulder, "see whether you can get into the back of the van and hold this guy's head."

"Will do," I said. Fortunately the back doors opened easily, and I climbed over loose piles of tools, pieces of pipe, and fixtures until I was behind the driver. I noticed that the post that held the steering wheel was shorter by six inches, probably caused by the impact of the driver's chest.

"Just hold still," Jack was saying, "until we get your head stabilized."

"I'm fine," the driver said. "I just got banged around some."

I placed one gloved palm on each side of the man's head and said, "Sir, I'm going to hold your head still. Don't move so that Jack can see how you are."

"I'm fine," he said, but held still while Jack leaned in through the windowless opening and carefully went over the man's body with his hands.

"You've got a few bad bruises," Jack said, "and your right knee's very tender. We need to get you checked out." He pulled back out the window and assembled the extrication gear Sam had brought from the rig.

I looked the man over. No bleeding that I could see. "Jack is getting ready to get you out of here," I said. "My name's Joan and that guy bringing stuff from the ambulance is Sam. We'll take good care of you and get you to the hospital."

"I don't need no hospital," the man said, although I didn't feel him putting up too much of a fight.

"What's your name?" I asked.

"Josh. Josh Rieber." He paused.

"How old are you, Josh?" I asked.

"I'm forty-three. Do I have to go to the hospital?"

"I think you should," I answered. "You've gotten a pretty good bouncing around in here. Were you wearing your seat belt?"

"I usually do."

"I assume that means no," I said as Jack pulled the driver's door open and placed an oxygen mask over Josh's face. He fastened a blood pressure cuff around his upper left arm and inflated it. He placed his stethoscope in the crook of Josh's arm and slowly released the pressure.

"His BP's 120 over 86," Jack said, "and his pulse is a bit rapid. About 90."

"I count respirations at 20," I added. "And strong AOB." In the warm confines of the van the smell of alcohol on Josh's breath was overwhelming.

Jack placed the bell of his stethoscope at the apex of Josh's left lung, just under his collarbone. "Take a deep breath," he said, and listened. Then he shifted to the right lung. "Again," he said, and again he listened. "He may have diminished sounds on the right, but I'm not sure."

I watched Jack fit a cervical collar around Josh's neck. "We can do a full immobilization," he said, pulling the dark green KED from its case.

"Okay, Josh," I said. "We're going to put this jacket-like thing around your chest and head. It won't be very comfortable, but it will protect your neck and back while we get you out of the car."

"I don't need this shit," Josh mumbled.

"I know it's probably unnecessary," I said, "but it's for your own protection." No blood and nothing obvious, I thought. Just another drunk who smashed up his car. "How did this happen?"

"I don't really remember the accident," he said. "I was on my way home from work."

"Did you have anything to drink?"

"Maybe one beer."

Maybe more than that, I thought. Lord, I hate drunks. At least this one hadn't taken anyone else with him. I started to ask the basic questions. "Do you have any medical problems?"

"Nothing. I'm healthy as a horse."

"Any allergies?"

"Nah."

Sam climbed into the passenger side of the van and together we shifted Josh's torso forward in the seat and placed the extrication jacket behind his back. "Do you take any medications on a regular basis?" I asked.

While Josh muttered negative answers to my questions, Sam and Jack fastened and tightened the KED's body and leg straps and secured his head inside the head flaps. We rotated Josh's body and slid him onto a long backboard. We strapped and taped him down and, with the help of Merve Berkowitz and Chuck Harding, another FPD officer, lifted Josh onto the stretcher and into the ambulance. With Jack and me in the back and Sam driving, we started toward Fairfax General.

Jack adjusted the non-rebreather face mask over Josh's nose and mouth. "Let's get another set of vitals," he said, inflating the BP cuff, which he'd left in place. I took Josh's wrist and looked at my watch. Puzzled, I caught Jack's eye. "Pulse is up to about 110," I said. "Respirations about 28."

"BP's still 120 over 84, but his color's lousy."

"Josh," I said, "how are you feeling?"

"Okay, I guess," he said. "A little weak and dizzy maybe. Fuzzy-like."

"Do you remember the accident?" I asked again.

"Not really." He took a breath. "I think I was on my way home from work." His eyes closed.

I counted his respirations again. "Respirations now 30," I told Jack.

"Shit." He hissed. "Get the BVM. We may have to bag him."

I pulled the bag valve mask from its plastic bag and hooked the oxygen tubing to it. I would remove the non-rebreather and hook the BVM to the oxygen if we needed it.

Jack pumped the BP cuff again and took Josh's wrist. "I get 100 by palp," Jack said a moment later.

Josh now appeared to be unconscious.

Since I was closer to the window to the driver's seat I yelled to Sam, "Take this code 3." Josh was going downhill fast.

"Okay, Joan," Sam said, flipping switches to start the lights flashing. An instant later I heard the siren begin its wail.

"Josh!" I said. Getting no response, I leaned close to his ear. "Josh! Can you hear me?" When he didn't answer, I shook my head to Jack. "He's becoming cyanotic. I'm going to bag him."

"I'll call in, then I'll cut his clothes. Maybe I missed something."

I hooked the BVM to the oxygen and turned the flow meter to fifteen liters per minute. "Josh," I yelled over the siren, hoping he could hear me, "I'm going to help you breathe." I held the BVM's mask over Josh's nose and mouth. "Try to take a deep breath when I say one, two, three, breathe." On the word *breathe* I squeezed the bag, forcing one hundred percent oxygen into Josh's lungs. "One, two, three, breathe." Again I squeezed the bag.

Jack wriggled past me, grabbed the radio, and toned for the hospital. "45–01 to Fairfax ER."

"ER on. Go ahead, 45–01."

"We are en route to your location with a forty-three-year-old man, the driver in a one-car motor vehicle accident. Patient has no obvious injuries, but his vitals are deteriorating. Last BP was 100 by palp, his pulse is 120, and respirations are up to about 30. We're bagging him with one hundred percent O_2 at this time. Our ETA," he said, staring out the window to see where we were, "is about three minutes."

"10–4, 45–01. We'll be expecting you. Fairfax ER is clear."

"45–01 is clear."

I continued to assist Josh's breathing as, lights flashing and siren blaring, we sped toward FGH. Jack used the heavy shears to cut Josh's jeans and did a full secondary survey for the second time. "His abdomen's rigid now," Jack said. "There could be internal bleeding or maybe those diminished sounds meant a collapsed lung or hemo- or pneumothorax."

The reason for Josh's deteriorating condition wasn't our problem. We just had to support his fight for life to the best of our ability and report whatever we could to the emergency room.

"He's cold and clammy," I said, so Jack pulled a heavy blanket over Josh's body to maintain his body temperature.

We pulled up to the wide ER doors and quickly unloaded our patient. He was rushed into an ER cubicle and a doctor, a physician's assistant, and three nurses struggled to save his life. While Jack finished the PCR, the state-required prehospital care report we fill out for every call, Sam and I put clean linen on the stretcher. Then Sam looked in the closet to see whether there was any equipment from previous calls that we could take back to headquarters.

"I found a longboard from that PIAA the morning crew had," Sam said, lugging the six-foot longboard toward the "dirty equipment" room. "It needs cleaning."

"Great," I said. "Is there anything more?"

"I didn't look any further, Joan."

I put a clean pillowcase on the pillow and strapped it to the stretcher. "Okay, I'll check for anything more." I pulled on a pair of gloves, went to the closet, and found a pair of head blocks, a KED, and a spider strap, all covered with dried blood.

When a patient is brought into the ER immobilized, unless the doctor is convinced there is no possibility of spinal injury, the patient will be X-rayed, still packaged. Then, when the X rays rule out injury to the vertebrae, the hospital staff will remove the equipment we have carefully applied and stash it in a "dirty closet."

To avoid the possibility of contamination, much of our equipment is now disposable. Everything from airways and oxygen masks to BVMs, cervical collars, and most of the suction unit gets thrown away after use. But splints, straps, KEDs, and longboards aren't disposable. They must be properly cleaned and decontaminated before they are put back into service. The Occupational Safety and Health Administration, OSHA, has recently handed down detailed, lengthy procedures that we have to follow to disinfect any reusable equipment to protect ourselves and our next patient from the danger of cross contamination.

While Jack finished the paperwork and checked on our patient, Sam and I took fifteen minutes to thoroughly disinfect the equipment we had found, first with Betadyne and then with sanitary-wipe towelettes. "I don't clean my house unless I'm having company, and often, not even then," I groused. "But we gotta clean this stuff. I can't win."

"That's why I like being crew chief." He motioned toward Jack. "The crew chief writes; we clean."

When we had washed, disinfected, and dried all the equipment, we loaded it into the rig and pulled off our gloves. "Yuck," Sam said, rubbing his gooey hands, now covered with a paste of sweat and the powder from the inside of the gloves. We returned to the ER and washed our hands thoroughly with more Betadyne. I raised my palm to my nose. "Double yuck," I said. "It takes me hours to get the plastic smell off of my skin. It's lucky I have long arms so my hands aren't close to my nose."

As the three of us were leaving the ER, Jack said, "I talked to Dr. Margolis. He suspects a ruptured spleen and several broken ribs, one of which probably punctured a lung. The guy's on his way to surgery, but he'll probably pull through."

"Steering wheel," I muttered.

"Yeah," Jack said. "I put in the report that the steering column was collapsed. And no seat belt."

"You know," I said, "I was really fooled on this one. There was no blood. I guess I feel that, when there's no blood, it can't be serious."

"Me, too," Sam said. "My bells and whistles don't go off as loudly."

"That'll teach me," I said. We climbed back into the ambulance and told the police we were back in service.

Carol Scuderi liked to say that she was just pleasingly plump, but in her heart she knew better. At five-feet-eight-inches tall she was more than one hundred twenty-five pounds over her ideal weight of one hundred forty-five. Her husband and three teenage children had become accustomed to her size and no longer noticed that she always wore double-extra-large sweatshirts and giant-size men's jeans.

Carol's main problem was that she didn't know which she enjoyed more: preparing elaborate, gourmet meals or eating what she prepared. She was a sensational cook, specializing in everything from her native Italian, to Chinese, French, and most recently, Greek and Indian. Since she didn't work outside her home, her family had multicourse, gourmet meals almost every night. To that end, nine years earlier, when they first bought their house in Fairfax, Carol's husband, Andy, had invested in the kitchen. He had a contractor raise all the counters to accommodate Carol's bad back and he installed a butcher-block island in the center with cabinets beneath and a baker's rack above, which Carol filled with saucepans of every size.

Late one spring morning, Carol was preparing crepes in two frying pans and combining several cheeses in a large bowl. Marinara sauce simmered on the back of the six-burner stove, and Carol was preparing to stuff the crepes with the cheese mixture and cover them with sauce. Later that afternoon she would pop the pan into the oven so that the homemade manicotti would be ready at precisely six. "Bread," she muttered. "Dill-and-parsley bread with oregano." Carol finished frying the final crepe and laid it out on the butcher block to cool. She turned off the stove and started toward the specially constructed shelves to get her bread cookbook.

As she turned, her foot slipped from under her and she fell backward, slamming her back into the face of the island's base cabinets, impaling herself on one of the upward-pointing handles and sliding downward. Her screams echoed through her empty house. "Oh, God," she yelled. "Help me." She landed on her bottom and started to cry.

It took several minutes before she had sufficient control over the pain and her tears to think clearly. She tried to stand but quickly discovered the heavy fat layer under the skin of her back was hooked on the cabinet-door handle and she was unable to move.

Slowly, and in tremendous pain, Carol uncurled one leg, reached forward with her foot, and hooked the receiver cord from the wall phone. It took another five minutes and several bouts of sobbing until she could maneuver the receiver close enough to get her hand on it.

The pagers went off. "Fairfax Police to all home units. An ambulance is needed at the Scuderi residence, 2343 Spring Valley Road, for a woman who fell. The caller is the one injured, and she says the doors are locked. The patrol unit at the scene will have to make forced entry."

When the duty crew had gone out on a "man with chest pains" call I had secretly hoped a second-rig call would come in. Dishwashing is a job I avoid at all costs. I turned off the water and immediately called the police. "It's Joan Lloyd," I told the dispatcher. "I'll go to the scene."

"Great, Joan," Mark Thomas said. "Fred Stevens is picking up the rig. The woman sounds like she's in bad shape, but you'll have to wait for an officer to force entry. Officer Flynn is on the way with an ETA of two minutes."

"I'm on my way," I said, dropping the phone and grabbing my pocketbook. As I dashed out the front door, I fumbled for my car keys, finding them at the bottom of my purse. I sped from my condo toward Spring Valley Road about four minutes away. Parking behind car 318, I grabbed a pair of latex gloves from my glove compartment and pulled them on. I saw Eileen Flynn start up the front walk and, crash kit in hand, I ran up behind her. Eileen pounded on the front door and yelled, "Police! Hello, police!"

"The dispatcher said she couldn't come to the door," I said.

"I just want to be as sure as I can that this is the right place before I break anything. Hello!"

When she got no answer, Eileen took her nightstick and banged out one small pane in the vertical window beside the front door. Carefully, she reached in and flipped the door's lock. As she opened the door, she yelled, "Police! Where are you?"

"Kitchen," a weak voice said.

With Eileen in the lead, we followed the sound of the voice to the back of the house and into the kitchen. Because of the central island, and the size of the patient, there was little room to maneuver. Eileen stepped aside, and I knelt beside the patient. "My name's Joan and that's Officer Flynn. What happened?"

"I fell," the woman said, holding her body rigid. "It hurt like a son of a bitch before, but I can tolerate it at the moment, as long as I don't move at all."

"What's your name?" I asked.

"Carol," she answered.

"Okay, Carol, let's see what's going on." I pulled out my shears and cut away the massive woman's sweatshirt. What I could see of her back was a mess. There was very little bleeding, but her flesh was laid open from her waist to her shoulder blades and the cabinet-door handle was deeply imbedded in the fatty tissue.

I looked at another cabinet handle and understood the enormity of the problem. The brass handle was shaped like a T, the central bar of which attached to the wood. One spur extended up and one down. When Carol fell, the upward-pointing one caught her just above her waist, ripped upward, and was now firmly embedded beneath her flesh.

How the hell am I going to get her out of here? I wondered. How am I going to get her off this cabinet in the least painful way possible? Bob Fiorella appeared at the kitchen door. "What can I do, Joan?" he asked.

"This is Carol," I told him, "and she's impaled on this cabinet." I hoped my expression and my slight shrug adequately expressed my consternation.

"Can we get her up?" Bob asked.

"No," Carol screamed. "It hurts too much."

"Can we take the handle off the door?"

"We'd need to get inside the cabinet and I don't think we can move her enough to get behind the door," I said.

"How about taking the door off the hinges?" Eileen suggested as she studied the brass hardware. "These might not be too hard to unscrew."

I looked at the brass hinges. "Okay. That might do it," I said. "Carol. Do you have a screwdriver?" I carry a lot of equipment in my crash kit, but I never anticipated the need for a screwdriver.

"Far right drawer," Carol said softly, motioning gently toward a row of drawers. While Bob looked for the tools, Carol said, "Hard to take a deep breath."

"Are you having trouble catching your breath, or is it just painful to inhale?" I asked.

Slowly, Carol took a breath. "Pain. When my ribs move it hurts really bad."

"Your color's good so just try to relax and take shallow breaths," I said, pulling out my stethoscope and BP cuff. "I'm going to take your pulse and blood pressure and I won't move anything except your arm. Bob will get you on some oxygen."

While Bob, screwdriver in his teeth, assembled the oxygen, I checked Carol's vitals. Although she was not an EMT, Eileen had her pad out, ready to do whatever she could to help us. "Pulse 84," I said as she took notes, "respirations 24 and shallow, BP 150 over 100." All results consistent with her injury and her size. With as little movement as possible I palpated her ribs and listened to her lung sounds. "Ribs seem okay," I said, "and her lungs are clear." Fortunately, for the moment, she didn't seem to have any serious chest injury.

Eileen asked Carol's name, address, phone number, and date of birth, making two copies of the information, one for her police report and one for us.

Bob put the oxygen mask over Carol's nose and mouth, then made his way around to the far side of the patient and set the blade of the screwdriver into one screw. "This might hurt," I told Carol, "but I can't think of any less painful way to get you out of here."

Carol gritted her teeth and hissed. "Do it."

As I held Carol's hands, Bob unscrewed one of the two screws that held the upper hinge. Then he did the same with the lower hinge. "I'll leave the second screw seated in the wood until I'm almost done. That should keep the movement to a minimum." He unfastened the third and fourth screws, but left the door loosely connected to the body of the cabinet.

"Carol," he said, "this is going to be the bad part. When I disconnect this door, the handle in your back will move and hurt like hell."

"45–01 is on location."

I recognized Fred Stevens's voice and keyed my radio. "45–24 to 01. We need the stretcher and a backboard." Because of Carol's size, once she was free we would need lifting help. Fortunately, two additional police officers had also arrived and were waiting in the living room.

"Are you ready, Carol?" I asked.

"As ready as I'll ever be," she said.

I supported the bottom of the door as Bob pulled the final screws from the wood. My EMT training says never remove an impaled object, but in this case, I had no choice. I couldn't immobilize the door against her back and, even if I could, we could never get her into the ambulance with the door still attached to her body. Reluctantly I gently lowered the door. Carol screamed as the imbedded handle loosened and the door came away from her back.

Freed from her awkward position, Carol slumped down and curled on her side. I quickly cut off the rest of her sweatshirt and examined her back. She had a deep, jagged laceration about ten inches long. There was very little bleeding, however, and her rib cage seemed unbroken. I covered the injury with a thick trauma dressing and taped it down.

Our next problem was how to get Carol, whose immense body filled the narrow pathway between the island and the side cabinets, out of the kitchen with as little movement as possible. "Carol," I said, "we need to get you onto a backboard."

"The pain's not as bad now," she said.

Fred came in with the longboard, and we carefully slid Carol, curled in fetal position, onto it and used four long straps to secure her. I placed the oxygen cylinder behind her raised knees, then tightened the immobilizing straps. "I'll try not to make these too tight," I told Carol, "but the better we can get you secured to this board the less your body will move as we get you to the ambulance and the less pain you'll have."

"It's okay," Carol said softly.

We finished strapping Carol's massive girth to the board and, as I started to grab one corner of the board,

Bob playfully slapped my hand. "Not with your bad back, you don't. You get all our equipment and we'll handle this." Most members are very solicitous of my back problem, which has laid me up on several occasions. I feel guilty, but not sufficiently so to put my spine in jeopardy.

Back problems are endemic in EMS. We work under stress, often disregarding the needs of our bodies. We climb around the back of the ambulance, and often do CPR for long periods of time, hunched and cramped, but unwilling to stop. We lift heavy patients and generally abuse ourselves under the influence of adrenaline and caring.

As I gathered the equipment, Bob and Fred, with the help of Eileen and the two other officers, lifted Carol onto the stretcher and into the rig.

In the rig, I took a second set of vitals and found them slightly better than the ones I had taken earlier. "She's in a lot of pain," I said to Bob, "but I don't think it's too bad."

"That's good to know," Carol said.

"I don't see any internal injuries," I told her, "but the doctors will take X rays at the hospital, just to be sure."

There was little either Bob or I could do as Fred drove, code 2—without lights or siren—to Fairfax General Hospital. Carol talked very little except to tell us that she had no significant medical history or allergies. At the hospital, we turned her over to Dr. Margolis and I stood beside him as he examined her. "We'll do an X-ray just to check, of course," he told her, "but I don't think there are any serious injuries. You'll need a lot of stitches and we're going to have a little talk about your weight."

Carol groaned. "I was afraid of that." Then she winked at me. "As a matter of fact, I'm more afraid of our little talk about my weight than I am of the stitches."

* * *

There was a TV commercial recently with a line in it that describes the following stories: You can't make this stuff up.

A middle-aged man wheeled a hysterically sobbing elderly woman into the emergency room. "My dad just died," the man said, "and my mother isn't taking it too well."

"We're so sorry," a nurse said softly to the older woman. "Let's see whether we can help you calm down a little." The doctor started an IV and, after she administered a light sedative, the woman calmed quickly. A nurse sat down next to the son in the waiting room. "She's better now and she should be able to go home in a little while." She handed the man a piece of paper. "And here's some information on several good grief counselors in the area who might give her support during this difficult time."

"Thanks. But what should I do with my dad?" the son asked, a bit bewildered.

"Excuse me?" the nurse said.

"My dad's body," he said. "What should I do with it?"

"Well, where is the body now?" the nurse asked.

"In the back of my truck. While we were hunting, Mom was waiting at the campsite, reading. Dad, well, he got a great buck. We carried it back near where Mom was, and as we started to dress the darn thing, Dad, he just collapsed. Mom went crazy, and I couldn't calm her down. So I put Dad's body in the back of my pickup and we drove here."

Most of the ER staff went out to the pickup and, sure enough, there was the older man, quite dead, laid out on the bed of the truck, next to the half-carved deer. Ultimately the body was moved to the morgue and the coroner was called. No one knows what happened to the deer.

* * *

One Super Bowl Sunday, a woman was carried into the ER by her husband and placed on a gurney. She had several contusions and a badly sprained wrist. When asked how she injured herself, she glared in the direction of the man, now giving information to the receptionist. "Harry was watching the game," she explained, looking at her watch. "About three hours ago, he asked me to get him a sandwich so I wheeled myself into the kitchen." She paused. "I'm wheelchair bound, but I get around just fine. Usually."

The ER doctor nodded his understanding.

"Well," the woman continued, "he'd left an old pair of shoes in the middle of the hallway, and when the wheel hit one, me and the chair went crashing down the basement stairs. Smashed myself up pretty good and ended up under the chair. I couldn't get up.

"Well, I yelled and yelled, but did he hear me? Not a chance. Too much noise on the TV."

"We're so sorry this happened," the doctor said, examining the woman's wrist. "We'll take an X ray and then decide how best to treat it."

The husband walked up and the woman shrieked, "Know when he found me? When I didn't come back with his sandwich and he got hungry. If it hadn't been for the bastard's stomach, I'd still be on that damned floor!"

Will we ever learn not to believe our dispatch information?

The ambulance was called to a local shopping mall for a woman in labor. The EMTs arrived at the scene and found a very large woman sitting in a spreading bright red stain. "How far apart are the contractions, ma'am?" one EMT asked.

"What contractions?" the woman asked, totally confused.

The EMT took a closer look at the obese woman,

removed his foot from his mouth, cleared his throat, and asked, "What seems to be the problem?"

"I slipped, twisted my ankle." She saw the EMT looking at the red stain. "Raspberry soda, young man," she said. "What the hell do you mean about contractions?"

Most of what EMTs do is psychological. Patients relax considerably when someone with a professional manner tells them that they're going to be well taken care of. Sometimes, the psychological first aid goes still further.

The police called the ambulance for a forty-year-old man sitting in the middle of Main Street in town screaming, crying, and claiming to be unable to walk. When the crew arrived, the policeman told them that, in his opinion, the man was faking his condition, not wanting to walk to the police car and be transported to the local crisis center. "Maybe you'll have better luck," the cop said.

"Sir," the crew chief said, walking over to the distraught man, "we need for you to get up and walk to the police car. They will take you to the local crisis facility where you can talk to someone."

"I can't walk," the patient said, tears flowing down his face. "I'll never be able to walk again."

"Sir," the crew chief continued, "if you don't get up, we're going to have to take you to the emergency room. And you'll probably be there quite a while. Wouldn't you rather go with the officer?"

"I can't walk."

The ambulance crew and the police gathered in a group, trying to decide what to do. Suddenly, the ambulance's EMT driver whispered, "I've seen this guy before and I've got an idea. Play along." He walked over to the man, still seated in the middle of Main Street, followed by the rest of the crew. "Do you believe in the power?" he intoned.

"Don't give me this shit," the man said, "I can't walk."

"He's a healer," the crew chief said, catching on quickly. "He works with us sometimes."

Several police and the crew of the fire engine that had also been dispatched surrounded the seated man. "Amen," they chanted, joining hands.

"Do you *believe*?"

"Amen." Over and over they chanted.

Finally, the patient was chanting "Amen" along with the rest of the group. When the group had reached the proper degree of fervor, the driver placed his hands on the patient's head. "Then arise and *walk.*"

Slowly the man rose to his feet and calmly walked to the police car. As the cop drove away, everyone shook their heads. "I guess we should give you a new title," the crew chief said. He placed his hands on the driver's shoulders and said, "I give you a new certification. EMT-H."

"H?"

"Emergency medical technician—healer."

"Whatever works," he said.

Chapter 4

For me, ambulance calls at nursing homes are among the most difficult ones. For automobile-accident victims or even victims of heart attacks, what I do as an EMT can make a profound difference in the outcome. If I do my job well, my patient may fully recover. But there is nothing that I can do against the ravages of advanced age or chronic debilitating illness. What is even more frustrating is the callousness and stupidity of some of the people who work in nursing homes.

The call had come in through 911 for a patient with difficulty breathing at the Mercury Nursing Home. I parked in front of the fifty-year-old building that had originally been an elementary school and Joan, Jack McCaffrey, and I walked up to the front desk, pushing the stretcher that carried our equipment. "Fairfax Ambulance. You have a patient for us?"

"I don't know anything about it," the woman said, glancing up from her paperback novel.

"We were called. Would you please find out what room our patient is in?" I suggested.

"Oh, yeah. Okay," she replied, obviously annoyed at being asked to do something. Looking bored, she picked up the phone and dialed. After a short conversation she hung up. "Room 203, West Wing," she mumbled.

"Do you have the patient's name?" I snarled.

"Blum."

"First name?"

"That's all I know." She returned to her book.

"Thank you so much," I replied sarcastically, already seething. The sarcasm was lost on the woman, already deeply into her reading. I felt Joan's hand on my shoulder, and I calmed a bit.

We rode up in the elevator and were, as usual, assaulted by the disinfectant and slightly urine-enriched smell of the upper floor. The walls were industrial green; the rooms beige and brightly lit.

Entering Room 203, we found a tiny, frail, old woman in a hospital gown, propped bolt upright, gasping for breath. She was barely conscious. Although her lips were blue, a sure indication of oxygen deprivation, she had a nasal cannula hooked over her ears, one tip in each nostril. Curious, I checked the liter flow and found it set for four liters of oxygen per minute. It was obviously providing far less oxygen than she needed, and her body was suffering from hypoxia—oxygen deprivation.

Whereas room air provides about twenty-one percent oxygen, a nasal cannula with the oxygen flow set for four liters per minute provides about thirty-six percent oxygen. A non-rebreather, the type of mask we normally use for a patient in respiratory distress, provides from eighty to ninety percent oxygen and can quickly ease a body starving for it.

"Let's get her on a non-rebreather, stat," I said to Joan, through my teeth.

"Take it easy, Ed," Joan said, sensing that I was nearing my boiling point. We quickly removed the nasal cannula and replaced it with a non-rebreather face mask supplied with high-flow oxygen from the oxygen tank that we had brought in with our stretcher. The woman's color began to improve almost immediately, but she was still struggling to breathe. Joan took the stethoscope out of the trauma bag and placed the bell against the woman's chest. "Her lungs sound like Niagara Falls," she whispered to me. "She's drowning in her own fluids." We were still alone in the room, with no details about our patient.

"Joan, why don't you and Jack get her on the stretcher while I try to find someone and get some information." Joan and Jack readied the patient for transport as I walked out of the room and looked up and down the hall. There was no one in sight other than residents in wheelchairs parked along the sides of the corridors. I walked down the hall and around the corner to the nurses' station. A woman behind the desk was concentrating on her paperwork. "Excuse me," I said, "could you please give me some information about the woman in 203, Mrs. Blum?"

The woman pretended not to hear me as she leafed through a pile of papers in front of her.

I slowly walked around the side of the counter, over which I had been talking, and came up beside her. I raised my fist and brought it down hard on the pile of papers under her nose. The desk shook with the impact of my hand and the pen fell out of the woman's hand. She stared at me, wide-eyed. I had apparently gained her attention.

"I want information about that woman, *now*," I snarled. "Do you understand me?"

"Oh, certainly sir," she replied. I had finally spoken a language she understood and she was now ready to be fully cooperative, possibly because the look in my eyes told her that her life was in danger. I'm a little guy and I'm almost always calm and reasonable, but people usually don't want to fool around with me when I'm angry.

"How long has the woman been having trouble breathing?" I asked.

The woman opened a chart. "Oh, yes. 203 started to complain at about five o'clock this morning, but we didn't want to disturb the doctor that early."

I looked at my watch. It was almost noon. "How long

has she been cyanotic?" I asked, referring to the bluish color of her lips and nail beds.

"Oh, that started about a half hour ago," she said pleasantly.

"Why didn't you give her oxygen?"

"Oh, we've been giving her oxygen like the doctor ordered. We wouldn't let her go without oxygen."

"A nasal cannula? For someone who's turning blue?" My voice started rising.

"Well," she said self-righteously. "*Doctor* prescribed a cannula for 203 and we don't go against *Doctor's* orders."

Realizing that there was not a shred of either intelligence or caring behind the vacant face in front of me, I forced myself to speak calmly. "Her name is Blum," I said through my teeth, furious that our patient was a number, not a person. "Please get her paperwork for us right now. We're going to get her to the hospital as fast as we can. The doctors there can decide about her oxygen dosage."

"Of course," she replied sweetly, as I turned and strode back to the room. "I'll have the paperwork for you in a moment."

With no help from the nursing home staff, Joan, Jack, and I rapidly moved the woman, now on our stretcher, toward the elevator. I quickly decided that, given the critical nature of the call, if the paperwork didn't appear, I was not going to wait. If necessary, the emergency room could call the nursing home and get whatever information it needed. I had no doubt that the nurse would have told the doctors whatever they needed to know. As the elevator doors were about to close the nurse with whom I had spoken caught up with us and handed us the paperwork.

As we rolled our patient toward the exit, no staff member said a word to our almost-unconscious patient. But an older man in a wheelchair, sitting in a sunny spot in the lobby said, "Good luck, Mrs. Blum," as we passed. I don't think Mrs. Blum heard.

We transported Mrs. Blum to FGH, lights and siren, and transferred her into the care of Dr. Margolis. He listened to her lung sounds and quickly connected her non-rebreather mask to the hospital's oxygen supply, with no thoughts of putting her back on a cannula.

We pick up patients at several nursing homes in our community and, unfortunately, I'm afraid that Mercury Nursing Home is not unusual. It's what most of the nursing homes are like, even the *good* ones. There are, however, a few exceptions.

At the Rutlandt Nursing Home, the walls are painted bright colors and there are crocheted bedspreads on many of the beds. The patients are in faded, but freshly laundered print gowns or pajamas, and they are always clean, combed, and cared for. I have never seen a resident neglected and, when we go there to transport a patient to the hospital, there is always a caring staff member present to wish the person well.

If I ever need a nursing home, I hope Rutlandt is still there.

I've never understood why almost every suburban male seems to haul a ladder out of his garage and climb up on the roof of his house during the first warm weekend of spring. What do they expect to find there other than squirrel shit and rotting leaves that have accumulated over the winter? It takes me forty-eight hours to recover from the terror of cleaning out my rain gutters, which I do as seldom as possible and only from as low a position on the ladder as I can possibly manage. But not so the rest of the population of Fairfax.

It was late March and on one Saturday the temperature was in the high fifties and the sun was shining brightly. I was on duty at headquarters with Heather and

Tom Franks, when the call came in for a man who had fallen off a ladder.

As we rolled to a stop in front of the Tudor-style house, the electronic siren of our ambulance suddenly cut off as if somebody had stuffed a sock in it. The old mechanical sirens used to sound so much better, I thought, as I grabbed the megaduffel and jumped out of the ambulance. Those old sirens had a much richer-sounding wail that would decrease in pitch and in volume, winding down as you approached a rescue scene. Much more dramatic than the new strangled-cat sound.

As we crossed the front lawn, we could see a man lying on the ground near the side of the house. An elderly woman stood beside his head and a middle-aged man was kneeling beside him. Fairfax Police Officer Chuck Harding met us as we approached. "He's seventy-seven years old and he fell about twenty feet," Chuck told us, pointing to the ladder resting against the side of the house. "He was staggering around when I got here but I convinced him to lie down. He doesn't remember what happened, or even being on the ladder, but he's alert and oriented. He let me look at his head when I first got here, but now he won't let anyone touch him. He's got some swelling and a minor laceration on the back of his head, but he's refusing medical attention."

Since I was crew chief, I knelt beside the man. "Hi, I'm Ed," I said. "What's your name?"

"Who the hell are you?" he growled, glaring at me.

"I'm an EMT with Fairfax Ambulance."

"What the hell are you doing here?"

"You fell off a ladder. I'd like to examine you."

"What ladder? I didn't fall off no goddamn ladder. That's bullshit."

I reached down to examine his head when he suddenly swung his right arm and none too gently batted my hands away. "Get your goddamn hands offa me," he barked.

"You really need to go to the hospital," I said, trying

to calm him down. This was becoming an awkward situation. Under most conditions a patient has the right to refuse treatment, but I was sure he needed medical care.

"For what?"

"You fell off a ladder."

"I wasn't on no damn ladder, and I'm not going to the hospital. Now get the hell off my property."

"Well, how about just letting me examine you?" I suggested.

"I don't need to be examined and I don't need no hospital," he screamed.

I turned to the man who had been kneeling next to him. "Are you related to him?" I asked.

"Yes, I am. I'm his son-in-law. My name's Jeffrey."

"And his name?"

"His name is Eric. Eric Cosgrove."

"Is this behavior unusual for him?"

"I'm afraid not. He's not the friendliest guy in the world on a good day and this isn't a good day. I'm sorry to say this is pretty much his normal self."

I stood up and walked over to the police officer. "Chuck, can you place him in protective custody? He may have a serious head injury." Under police custody, he could be forced to accept treatment.

"Sorry, Ed," he replied. "He's alert. He knows who he is, where he is, what day this is. His son-in-law says he's always a pain in the ass. I have no grounds for claiming that he's incompetent. If he doesn't want help there's nothing I can do."

"But, Chuck, his brain is obviously scrambled. He doesn't remember the accident."

"I know, but that's not enough. I ticketed a woman recently for doing seventy-five in a thirty-mile zone. Now she claims I was harassing her because she's a woman. I don't want to do anything nowadays without an absolutely solid legal basis."

Turning back to the man on the ground, I picked up the metal box containing the prehospital care reports that we had brought from the ambulance. "Sir," I said, "I think you may be seriously injured, but I can't force you to go to the hospital if you don't want to." I filled out the man's name and address on the front of the PCR and turned it to the "refusal of care" statement on the reverse side. I held out the box with the PCR form clipped to it. "If you'll just sign we will be on our way. This just says that we offered to treat you and take you to the hospital, and advised you of the dangers of not being treated, but you are refusing treatment and transport."

With a swing of his right arm, the man knocked the PCR box out of my hands. "I'm not signing a goddamn thing," he snarled. "Get the hell out of here. Why the hell are you here anyway?"

"Sir," I said to the man's son-in-law who had been listening to our conversation, "will you witness his refusal, please?"

The man signed his name.

I picked up the PCR box and brought it over to Chuck. "Would you also witness this?" I asked.

"Sure," he replied, scrawling his name on the back of the form.

As my crew members started to wheel the stretcher away, I knelt next to Mr. Cosgrove one more time. "Look, if you change your mind later, just call us. We'll be glad to come back."

He looked at the stretcher being wheeled away, then back to me, and winced.

"Does something hurt?" I asked.

"Yeah, maybe. My left shoulder's kinda sore."

"Do you want me to look at it?"

He hesitated, then nodded. "Yeah. I guess so." He winced again, now obviously in pain. "But nothing else. Keep your hands off the rest of me."

I cut his shirt off and saw that his shoulder was swollen, discolored, and deformed. "It looks like you may have broken your shoulder," I said. "But I really need to examine you to see if you have any other injuries. Okay?"

"Yeah, I guess. My back hurts like hell. What happened?"

"You fell off a ladder."

"I wasn't on a ladder. Who are you?"

"My name is Ed, and I'm an EMT with Fairfax Ambulance. What's your name?"

"Eric," he answered. "Can you do something for this shoulder? It hurts like hell. What happened?"

Other than a few perfunctory snarls of "get the hell away from me," Eric gave us no further resistance as we examined him, stabilized what turned out to be multiple fractures, immobilized him on a backboard, and transported him to Fairfax General Hospital. I found out that he remained in the hospital for two weeks.

Joan and I often chuckle about how, on a currently popular TV emergency-medical program, patients always meet and thank the EMTs who helped them, and frequently become close friends with their rescuers. I ran into Eric in the Fairfax Diner recently. "Hey, Eric, how are you doing?" I asked.

"How I'm doing is none of your goddamn business," he snarled, turning back to his stack of pancakes.

I shook my head. "I guess his son-in-law was right," I said to Joan. "It really wasn't a head injury that made him behave like that."

Though we may not use tobacco, alcohol, caffeine, or any other type of drug, those of us who routinely deal with emergency situations have to learn to deal with the effects of a very powerful chemical. It's called adrenaline or epinephrine and it's part of every animal's "fight or flight" response to a stressful circumstance. When an animal is confronted with a situation that requires immediate action, its body automatically produces large quantities of the hormone and releases it into the bloodstream, which carries it throughout the body. Among other things, adrenaline speeds up an animal's heart and breathing rate, and makes the animal more alert, enabling it to run faster and fight harder than it normally could.

Like an animal confronting a challenge or danger, we emergency medical workers feel the effect of our body's secretion of adrenaline in a crisis situation. It increases our alertness and can help us to act more effectively. However, unlike animals, we don't normally fight or run in the course of dealing with emergency medical situations. As a matter of fact, it is usually critically important that we act calmly and deliberately in dealing with the stress of a serious illness or injury, despite our racing hearts. It isn't always easy.

When driving an ambulance under emergency conditions, we are exempt from most traffic laws. We are required, however, to exercise reasonable caution in driving, despite the excitement, the adrenaline, and the stimulating, almost hypnotic effect of the siren. Responding to an emergency in a personal vehicle can be the most difficult driving situation of all.

In our state, active ambulance corps personnel are permitted to mount a flashing green light on their vehicles. Fire department volunteers use blue lights. Both of these are called courtesy lights and they give us no driving privileges whatsoever. When we respond to an emergency call, we may turn on our green or blue light, but we are required to obey all traffic laws without exception. Despite the adrenaline in our blood and our sense of urgency, we stop at all traffic lights, yield the right of way, and obey speed limits. We can only hope that other drivers see our light and pull over to the right so we can pass safely and get to the scene of the emergency as quickly as possible.

Even more frustrating than trying to get to the scene of an emergency and fighting with our adrenaline, is an emergency situation in which the wisest thing to do is absolutely nothing.

* * *

It was one of the first of the summer's dog days. The temperature was in the nineties and the humidity over ninety percent. I had run out of cold soda and was on my way to the local grocery to pick up some soft drinks. Suddenly the pager of my FVAC portable radio began to beep. "GKL–642 Fairfax Volunteer Ambulance Corps to all portables and pagers. An EMT is needed to meet the ambulance at 1510 Leroy Court, Apartment 2E, the Feinstein residence, for an unresponsive male. Please call in."

Leroy Court was in the retirement community of Hamilton Village, a sprawling collection of condos about a mile away from where I was. To get there, I would have to take Fremont Street, a winding two-lane road. But with little traffic, I would arrive well before the ambulance. I keyed the microphone on my radio. "45–22 to GKL–462."

"Go ahead, 45–22."

"I'm responding to 1510 Leroy Court. My ETA is zero-two to zero-three."

"10–4, 45–22. GKL–462 clear."

"45–22 clear."

An unresponsive patient could mean anything from someone who's fainted to a person in cardiac arrest. Considering the elderly population of Hamilton Village, a cardiac arrest was a distinct possibility. If it was a cardiac arrest, any delay in getting to the scene could cost a life. With my heart pounding, I switched on my green, ambulance corps courtesy light, turned onto Fremont Street, and found myself behind a car doing twenty-five in a forty-miles-per-hour zone.

Although there was plenty of room for the driver to pull over and let me pass, he continued doddering along in the center of the lane. Since he seemed unaware of my presence behind him, I flashed my headlights. No response. Well, perhaps he doesn't use his rearview mirror, I thought. I beeped my horn. The driver looked up into his rearview mirror, obviously saw my flashing green light, and just as obviously ignored it, refusing to allow me to pass. I've never been able to understand why anyone would deliberately delay a volunteer who is responding to a medical or fire emergency, but they do. Often.

I was able to pass just before the junction of Fremont and Barton streets, and found the traffic light at the intersection turning red. Difficult though it was, I resisted the temptation to run the light. The ten or fifteen seconds that it took for the light to turn green seemed like hours. Finally, I turned into Hamilton Village. The delay had only cost me about a minute. I hoped that it wasn't critical.

I parked behind two patrol cars, popped the trunk, and grabbed my crash kit, knowing that the cops would have already brought oxygen to the scene. As I trotted around the back of the building to the stairway leading to Apartment 2E, one flight up, I could see a woman and two Fairfax police officers at the top of the stairs. Officer Will McAndrews was banging on the door. "Mr. Feinstein, are you okay?"

There was no response from inside the apartment.

Officer Eileen Flynn turned to the woman beside her. "Are you sure he's inside?"

"Yes. He asked me to bring him some water, but I couldn't open the door."

Will knocked and yelled again. "Mr. Feinstein, can you hear me?"

No response.

I clenched my teeth in frustration. Why the hell don't they just break down the door? I thought. The guy's probably in cardiac arrest. By the time the cops finish diddling around it will probably be too late to save him. I remembered that each of the apartments on this side of the building had a tiny deck outside the living room. "Can we get in through the deck?" I asked Eileen.

"The fire department is on its way with a ladder," she replied.

"Mr. Feinstein, this is the Fairfax Police," Will hollered. "Are you okay?"

This time a faint voice answered. "I'm okay. I just want some water."

"Mr. Feinstein, can you open the door?" Will continued.

"Yes."

"Please open the door."

"I just need some water."

"Mr. Feinstein, there are police and ambulance people here to help you. Can you open the door to let us in?"

"Yes. Please bring me some water."

There was no sound of movement from within, and the door didn't open.

"Mr. Feinstein, do you need us to break down the door to get in?" Will asked.

"Do you have some water?"

Why the hell don't they just do it? I thought. Will is a big guy. He could probably break down the door with one or two good kicks. What the hell are they waiting for? First that creep on the road, then that damn traffic light, now these damn cops, I raged silently.

Although I wanted to, I knew better than to say anything to Will or Eileen. I had a good working relationship with the police and I wasn't about to jeopardize it by telling them how to do their job. Still, this was infuriating.

At last I heard the sirens of the approaching fire engine as it pulled up in front of the building. Unwilling to wait an extra second at the Feinstein front door, I grabbed my crash kit, ran back down the stairs, and followed the firefighters around to the back of the building. They put a hand ladder against the edge of the deck and firefighter Mike DeVito began to climb. "Coming, Ed?" he yelled.

I was between a rock and a hard place, between my impatience to care for the patient and my fear of ladders. It's not too high, I told myself. Just one story. And Mike can help me over the balcony. After only an instant of indecision, I climbed, sweat pouring down my face from the heat and the terror. Don't look down, I told my eyes. Don't think about the height, I told my brain. I just stared at Mike and suddenly I was on the balcony, and Mike was working on the sliding door.

In just a moment, the door opened and we walked inside. It was difficult to breathe. All of the windows in the apartment were closed, and the temperature must have been well over one hundred degrees. Mr. Feinstein was lying on his back next to the front door. He was flushed and, as I knelt beside him and felt his face, his skin was hot and dry. "Sir," I said. "Did you fall?"

"I'd like some water, please," he said.

"Let's get him away from the door." Mike and I carefully slid the wizened old man along the tile floor. I knelt beside him as Mike opened the door to let in the police and my crew members.

"My name is Ed. I'm an EMT with the Fairfax Ambulance Corps. What's your name, sir?"

"I'm Sam Feinstein."

"Mr. Feinstein, can you tell me what happened?"

"Nothing happened. Can you get me some water?"

"I need some information first, Mr. Feinstein. Why are you on the floor?"

"I'm not on the floor," he replied indignantly.

"Well, where are you?" I asked.

He stared at me silently, clearly troubled and unable to answer my question.

"Mr. Feinstein, what is your date of birth?" I asked.

"I can't remember."

"Do you know what day today is?"

Mr. Feinstein was disturbed by my questions and couldn't provide any information except his name and the name of his doctor. "All right, sir. We'll just check you out. You tell me if anything I do hurts."

While I checked his head for injury, my crew members, Pete Williamson and Marge Talbot, who had just arrived, checked his blood pressure, pulse, and respiration and surveyed the rest of his body. His vital signs were all within normal limits, but his skin had lost its resiliency. He was dehydrated and suffering from the heat, but other than that, he seemed all right.

"Please. Just a little water."

Since his mental status was not normal, our protocols did not permit us to give him fluids by mouth. We would need to quickly transport him to Fairfax General where his body's fluids could be replaced intravenously. I took a towel from the stretcher and wet one corner in the sink in the kitchen. "Here, Mr. Feinstein. I can't give you a drink because it will probably make you sick but you can suck on this. It should help."

"Thank you so much, my boy."

My boy? I'm almost sixty and haven't been called anything like that in many years. Smiling, I helped the rest of the crew to get Mr. Feinstein settled on the stretcher.

As my crew, assisted by two firefighters, carried the stretcher down the steep flight of stairs, I collected our equipment. Walking out the door, I paused and looked down at where Mr. Feinstein had been lying. With a sinking feeling I suddenly realized that the old man's head had been right next to the front door. If Will had acted as urgently as I had wanted him to and had kicked down the door, Mr. Feinstein might easily have been seriously injured. I thanked God for Will's restraint. But then again, I thought, if he had been in cardiac arrest, by the time we got in, it would have been too late.

Adrenaline or not, sometimes our decisions are a crapshoot.

* * *

I have a great relationship with my younger daughter, Arielle, and sometimes there seems to be little or no generation gap between us. But at other times the gap seems enormous.

During her senior year of high school, two members of her class were killed in an automobile accident. I was shocked by her matter-of-fact attitude toward the event. It wasn't that she was uncaring about it; she was deeply disturbed. But these were not the only friends and acquaintances that had died or been killed during her teenage years. She seemed to accept the deaths of teenagers like herself as normal.

"You know, Ari," I said to her, "when I was a high school senior, none of the kids that I went to school with died. I always thought that death was something that happened to old people, not to kids."

Arielle looked at me with obvious disbelief. "I certainly don't think that," she said.

I felt a great sadness for her. When I was growing up in the northern Bronx in the forties and fifties, kids didn't do drugs and kids didn't drive cars, and kids didn't die.

Tim Osgood was feeling great. It must be my lucky day, he thought. His girlfriend Sally had been with him an hour earlier when he had opened his mail and learned that he had been accepted to his first-choice college with a good financial-aid package. He had dropped Sally off at her house and was now carefully negotiating Maple Road, a narrow, winding road that led down the hill through Prescott. Knowing that this was a particularly dangerous section of road, he kept his five-year-old Jeep toward the right side of his lane.

As he rounded a curve, a car coming toward him struck the roadside guardrail and careened off. It headed straight for him. Tim never felt the steel fragment that sliced off the left side of his head.

* * *

I was concentrating on an article I was writing for my newsletter, so I only tuned in to the Prescott dispatcher in midsentence. ". . . are needed for a personal-injury auto accident on Maple Road, half a mile past the old stone church." Not today, I told myself. It's Saturday. There are lots of squad members around and I need to finish this. Weekdays, yes. Weekends, no.

A few moments later an excited voice came over the fire radio. "Engine 21–31 is on location. Dispatch, tell the rescue to expedite."

"Shit," I muttered, pressing the save key on my computer. I phoned in to tell the dispatcher that I was responding and I was out the door.

It was quite a distance to Maple Road, so a Prescott Engine, Rescue 1, and the paramedic fly-car were already at the scene by the time I arrived. Two cars had been involved in a head-on collision and the front ends of both vehicles were demolished. One, a Jeep-type vehicle, was partway up an embankment, leaning toward the road. There was nobody near that vehicle. A yellow tarpaulin covered the front seat and blood was dripping and pooling on the ground beneath the front door. I took a deep breath and turned my attention to the other car.

The crushed hatchback was about twenty feet up the road, surrounded by firefighters attacking the driver's-side door with the Hurst Tool—the jaws of life. Jack Johnson, a Prescott EMT, was watching the driver over the shoulders of the firefighters. In the center of the roadway, a jeans-clad figure lay on a backboard. Several firemen were securing him to it with heavy canvas-and-Velcro straps. Paramedic Amy Chen was in the process of starting an IV line in his arm. As I walked over to Amy, I could hear her patient moaning.

"Need any more help, Amy?" I asked.

"Hi, Ed. The kid in that car"—she nodded toward the Jeep—"was a 10–45." Not wanting to further agitate the backboarded young man, she used the code for obvious death. "This kid was the passenger in the hatchback with the one that's pinned. He walked out of the car, and doesn't seem to be badly injured. His vitals are okay, too, but he doesn't respond to my voice." The boy moaned, and although his body was tightly fastened to the board for his own protection, he moved his hands and feet almost continuously. Brenda Frost was securing the boy's head. "Hi, Ed," she said. "Glad to see you."

"While Brenda gets a second set of vitals, Ed, would you check the boy's pupils?" Amy asked.

I reached into Amy's trauma bag, took out a penlight, and moved up to the boy's head. I looked down at his closed eyes, wondering at the lack of any serious bleeding or broken bones. With my thumb, I gently pulled up his right eyelid and pointed the penlight at the pupil. I didn't bother to turn on the light. Although we were in the shade, the boy's right pupil was constricted to the size of the point of a pin. Lifting the left eyelid, the same thing. Shit, shit, shit. I glanced at the Jeep and the yellow tarp draped over the driver's seat. Shit, shit, shit.

"Amy," I said, "looks like this kid is high on something. Narcotics, probably, because his pupils are pinpoint."

"Yeah, I had a feeling," Amy said, fastening the IV tubing to the boy's arm with thin strips of tape.

A firefighter leaned down and said, "The chopper's airborne. They have an ETA of eight minutes."

"Okay," Amy replied. "Let's get this kid into the ambulance and over to the LZ. I'll give him some Narcan in the rig and see if that helps, but right now I want to get him to the helicopter."

"Where's the LZ?" I asked, asking for the location of the landing zone.

"The ball field at the foot of Maple," Amy replied. "It will take us a few minutes to get there."

"Do we have another chopper coming for the other kid?"

"The state police helicopter is coming but they aren't

airborne yet. They'll probably be here by the time he's extricated, though. He's pinned under the dashboard and they've got a lot of cutting to do. Hugh's on his way." Hugh Washington was another paramedic and, when he arrived, he would start an IV for the driver. Thank god for backup paramedics, I thought.

We loaded the boy into the ambulance for the short ride to the helicopter LZ. "Do you want me to come along?" I asked Amy as she climbed into the rig.

"No, I'm fine. Max'll drive and Brenda's moving my stuff. Why don't you stay here with Jack? Hugh'll probably need both of you when they get the other boy out. Tell him we'll be back to ferry him to the LZ."

"Sure, Amy." As the ambulance rolled away, I turned toward the wrecked car in which the boy was still pinned. I heard the popping of the hinges as the jaws forced the door away from the body of the car. The boy could probably now be freed, I thought. With a groan of metal, four firefighters pulled the door back until it rested against the front fender.

Suddenly Jack dove into the driver's-door opening and yelled, "Ed, get me some trauma dressings, stat!"

I grabbed two of the large, bulky trauma dressings from the crash kit the rescue had left with me and bounded over. As I pulled the wrapping off the large squares of sterile material, I leaned over Jack's shoulder. "Shit," I said. There was fresh blood everywhere. Jack leaned back so I could see that his gloved hand covered a huge wound on the boy's thigh just above the knee, slowing the flow of blood that had been spurting from it. A section of the smashed dashboard protruded from his leg.

"I need those dressings, stat," Jack yelled over the boy's screams.

I handed him the bulky dressing and, as he lifted his hand to place the sterile material against the wound, I saw that metal had almost severed the boy's leg at the knee. Blood spurted from the wound and sprayed the dashboard and the passenger seat.

"The door must have been applying just enough pressure to stem the bleeding. When the pressure was released . . ."

The patient was impaled on the piece of dashboard, his legs entangled in several layers of metal. "We're going to be here a while," I muttered. Jack nodded and, as he pressed, the spurting stopped. With his free hand and my help over his shoulder, Jack cut away as much of the victim's jeans as he could. I handed him several more trauma dressings, rolls of gauze, and lengths of tape. As Jack did his best to bandage the injury, I attached an oxygen mask to a portable cylinder and fastened it over the boy's face.

The extrication became a case of "hurry up slowly." In every decision the firefighters made, two factors had to be weighed. One wrong move and the metal in his leg would shift, setting off more life-threatening bleeding. But time was the enemy. While the firefighters worked, Jack checked and rechecked the boy's breathing and pulse rate. Although he was semiconscious, screaming at intervals then slipping into silence, his vitals remained steady. There was no way of knowing, however, how long his vitals would hold. I was glad that I wasn't the one to have to decide how to proceed.

Quickly, but carefully, specially trained firefighters cut away piece after piece of twisted metal that trapped the boy in the vehicle. I've never appreciated the skill of those firefighters more. A bucket brigade of sorts carried sections of twisted metal to the far side of the road and piled them for the wrecker to remove later. It was an agonizingly slow race against time.

Hugh Washington arrived, started IV lines in both the boy's arms, and then, like myself, could do nothing but stand by and wait. It was torture for us to listen to the boy's cries while the firefighters carefully did their job of cutting away the car from around him. We could do nothing.

After almost an hour, they had managed to cut away most of the dash while leaving the one impaled shard in place. The boy was finally pulled out of the vehicle, immobilized on a backboard, and rushed to the waiting helicopter.

Two days later the newspaper gave details about the funeral for the boy in the Jeep. It said the passenger in the hatchback had been kept in the hospital for twenty-four hours and then released. The driver was admitted in critical, but stable condition. I never learned whether drugs had indeed been involved. It makes me so angry that I'm just as glad not to know.

Marilyn Barnett and her married daughter, Hillary Smith, met at the Mid County Mall one Saturday morning to shop for new clothes for Hillary's two children, eight-year-old Alyssa and six-year-old Jimmy.

"What do you think about this, Mom?" Hillary asked, holding up a pair of jeans with plaid patches on the knees and a short-sleeved shirt in a matching plaid.

"Who's it for, Alyssa or Jimmy?" Marilyn replied.

"You wouldn't catch Jimmy in a shirt like this," Hillary said, grinning. "Polos and short-sleeved sweatshirts. That's it. And if the shirt has anything written on it, he has to approve of what it says."

"You're kidding." Marilyn sighed, regretting that she could visit Fairfax only twice a year, when she took her vacation from the Michigan law firm where she worked.

"Now that he reads," Hillary said, "he's impossible. He found out that one shirt said 'My parents went to Aruba and all I got was this lousy shirt' and he stuffed it into the garbage."

"I remember when you brought that one back. Why on earth won't he wear it?"

"He doesn't want anyone knowing he didn't go along." She hung the plaid outfit back on the rack.

"Kids are impossible." Marilyn took a deep breath, trying to quiet her aching stomach.

"Are you all right, Mom?" Hillary asked, noting her mother's pallor and obvious discomfort.

"I'm fine, dear. Just a bit of indigestion."

Hillary reached into her purse and pulled out a container of Di-Gel. She dropped two tablets into her mother's outstretched palm. "Chew these and let's go over to the food court and get you some club soda."

"I'm okay, darling. I just need to swallow these. And maybe sit down for a moment."

The two women made their way through the crowds of shoppers to the food court where, because it was still early, Hillary found a small table and two unoccupied chairs. She got her mother a glass of ginger ale from a Greek fast-food shop and watched the older woman sip the golden liquid. Then the two women sat for a few minutes and chatted about the children and about James Sr.'s most recent promotion. Finally, Hillary asked, "Are you feeling better, Mom?"

"Actually, not really." She rubbed her breastbone with the heel of her right hand. "If I could just belch a few times."

"Didn't the ginger ale help?"

Marilyn took a deep breath, trying to bring up gas. "Maybe we'd better go back to the house. I really don't feel so well and I could use the bathroom."

When the two women reached the sidewalk outside the mall, Hillary took a good look at her mother. "Mom, you don't look well. Maybe I should drive you over to Dr. Steinberg's office and let him look you over."

"Don't be silly. I'll be fine." After walking to the car, however, Marilyn wasn't so sure she was feeling all right. "You know," she said, climbing into the passenger seat of her daughter's BMW, "maybe I'd better have someone check me out. I'm not feeling well at all. A couple of years ago, a doctor said I might have a hiatal hernia. That's what's acting up, I guess."

By the time Hillary drove into the medical complex, Marilyn's face looked ashen. "I'll drop you off in front, then park," she said. She pulled up in front of building B, shifted into park, got out, and came around to let her mother out of the car. Opening the door, she saw that her mother's eyes were closed and her head had dropped back onto the headrest. "We're here, Mom," she said. When her mother didn't move, she reached in and touched her shoulder. "Mom!" She stood up and screamed. "Someone call 911!"

Twenty-seven-year-old Sue Sheridan was standing in Phil's Pharmacy, a store situated in one corner of building B. "Do you hear someone yelling?" she asked the older woman standing next to her.

"I think I do," Geri Walters said. The two walked out toward the parking lot and saw Hillary screaming for help. "Call 911," Sue said to Geri. "Hurry."

While Geri ran back into the pharmacy, yelling to the pharmacist to call an ambulance, Sue ran over to Hillary. "Someone's calling an ambulance. What's wrong?"

"My mother," Hillary sobbed. "She's not moving."

"Her name?"

"She's Marilyn and I'm Hillary."

Sue, who used to be a lifeguard and had learned CPR many years earlier, reached into the car and felt Marilyn's neck. Feeling no pulse, yet not wanting to further alarm Hillary, she said, "Let's get her out of the car so that she's more comfortable." She shook Hillary's shoulder, trying to get attention from the hysterical woman. "Ma'am, can you help me?"

"My mother. She's my mother. She's not breathing. I know it. She's going to die." She started to sob louder.

"Ma'am," Sue said, "please help me."

* * *

"325 to 715," the police dispatcher said into the microphone.

Stan Garth picked up the mike in his patrol car. "715."

"Respond to a report of a woman down in front of the Grant Boulevard medical complex, building B."

"10–4." As he flipped on the lights and siren, Stan nodded to Bobby Harding, a new member of the Prescott Police Department, riding along before beginning his class at the police academy. "That's only two blocks from here. Let's go."

The dispatcher's voice continued. "325 to 706. Back up 715."

"10–4," Stan and Bobby heard Officer Roy Zimmerman say.

It took only thirty seconds for car 715 to arrive in front of the medical complex. "Over there," Bobby said. Stan also saw the knot of people standing on the sidewalk.

"Got it," Stan said. As he pulled the car in behind Hillary's BMW he saw three or four people trying to get someone out. "Call it in," he said to Bobby.

As Stan darted toward the crowd, he heard Bobby call the dispatcher. "312 is out."

The crowd parted as Stan made his way toward the passenger side of the car. "What's the problem?" he asked.

"I don't think she's got a pulse," Sue answered.

"Who is she?" Stan asked, taking the woman's legs and placing her gently on the pavement.

"Her name's Marilyn," Sue said, "and that's her daughter." She pointed toward the now-hysterical woman.

Stan, who had been recertified in CPR just a month earlier, lifted Marilyn's chin and placed his ear near her open mouth and his fingers on her carotid artery in her neck. After five seconds, Stan said, "She's not breathing and there's no pulse." He lifted his head. "Bobby!"

"Yeah," Bobby said.

"Call in and tell them we've got a code 99. Then get the oxygen and the BVM."

"The what?"

"The oxygen and the large blue bag in the trunk."

"Okay."

"I can help," Sue said. "I know CPR."

"Good. You can do compressions." Stan took a four-inch-square clear plastic face shield from his pocket and placed the small plastic cylinder in Marilyn's mouth. He spread the heavy plastic shield over her nose, pinched, and gave her two full breaths through the tube. He nodded to Sue, who began chest compressions.

Moments later, Bobby returned. "Prescott Rescue has been dispatched," he said, puffing, "but the paramedic is out on another call. The rescue squad is going to have to handle it alone." He handed Stan the oxygen and the BVM.

"Take out the oxygen cylinder and the BVM," Stan said, pausing to give Marilyn a breath. When Bobby had done that, Stan continued, "Now attach the face mask to the bag and connect the tubing to the cylinder."

With the help of two bystanders, Bobby connected all the pieces and handed everything to Stan. Stan opened the main valve on the oxygen cylinder and set the flow to fifteen liters per minute. He fitted the mask over Marilyn's face and, when Sue had completed her five compressions, he squeezed the bag, forcing oxygen into Marilyn's lungs.

"GRQ–325 Prescott to the Rescue Squad. An EMT is needed for a report of a woman down in front of the Grant Boulevard medical complex, building B. Will an EMT please call in?"

I ran to the phone just inside the main entrance of the mall, where I had been looking for a Fairport Convention album. The folk-rock group had been making records for more than twenty years, but I had heard them on the radio for the first time only a week earlier and wanted to get one of their albums. I dialed the firehouse number.

"Prescott Fire Department. McCann speaking."

"It's Ed Herman," I said. "Do you have a driver and attendant in quarters?" I asked.

"Yeah, Sally Walsh and Max Taylor are here."

"OK, tell them to roll and I'll meet them at the scene. I'm at the mall. My ETA is about zero-one."

"Okay, Ed. The medic is unavailable. He's on another call. He doesn't know yet whether this call's going to be ALS or BLS, but he'll try to get to you if he can."

"Okay," I said, dropping the phone none too gently into its cradle and dashing for my car.

As I pulled into the medical complex I could see the Prescott patrol car and, nearby, Stan Garth and a young woman doing CPR on a woman lying on the ground. I parked, switched off my blue light, clipped my Prescott Rescue Squad ID to my shirt collar, and got out of the car.

"What have you got, Stan?" I asked.

"Sixty-year-old female. She was on her way to her doctor's office and coded in the car. Sue here and I got her out and started CPR," he said, nodding at the young woman who was doing chest compressions.

I knelt at the prostrate woman's side and pressed two fingers against the side of her neck until I could feel the pulse that was being generated by Sue's compressions.

"Good compressions," I told her, "I can feel the pulse. Stop CPR for a minute."

Sue rolled back on her heels and Stan stopped squeezing the bag. The pulse disappeared. "Continue CPR," I said.

I could hear the siren of the approaching ambulance as I looked down at the woman's face. Her color was good. I lifted one eyelid, then the other. The pupils of both eyes contracted when they were struck by light. "You guys are doing a great job," I said. "Her color is good and her pupils are reactive to light. Can you keep going for a few minutes?" I asked. Since I was the first on the scene, I would act as crew chief, so I needed to be free to operate the defibrillator when the ambulance arrived. Stan and Sue both nodded.

The ambulance pulled into the parking lot and Sally trotted over carrying the defibrillator and crash kit. I quickly selected and measured an oral airway, then inserted it in the woman's mouth to assist ventilation. Sally opened the briefcase-sized device and pulled out the leads and a package of adhesive electrodes and handed them to me. While Sally turned on the machine, I attached an electrode to the white lead and pressed it in place under the woman's right collarbone. Then I attached an electrode to the red lead and placed it against her left lower ribs. "Stop CPR," I said.

The defibrillator screen showed the zigzag pattern of vertical lines characteristic of ventricular fibrillation, a type of cardiac activity in which the heart muscle quivers but is unable to pump effectively. I pressed the button marked *analyze*.

"Stand clear, stand clear," the mechanical voice of the defibrillator ordered, then began to whine as it charged up in preparation for delivering a shock.

"Press to shock, press to shock," the machine said.

I pressed two fingers against the side of the woman's neck, searching for a carotid pulse, but could find none. "Stand clear," I yelled, then pressed the *shock* button. The woman's body convulsed as electricity surged through it, causing her muscles to contract. For a second or two the defibrillator screen showed a flat line, then, again the zigzag lines indicating v-fib.

I administered a second shock, hoping to convert her heart rhythm to a normal one or, at least, to one that could keep her alive without CPR. After the second shock, however, the defibrillator screen showed a flat horizontal line.

"Shit," I said to Sally. "She's in asystole."

Instead of converting the woman's ineffective heart rhythm to a normal rhythm, the second shock had caused her heart to stop completely. She was no worse off than she had been before the shocks, but now there was nothing more that we could do except CPR, and time was critical. Even with CPR, her blood chemistry was deteriorating rapidly, and by the time we got her to the hospital it was unlikely that they would be able to save her.

"Let's move," I said to Sally. "Does anyone have her name?"

"It's Marilyn Barnett," Stan said.

"Thanks," I said.

Max, Sally, and I took over CPR and quickly loaded our patient into the ambulance. As we were about to roll, the ambulance radio started: "Medic Washington to Rescue 1."

Max picked up the mike. "Rescue 1 on."

"I'm clear at this scene and available to respond to your location," Hugh Washington said. "My ETA is about four minutes."

Fairfax General was only about two minutes away from us and our protocols were very specific. We were not permitted to delay transport to wait for a paramedic. Although a paramedic could do a lot for the patient, the emergency room could do more. And, at this point, every second counted.

"Tell the medic that we're ready to roll. We'll have to go without him," I said, squeezing the BVM while Sally did chest compressions.

Max keyed the mike. "You can discontinue your response, Hugh. We're going to transport without you. We'll have to take it BLS." We'd use our basic life support techniques, CPR, and rapid transport, rather than wait for the medic's advanced life support.

"10–4. Good luck," Hugh responded.

Max drove the short distance to FGH. Although he had the siren wailing and the lights flashing, he drove slowly enough to allow us to do effective CPR in the back. Sally continued compressions and, between breaths, I talked to Mrs. Barnett and prayed that what we were doing might matter.

It had been fifteen minutes since we had delivered our patient to the emergency room. While Sally and Max made up the stretcher and replaced equipment that we had used, I completed the PCR in the back room. The emergency room team had been ready for our arrival and were working the code aggressively. I had no expectation, however, that our patient could be saved.

Suddenly Sally ran in. "Hey, Ed, she's alive," she shouted.

"Who's alive?"

"The woman we just brought in."

"You're kidding."

"No, Ed. She's alive. They've got a good rhythm and a BP of 130 over 90. She's even breathing on her own. Come and see."

I followed Sally into the ER and saw Mrs. Barnett's daughter with tears streaming down her face.

"They say she's going to go to CCU," she said, grasping my arm. "We're not out of the woods yet, but the doctor says she might be okay. Oh, God, thank you."

"Hey, guys," Dr. Margolis said over his shoulder, "nice job."

Because of the effective CPR that had been done before our arrival, and because of the combined efforts of the police and my crew, Mrs. Barnett's heart had been in good enough condition to respond to the drugs that were administered upon her arrival at the hospital. She went home three weeks later.

Short Stories

These are sad, but true.

Early one afternoon, a crew arrived at the home of a thirty-five-year-old male who was experiencing severe pain and a high fever. They were led into the living room by the man's sister.

"What seems to be the problem?" the crew chief asked.

The woman pulled back the blanket and showed the crew the man's penis, securely bound with a tourniquet. "What happened?" an EMT asked as they rapidly loaded the moaning man onto the stretcher.

"He had laser surgery yesterday morning in the doctor's office to cure a urinary blockage," the woman explained. "He called me last night, saying that there was blood squirting from his penis and he was running a fever. I'm a nurse," she told the crew, "so I knew what to do. I came right over and tied the finger from a latex glove as a tourniquet. I gave him some Tylenol and told him to get some sleep."

"Last night?" the crew chief said, incredulous. "Don't you know never to use a tourniquet?"

"Except in extreme cases," the nurse said. "This seemed extreme to me."

Although the crew was tempted to strangle the woman, they quickly transported the man, whose penis had started to turn black, to the emergency room. They were later told that the doctors were barely able to save the member.

Late one evening, a twenty-six-year-old woman staggered into the emergency room, stating that she had been the victim of a sexual assault. Motioning for the triage nurse to notify the police, the ER doctor asked, "Where did this happen?"

The woman lifted up her skirt and showed him.

* * *

One crew responded to a sixteen-year-old with a possible seizure. When they arrived, a female EMT questioned the girl.

"What happened?"

"I shook uncontrollably. It was so weird and scary."

"How long did this shaking last?"

"Only about, maybe, half a minute. Maybe less. But it felt like it lasted forever."

"I'm sorry it happened," the EMT said. "Has anything like this ever happened before?"

"No, ma'am."

"What were you doing when this happened?"

"Well . . ."

"It might help us to figure out what the problem is."

"I was making out with my boyfriend. He was rubbing me . . ." She motioned to her groin. "Well, you know. This is very embarrassing." Suddenly comprehending and struggling not to laugh, the EMT explained about intercourse and orgasms.

The girl was amazed, then grinned. "Oh," was all she said.

A crew had immobilized a fifty-six-year-old woman, the victim of a motor vehicle accident. Since she had been placed on oxygen while still inside the vehicle, she was connected to the small portable tank. "Ma'am," one of the EMTs said, "while we lift you into the rig, I'm going to put the oxygen between your legs."

"Okay, son," she said. "Anything you say. But don't you think it would do more good on my face?"

One crew was examining an unresponsive adolescent female with severe abdominal pain. Suspecting an ectopic pregnancy—a life-threatening condition—a crew member asked the patient's mother, "Has she ever had intercourse?"

"I don't know," the seriously distraught woman answered, "but if she needs it, give it to her. We have insurance."

Chapter 5

Rocco Guarneiri and Maria Del Greco were married at St. Patrick's Roman Catholic Church in Fairfax at four in the afternoon one Sunday in the early spring. The wedding was spectacular. The bride was radiant in ivory satin and lace, and the groom was handsome in a black tuxedo with a light green cummerbund. Maria's sister, Lucy, in dark sage green, was maid of honor and Rocco's brother, Bill, was best man. Six bridesmaids, all dressed in slender dresses of pale sage, walked down the aisle beside six tuxedo-clad ushers. Maria's four-year-old niece, Jenny, dressed in a pink-and-green floral-print dress, walked down the aisle just before the bride and sprinkled pink rose petals for her to walk on.

After the ceremony, the bridal party and one hundred twenty-five guests adjourned to the largest room at the Manor House for the reception. The party was a sensation and, as the guests celebrated, everyone said they couldn't remember a better affair.

Lucy Del Greco Franelli, the maid of honor, had a wonderful time, although she regretted the fact that she hadn't been able to find a baby-sitter for three-month-old Andy Junior. Her husband, AJ, was a tremendous help with both the baby and four-year-old Jenny, as were Lucy's mother and the oldest of her three children, nine-year-old Grace. But, by about ten o'clock, the baby was fussy, Jenny was overexcited and overtired, and Lucy had just caught one of her uncles letting Grace drink an entire old-fashioned from his glass. "Okay, everyone," Lucy said. "I think it's time to go."

"Me, too," her mother said in Italian. "I'm really tired. Could you drive me home?"

"Of course, Mama," Lucy answered, slipping easily into Italian. "Help me gather up the family."

By the time they climbed into AJ's van, there were nine of them. Besides AJ and his family, Lucy, Grace, Jenny, and baby Andy, Lucy's mother, Lucy's sister Patsy Taglione, and her eight-year-old twins, Ricky and Carol, were all seated in the van. "Thanks so much for the lift, AJ," Patsy said in Italian so her mother could understand. "Carl wanted to stay and, frankly, I didn't want to let him drive us anyway. He's put away at least a gallon of Uncle Julio's rotgut red wine."

"It's no problem," AJ answered. "That's why I got this van, so we'd have room for everyone."

Lucy sat in the passenger seat with Patsy behind her, baby Andy's infant seat on her lap. Jenny cuddled on her grandmother's lap behind AJ, and the three other children climbed onto the rear seat. AJ drove one exit on the parkway, then through town toward Floral Court, where he would drop Patsy, her mother, and the twins. As he made the left turn onto Back Street, the two-lane road behind the Home Depot parking lot, a car came toward him, momentarily blinding him with its bright headlights. AJ swerved to miss it, bounced onto the right shoulder of the road, and struck an electric pole.

Thirteen-year-old Kendra Brown had spent Sunday evening at her friend Joellen's house, finishing their science homework, two bags of Doritos, and a large bottle of Coke. At 10:35, Joellen had looked at the clock. "Shit, it's almost eleven. You gotta get home."

Kendra threw on her jacket, glad that she'd have something to turn in to Mr. Hoskiss the following morning. "My mom'll yell, but when I tell her that I've got all my work done, she'll chill." Kendra threw on her sweatshirt and, brandishing her completed pages, climbed on her bicycle and pedaled toward home.

As she turned onto the shortcut through the well-lit parking area behind Home Depot, she heard a tremendous crash. Without much conscious thought, she rode toward the sound. A large white van was tilted at an angle toward the passenger side. Smoke and a small handkerchief of flame rose from under the hood. Kendra saw a woman in a bathrobe emerge from one of the houses on Back Street. "It's on fire," Kendra shouted, "call 911." The woman disappeared back into her house.

As Kendra approached the passenger side of the van, she saw a woman climb out. The woman pulled on the sliding rear door of the van and, with Kendra's help, dragged it open. "The kids are in the back," another woman's voice screamed as she struggled out through the sliding door. "Open the hatch. And find the baby!"

Kendra ran to the back of the van and pried the back hatch open. Two girls clambered out, and Kendra climbed inside over the rear backseat. She saw a boy, screaming and holding his right arm. She grabbed him, passed him over the back of the seat, and the two girls pulled the boy the rest of the way.

Kendra glanced at the front seat and saw the driver unfasten his seat belt and struggle to open his side door. Two screaming women pulled the baby, whose car seat had been torn from Patsy's arms at impact, from the floor on the passenger side.

From the seat behind the driver, an older woman screamed in a language Kendra didn't understand. "Get out," Kendra yelled. "There's a fire." Smoke began to fill the van and Kendra started to cough. The older woman continued to scream words Kendra didn't understand. "Get out!" Kendra yelled again, coughing, her throat beginning to hurt.

She climbed over the second seat, and shoved the moaning older woman through the sliding door. Then she felt around on the floor between the two seats and found a lump of cloth. "Help me," she yelled to the two girls who stood peering in through the open hatch. A girl climbed in and, between the two of them, they lifted an unconscious child out through the hatch.

"How many were in here?" Kendra called from inside the van. "Is everyone out?"

The girl thought a moment, then called, "We're all out." Kendra climbed back out the hatch as the first fire truck, lights flashing and siren screaming, rounded the corner. "Get back," she said. "Back away." The group backed up, away from the van, now belching smoke and flame from under the hood. Smoke poured from the open doors.

Suddenly, over the siren's wail, a woman shouted, "AJ! AJ! Where are you?"

Nine-year-old Grace looked around frantically, then shrieked, "My daddy's still in there! He's burning. Get my daddy out!"

As the first fire truck pulled up, Kendra held the children and kept them from running back toward the van. "We'll tell the firemen, and they'll get your daddy," she said softly. Then, more forcefully, she added, "You stay safe!" She pointed to the boy lying on the ground screaming. "Stay with him," she said.

Ken Stavitsky, a longtime Fairfax firefighter, and Andy Johansen, a young man who had only been with FFD for about a year, were at the firehouse when the radio squawked. "Fairfax Police to GCC–905, Fairfax Fire Department. We have a report of a car fire on Back Street behind Home Depot."

"10–4," Ken said into the mike. "Engine 44–31 will be responding to a car fire behind Home Depot." He yelled to Andy, "Going with me?"

"Yeah," Andy said, heading down the stairs toward the large, lime yellow engine. Enough firefighters to fill out the company would respond directly to the scene. Others would pick up a second engine and respond as well. Actually, Andy thought, for a small car fire, the second engine probably wouldn't even be needed. Well, someone would figure that out later.

He dashed to where he had hung his gear an hour earlier, grabbed the bunker pants with his gear number on the thigh, then pulled on the jacket that had the same number on the sleeve and his name on the back. Finally, he grabbed his helmet. He remembered that his boots were still in the trunk of his car so he ran outside, retrieved them, then jumped into the passenger seat of the engine to wait for Ken.

Upstairs, Ken hit the button that would set off Fairfax Fire Department's distinctive pager tones, then keyed the mike. "GCC–905 to all responding men and apparatus. We have a report of a car fire behind Home Depot." He left the mike on the table, waiting for the next nondriving firefighter to arrive and dispatch. Then he galloped down the stairs, grabbed his gear, and climbed into the driver's seat of the waiting engine. As Ken drove out through the wide garage doors and flipped the light and siren controls, he watched Andy pull on a pair of heavy boots.

"GCC–905 is on the air at 22–45 hours. We have a reported car fire behind Home Depot." Jimmy Marcus had arrived and was dispatching. "GCC–905 standing by."

Another voice responded, "Car 44–11 is 10–17." Good, Ken thought. Chief Bradley is coming. Always known as Chief, he had twenty years experience and was calm and extremely efficient in everything he did.

It took only two minutes for the engine to arrive at the scene. As the rig pulled to a stop, Firefighter Stavitsky, well trained and experienced, took in the whole picture. The pole that the van had struck was listing at a slight angle, seemingly held up by a tree and supported by the electrical wires. He noted that, fortunately, there was a hydrant across the street near the outside lumber-and-building-materials' storage area. He remembered when the town planning board had insisted on its installation before the Home Depot was built. "Too much wood and stuff stored there," someone had said. "It's a fire hazard."

Then he saw a girl holding people away from the back of the van. The distinctive shape of a body lay on the ground about five feet from the back of the burning vehicle.

Ken immediately realized that the situation was far more serious than the caller had indicated. He grabbed the mike from its holder and pressed the *send* key. "Engine 44–31 is 10–19. GCC–905, we have a working car fire with injuries. Unknown whether anyone's entrapped. Dispatch the ambulance, the rescue, and additional manpower to this location." The Fairfax Fire Rescue Unit, although not an ambulance, was equipped with extrication equipment and forcible entry tools to disentangle anyone trapped in the vehicle, backboards for carrying victims who couldn't walk, extra air bottles for the Scott Pack breathing apparatus, additional communications gear, and other things the firefighters would need.

"10–4, Engine 44–31." Ken heard the dispatcher radioing to other units. He pulled the engine nearer the hydrant, blocking as much of the street as possible so no traffic would drive through and endanger the rescuers. He set the brake and engaged the engine's thousand-gallon-per-minute pump.

Having positioned the engine, he climbed out and assessed the fire danger. The fire was small, but it would be hard to get at with victims scattered around on the ground. They'd have to figure out an angle of attack.

"Let's pull the Mattydale," he told Andy, knowing that any fire suppression would have to wait until more manpower arrived. As they payed out the Mattydale, a preconnected attack hose, Ken saw several cars with flashing blue lights approaching. In addition, Chief

Bradley's small red vehicle pulled to a stop and the chief turned off its siren. He climbed out of his car and trotted up to Ken.

"Glad to see you, Chief," Ken said. "Fire's in the engine compartment and there are people on the ground all around the car. Pole's off plumb, too," he added, indicating the tilted electrical pole. "I've requested FVAC, 44–61, and additional manpower."

The chief took a deep breath. He was in command now and it was his job to stay back and assimilate the entire picture. The ambulance and the rescue should be arriving shortly, and he had to decide where to position all the incoming vehicles.

A young, black girl with a head full of tiny braids ran up to the firemen. "Help him," she said. "The driver's still inside. He couldn't get out." Tears ran down her sooty face. "I didn't know he couldn't get out. Help him!"

"We will help him. First we have to put out the fire. Just stay back. We'll get him out. I promise."

The girl ran back to a cluster of people by the side of the road.

Gerry McCarthy ran up, pulling on his turnout coat and plopping his helmet on his head. "Gerry," the chief said, "stay with 44–31. You're MPO." The motor-pump operator would stay with the engine at all times, operating the pumps and overseeing the operation of the engine. "Ken, pack up and take the knob and get ready to attack the fire from the driver's-side front. Andy, back him up. The driver's still entrapped so half fog the driver's seat as soon as you're ready."

Ken and Andy pulled on their Scott Packs to protect them from any toxic fumes from the fire. Ken adjusted his mask, pulled on his gloves, and ran to the nozzle of the one-and-a-half-inch attack hose with Andy right behind.

As the two men prepared to attack the fire, the chief looked at the tilted electrical pole and yelled, "I want everyone who can move to get over to this side of the street. *Now!*" As the growing crowd flowed toward the parking lot, the chief shouted, "I need to talk to someone who was in the car."

A woman in her thirties in a slender medium-green dress ran up to him, crying. "I was in the car. And my husband's still in there. I thought he was getting out his side. I had to get the kids." Her accent got thicker as she got more excited. "Get him out. It's burning. Get him out!"

"We're already working on it."

The woman grabbed his arm and tried to pull him toward the van. "Get him out!"

"It's more important that we protect him by putting out the fire. Please stand back and let us do our jobs."

Choking back sobs, she backed away.

The chief instructed two of the rapidly assembling firefighters to pull a second attack line from the engine and back up Ken and Andy. Relieved, he saw a welcome face. "Pat," he yelled to Lieutenant Connoly, "take over fire suppression. I'm told the driver's still inside. We've got one line working, and a second backing them up. Let me know as soon as the fire's knocked down so we can get rescue in to free the driver."

"Will do, Chief," Lieutenant Connoly said.

Now that he could concentrate on other matters, he turned to the weeping woman and his voice got louder and more commanding. This woman had information he needed, and he wasn't going to let her fall apart. "What's your name, ma'am?" he asked.

"Lucy Franelli."

"Lucy, is anyone else still in the car? Look around and account for everyone who was with you. Do it for me right now!"

"Yes. Yes. Okay." She scanned the area. "My mother's on the ground over there, and she's hurt her legs and her head." She pointed to the grassy verge just behind the car.

The chief knew that she would have to be moved as soon as they could do it more safely. Not only was she in the path of the hoses, but she was directly under one set of drooping primaries.

The woman continued, "The girls are with Ricky, who's unconscious now. Some girl pulled him out. My sister's got the baby and I think they're okay. Where's Jenny? Where's Jenny?"

"How many people were in the car?"

Lucy shook her head as if to clear it. She ticked people off on her fingers. "AJ, me and the kids, Mom, Patsy, and the twins. Nine. We were nine. Oh, God, where's Jenny?" Through the fog of water, she looked at the fingers of flame still coming from the car's engine.

"Who's Jenny?" the chief asked, giving his voice even more authority to counter the woman's rising anxiety. "I need you to help me!"

"Yes, yes. Jenny's my four-year-old!"

More vehicles were arriving each moment and soon Chief Bradley heard the siren of the rescue truck. As it slowed to a stop, the chief considered where to position the vehicle. He wanted to be able to use the PTO, the power take off, to run the Hurst Tool and he knew there was only one hundred feet of hydraulic hose. He weighed that against the need to keep the rescue away from the damaged pole's power lines.

Having made the decision, he pointed to the roadway about fifty feet down the road, upwind of the fire. "Put it there, Brad," he said to Lieutenant Brad Stark, who was driving 44–61. He quickly identified four of the newly arrived firefighters. "We've got the driver and maybe a four-year-old inside. You four get ready to go in as soon as Pat says the fire's under control."

He watched as Brad positioned the rescue and the men assembled their gear. He had three more men, as yet unassigned. Of that group he knew that Sam Middleton also rode with FVAC. "Sam, take charge of triaging the victims we have and get them over on this side of the road as quickly as you can. You can pull a backboard from the rescue. The pole's not stable." He pointed to the tilting electrical pole. "Check with the other victims and see whether anyone's seen the four-year-old. Her name's . . ." He looked at Lucy.

"Jenny. Her name's Jenny. Oh, God. Oh, God," Lucy said.

"Her name's Jenny, Sam. I'll call for a second ambulance. Let me know whether you'll need more." He watched Sam stride across the street as he called the fire dispatcher and asked him to have FVAC dispatch a second ambulance to the scene.

The chief then moved so he could assess the tilt of the pole. He lined it up against the edge of one of the buildings across the street and saw that the pole was now leaning at about a ten-degree angle. Three 13,800-volt primaries were in danger of coming down right in the middle of the group of victims, and the drop line to the pole on the Home Depot side of the street looked stretched as well.

"Eileen, Chuck, Stan," he called to the three police officers trying to maintain order, "get everyone into the Home Depot parking lot. Those wires might come down."

"Sure, Chief."

Chief Bradley took a deep breath. "Anyone got a pole number?"

Someone yelled, "Power company pole number 3658–3, Chief."

The chief climbed into the cab of the engine and picked up the mike. "44–11 to dispatch."

"905 on, Chief."

"Get another FVAC rig here. We've got multiple injuries. Also, get the power company. Tell them it's their pole number 3658–3 and get their ETA. And put the helicopter on standby."

"10–4, Chief."

Sam Middleton returned. "We found the kid. She's not in the vehicle."

The chief quickly relayed the news to the rescue. It meant that there was only one person inside the car. He turned back to Sam. "How many?"

"Best guess first off, besides the driver, we've got a red—an unconscious boy. The older woman's a yellow, and there are two greens." Sam used the triage designations indicating that there was one critical injury, one serious, and two "walking wounded."

"One more rig?" the chief asked. "We've got two coming from FVAC. Do you want the chopper for the older woman?"

"905 to 44–11."

"44–11 on. Go ahead."

"Be advised that the bird's unavailable. There's a bad accident on the interstate."

"10–4, 905."

"Okay. That's that. Let's call for a third rig, mutual aid from Prescott," Sam said. They would need one ambulance for each serious injury and probably one for the driver. The rest would depend on whether the ambulances could take one of the less serious injuries with a critically injured patient. In addition, in situations like this, people often don't realize they're hurt until the immediate excitement lessens.

He rekeyed the mike. "905, get one additional ambulance from Prescott and put Davenport on standby." He released the *send* key. "Just in case." Sam nodded.

"10–4," the dispatcher said. "905 clear."

As Sam ran to the rescue to get backboards to move the victims, the chief reviewed the situation. The fire suppression was proceeding well, and Sam was taking charge of the injured. The chief heard the FVAC tones and the dispatcher requesting a second rig. Fortunately it's a Sunday night, he thought, and there'll be plenty of people around.

* * *

"Fairfax Police to the ambulance corps. The fire department requests you respond to a personal-injury auto accident on Back Street, behind Home Depot."

"10–4," Nick Abrams's voice said. "45–01 is responding to Back Street for an MVA."

Ed was at his house, working late, and I was watching a movie on TV when I heard the ambulance dispatched. I was confused as to why the fire department rather than the police was requesting the ambulance. I live only a mile from town and it was a boring movie, so I decided to drive over to the scene, just in case. As I drove, I heard the second rig dispatched.

When I arrived at the scene, I parked my car in the Home Depot parking lot and looked around. There was a cluster of firefighters spraying water on the front end of a crunched white van and another group in full turnout gear gathered around the rescue truck. The police were trying, with limited success, to move all the bystanders to the Home Depot parking lot and several firefighters were assisting victims. I spotted Sam Middleton in the crowd.

"Sam," I called, trotting up to him. "What can I do?"

"Glad to see you, Joan," he said. "Check out the older woman." He pointed to someone lying on the ground. "She's not doing well, and she doesn't seem to speak any English. See what you can do. And we need to move her ASAP. She's right under those wires." He pointed to the hanging lines, now about five feet lower than they should have been.

"Will do." As I walked over to the woman, I saw that two firemen were trying to keep her from moving. I knelt beside her. "Hello," I said calmly. "My name's Joan."

"She doesn't speak English," one of the firemen said. "And I can't get her to hold still."

Without thinking I said to the woman, "You've got to hold still and let us help you." Feeling sheepish, remembering that she didn't understand, I called over a girl of about ten who seemed to be uninjured. "Are you all right?" I asked her.

"I'm fine, but Ricky's not moving."

"But you're sure you're okay? Nothing hurts?"

"Nothing hurts at all."

I looked over and saw that Sam was crouched over the unconscious boy. "Okay. That's Sam who's taking care of your brother. He's an EMT like me and he's the best. He'll take the best care of your brother. I need you to help me. Can you do that?"

When the girl nodded, I asked, "What's your name?"

"Grace."

"And who's this?" I asked, indicating the woman on the ground.

"That's my gramma."

"She doesn't speak English. Can you talk to her?"

"She speaks Italian. Sure. I can talk to her."

"Great. Tell her to lie still. She mustn't move her head or neck." The girl translated and the woman calmed. "Now ask her where it hurts." The two spoke, then Grace said, "She says her knees and her head and her neck."

"Can you hold head stabilization. . . ?" I asked the fireman who was kneeling at the woman's head.

"Brian," the fireman said.

"Okay, Brian?"

He nodded and placed one hand on either side of the woman's head.

I heard the siren on the first ambulance stop, then someone dropped a collar bag beside the longboard and went to care for other victims.

"That's fine, Grace. You're doing great and helping your gramma. We need to put a collar around her neck to protect her. Can you tell her that?"

The girl spoke to her grandmother, who was obviously very agitated. "She wants to know how everyone is," Grace said. "She's very confused. She keeps asking about my grandpa."

"Was he in the car with you?"

"My grandpa's been dead since I was a baby."

"Is she usually like this? Confused?"

"No. She's great. She's my gramma."

"Ask her to tell you her name."

"Why?"

I started to answer impatiently, then reminded myself that this was a little girl, not an EMT. "I need to know how well her brain's working. Will you ask her?"

The girl spoke a few words and the woman looked confused. "She can't answer." The child looked worried.

"That's okay," I said to Grace. "She's very upset right now." And probably has a closed head injury, a possibly life-threatening condition, I thought. I mentally downgraded her from a yellow to a red.

"She wants to know how everybody is. She's very scared."

"Tell her we don't really know how everyone is yet. We'll tell her whatever we know as soon as we know it. Right now, we have to take care of her and she has to stay calm and relax as much as possible." As the girl spoke, I could feel the woman relax slightly. I sized her for the collar, grabbed a short, slipped it beneath her neck, pulled it closed, and fastened the Velcro.

Jill Tremonte knelt at the woman's side. "What can I do?"

"We need to logroll her and get her out of here. I've downgraded her to a red." I caught Jill's eye and she understood. "And she speaks no English. I've got my very efficient translator here to help us." I turned to the girl. "Grace, this is Jill."

"Hi, Grace," Jill said. "Thanks for helping." Jill understood immediately the need to keep Grace calm so we could keep her grandmother calm.

"Okay, Grace," I said. "I'll tell you what we're going to do and then you tell your gramma. Okay?" She nodded, so I continued. "We're going to roll her onto this board. She needs to relax and let us do the work." As I spoke the girl kept up a running translation. "I'm going to let this nice man at the head count and on three we'll roll."

"One, two, three," Brian counted. We rolled the woman onto her left side and slid the board beneath her.

"And back," I said.

"One, two, three," Brian repeated as we rolled the woman back onto the board.

As we moved her, the woman screamed. "She says her leg hurts real bad," Grace said. "But she's not talking too good."

"What does that mean, Grace?" I asked.

"She's all fuzzy-like. Kinda confused."

I quickly palpated her leg and discovered that the femur—the large thigh bone—was probably broken. I thought about taking the time to use a traction splint to immobilize the broken bone, but decided that we would do what we could in the rig. We needed to get the woman to a hospital quickly.

"Tell your gramma that we're going to put some straps on her to hold her still." As we worked, the girl translated. I looked up and saw that the second rig was just pulling into the Home Depot parking lot across the street with Pam Kovacs on board. Since the captain wasn't around, Pam, as first lieutenant, would be in charge.

As we strapped, I watched Pam walk calmly from victim to victim. "What have you got?" she asked when she arrived at my patient.

"Closed head injury, neck, and legs. She's asking about a long-dead husband so I'd assess as a red. It's hard to assess too much else since she speaks no English. I've got Grace here translating."

"Okay. Get her into 45–02 with the girl. You and Jill can go as soon as you're ready. I've already put a woman with a baby in the crew seat."

Jill, the firemen, and I carried the woman on the backboard to the waiting rig, then placed her on the stretcher and loaded it into the ambulance. "Grace," I said to the girl, "stay with us so you can help your gramma. Okay?"

"I haven't seen where my dad is. And what about my mother and Jenny?"

"I'll have Brian here tell them that you're with us, taking care of your gramma so they won't worry. Climb in."

"If you're sure it's okay . . ."

I gave her shoulders a squeeze. "I'm sure. And your gramma needs you."

As I set up oxygen for the older woman and then started to take a quick set of vitals, Jill scrambled over to the woman with the baby. "Are you hurt?" she asked the woman.

"Check the baby," she said. "I'm fine but the baby's got a cut on his head." She showed Jill the one-inch laceration on the baby's forehead. The bleeding had stopped and the cut didn't appear to be serious.

Grace climbed in. "Aunt Patsy," she yelled. "Is Andy okay?"

"He's got a cut on his head," Patsy said. "Did you see Ricky?"

"I think he's in the other ambulance."

"Oh, God, Ricky. I should be with him."

"We're all going to the same place," Jill said. "You'll see everyone when we get there. Let's check the baby."

"Grace," I said, turning her away from the baby and helping her to sit on the crew bench, "let Jill take care of your aunt and the baby. You sit here and talk quietly to your gramma." I needed to keep the chaos to a minimum. I explained about taking vitals so Grace could reassure the older woman in Italian. While I worked, I half listened to Jill caring for the aunt and the baby.

"Your name's Patsy?" Jill said.

"Yes."

"Is this your baby?"

"No, he's my nephew."

"Was he in a car seat?" Jill asked.

The woman indicated a baby seat, now on the floor of the rig. Then she started to cry. "I was holding his seat."

I heard Jill sigh and glanced at the seat, a flimsy contraption meant for use in the house. It wasn't a car seat and shouldn't have been in the car at all.

The baby lay quietly in Patsy's arms, his thumb in his mouth. "He seems quiet and comfortable. Is he acting strangely?" Jill said, carefully palpating his tiny body.

"No. He seems fine. I just wasn't sure." Tears streamed down the woman's face. "I was holding him and I couldn't hold on. He was just pulled out of my arms and he bounced off the windshield and landed on the floor at my feet."

Jill carefully checked his neck and head, but found no evidence of head injury. She retrieved a short backboard from one of the ambulance compartments, had Patsy lay the baby on it, and put a pediatric collar around his neck. She used a rolled towel to secure his head and strapped him down. He was still quiet.

Surprised at how quiet the infant was, Jill asked, "Is he usually this quiet?"

"Oh, yes. He's such a good baby." The two women watched as Andy stuffed his left thumb back into his mouth and closed his eyes.

Jill checked the brachial pulse in his right arm and counted his respirations. She picked up the PCR box and jotted down the results, all within normal range. It seemed that the baby had been lucky. "From now on, you'll see that he's in a proper car seat?" Jill said.

"Oh, yes," Patsy said. "We'll get one tomorrow."

I took a second PCR form from the box and noted Mrs. Del Greco's vitals on it. Although her pupils were normal, her BP was high and her pulse rate was decreasing. I heard someone slam the driver's door of the rig. "Are we ready to go?" I yelled.

Jill looked into the cab. "Yeah, Fred's driving."

"Okay. Let me get the doors, then let's roll, code 3."

As I grabbed the rear doors of the rig and pulled, I glanced out and saw other EMTs loading what must have been Grace's brother into the other vehicle. I saw a Prescott rig pull up, and as I watched Ed get out, I waved at him, then closed the back doors of 45–02. Fred flipped on the siren and we drove toward St. Luke's Trauma Center.

As I got out of Prescott Rescue 1, I saw Joan wave at me, then she closed the doors and the rig drove away.

I watched them load a boy on a long backboard into 45–01 with a girl of about ten and one of about four with a bandage around her forehead. Then 45–01 followed 45–02 toward St. Luke's.

I walked toward Pam Kovacs. "Hi, Ed," she said. "The driver's still in the vehicle. We got all the other injured into those two rigs. Now we just wait for the firemen to get the fire out and bring us the driver."

Brenda Frost, Max Taylor, and I took the stretcher out of the back of the rig. Brenda set up a nonrebreather mask and I found the water gel packs we would use for burns. We placed them on the ground beside the crash kit. Then, together with Hugh Washington, who had arrived in the paramedic fly-car, we waited.

"Fire's knocked down," someone shouted.

I watched several turnout-geared firefighters use pry bars to open the driver's-side door and pull it back against the front fender. Then they attacked the driver's compartment with the cutters of the Hurst Tool. Only minutes later, they were lifting the driver onto a longboard. Three firefighters carried the coughing man toward the rig and placed the soot-covered body on the stretcher. He was gasping and fighting to breathe. "Were you wearing your seat belt?" I asked him, placing the oxygen mask over his face.

He nodded, holding the mask pressed against his sooty nose and mouth.

"Any loss of consciousness, or pain in your neck or head?" I asked, palpating his neck and as much of his back as I could reach. If I could be reasonably sure he had no spinal injury, I could place him sitting up to make it easier to breathe.

"No," he said, gasping.

"Why didn't you get out of the car?"

One of the firefighters answered for him. "The door was jammed and his ankle was caught under the gas pedal."

"Does anything hurt beside your ankle?"

"No."

A woman ran up. "Oh, God, AJ," she shrieked. One of the firefighters held her back as she attempted to hug the man. "You're alive."

"Ma'am," I said to her. "Calm down. I need your help."

"He's my husband. He's alive."

"Please try to stay calm," I said again. I watched her entire body shake, but she looked at me so I continued, "Let me do my job and help him."

She took a deep breath, her shoulders slumped, and she nodded. "Mary and Joseph, he's alive." Then she began to mutter in Italian.

AJ was struggling to sit up. "Let him sit," I said. I had found no evidence of spinal injury and decided that his respiratory problems were of primary importance. I moved so that I was in his line of sight. "Breathe gently, AJ. My name's Ed and we're going to take you to the hospital." We slid the long backboard from under him, raised the back of the stretcher, and propped several pillows behind his back. "We'll check your ankle on the way."

Hugh Washington looked him over, checked his pulse, and listened to his chest sounds. "His lungs are clear and his color is good, what I can see of it through the soot. There's really not too much I can do that you can't, Ed," he said. "You want me to come?"

"Not if you don't think you can help."

"Nah. You're doing everything that can be done right now. Lots of high-flow oxygen and transport. I'm going to take off and get back into service."

"Okay, Hugh," I said and watched his retreating back.

We lifted AJ into the rig and I suggested that his wife ride up front with Max. Brenda and I climbed into the back. "FGH?" Mac asked.

"My babies are at St. Luke's," the woman said. "I need to be with my babies."

"Okay, then, let's go to St. Luke's. They'll need your permission to treat anyway."

I removed AJ's black loafer and cut his black sock. Although his ankle wasn't lacerated, it was seriously swollen and beginning to turn colors. "Can you wiggle your toes?" I asked the coughing man. The toes wiggled. I squeezed his great toe and released. The whitened skin returned to its natural color quickly. Good capillary refill. "Can you feel me touching you?" The man nodded again. I found a strong pulse just behind his anklebone.

"Your ankle is injured, but your pulses and nerve functions are good. After X-rays at the hospital they'll be able to tell you more." I took another pillow from the well under the counter. "I'm going to use this to immobilize your ankle," I explained.

As Max drove to the trauma center, code 2, I wrapped the pillow around AJ's ankle and tied it tightly. With the oxygen, AJ's breathing became easier and his coughing lessened. I checked his lungs again and found them still clear. By the time we pulled into the ambulance bay, he was breathing almost normally.

When we arrived in the ER, the staff was busy, but

organized. A nurse took our report on AJ and we wheeled him into Room 6. I saw Joan in the report room, writing her PCR. "Hi. What did you have?"

"The grandmother's already headed for surgery. I think she's got a closed head injury and a femur fracture. The little boy is in Trauma 1 with the door shut. We had a baby with a minor head laceration and the girl has a broken collarbone. You?"

"We transported the father. He had breathed a lot of smoke, but he seems much better now. We splinted his ankle, but I think it's probably not broken."

"No seat belts," Joan said. "The baby wasn't even in a car seat."

"Figures," I muttered.

A few days later the paper carried a short article about the accident:

HEROIC RESCUE OF NINE FROM VAN ACCIDENT

Late Sunday evening, 13-year-old Kendra Brown of Fairfax was riding her bicycle when a van driven by Andrew Franelli was involved in a one-car accident and resulting fire. Heedless of her own safety, Miss Brown climbed into the van and assisted the occupants to safety.

As of this writing, Mrs. Salvatore Del Greco, 72, is still in intensive care in guarded condition with a severe head injury and leg fracture. Ricky Taglione, 8, nephew of the driver, is listed in good condition with a ruptured spleen, other internal injuries, and multiple fractures of his right arm. It is unclear whether he will regain full use of the limb. Both were transported to St. Luke's Trauma Center by Fairfax Ambulance.

Andrew Franelli, the driver of the vehicle, was rescued from the burning automobile by members of the Fairfax Fire Department and transported by Prescott Rescue. Suffering from smoke inhalation, Mr.

Franelli was kept overnight for observation, then released. He was ticketed for seat-belt violations and for transporting a child under four without a proper safety seat.

Miss Brown will be honored by Mayor Conklin for her bravery with a ceremony at Town Hall at 7:30 on Monday evening.

Chapter 6

Harry S. Truman State Park is a huge facility just off the parkway in Fairfax. It boasts seven large parking lots adjacent to picnic areas and ball fields, a greater-than-Olympic-sized swimming pool with huge locker rooms and eight lifeguards on duty at all times, miles of bike paths and walkways, and a large lake with rowboats for rent. On hot, sunny weekend days, the park fills rapidly as cars and buses discharge city dwellers anxious to "go to the country" for a day of recreation. Most of them have a wonderful time and return to the hot city with nothing more uncomfortable than a bad sunburn and memories of a losing softball game.

Joey Porter and his girlfriend Kenisha Weaver had been going together for nearly three months. Although they were only sixteen, they were already thinking about marriage and starting a family.

One particularly gorgeous Sunday in August, Joey's car, with Joey driving and Kenisha in the passenger seat, led a caravan of family and friends northward on the parkway toward Truman Park. As usual, the conversation turned to their favorite subject. "I'd love a boy first," Kenisha said. "One who looks just like you." She squeezed Joey's heavily muscled thigh. *Joey's sure a good lover,* she thought. *I hope we can find some privacy later today.* She pictured the tiny bright green suit she wore under her tank top and shorts. *If this bikini doesn't make him hot, nothing will.*

Joey grinned. "And a girl who looks like you." He opened the window of his 1993 Toyota and let the wind blow his shirt open. He wore only a light short-sleeved shirt and his sexiest black trunks. He checked his rear-view mirror to be sure he was being followed by his cousin's Bronco, which, in turn, was followed by several other cars, packed with members of his family. He looked down at Kenisha's dark hand on his bare thigh. I wonder whether Kenisha and I'll get any time alone, he mused.

The caravan entered the park and found four parking spaces in lot 2. "Hey, Ma," Joey said. "Kenisha and I are going to the pool."

His mother nodded while continuing to unpack a giant cooler filled with more food than any two-dozen people could eat in a week.

Joey and Kenisha sat beside the pool for a few minutes taking in the mobs of people. Most of the swimmers and waders were between five and twelve years old, filling the shallow end. "You could walk across the pool and never get your feet wet," Joey said. "There's not even any space to breathe."

"Yeah," Kenisha agreed, "but it's too hot to just sit here." She stripped off her shorts and tank top and enjoyed the looks her gorgeous body got from Joey and a few guys hanging out nearby. She walked along the concrete edge of the pool, jumped into the five-foot area, and paddled around for a minute. "Come on, Joey."

"Okay, babe," he said, removing his shirt and posing to show off his well-developed body. "But I'm going off the diving board. Watch me?"

Kenisha pulled herself out of the water and squeezed between a pair of young mothers who were watching a group of school-age children, and a trio of teenage girls. Dangling her feet in the cool water, she yelled, "Sure. Do something fancy, just for me."

After waiting in line for almost five minutes, Joey

climbed onto the three-foot board and dove off the end. He surfaced beside Kenisha. "How was that?"

"Nice."

"Okay," Joey said. "One more for my girl." He returned to the line and finally mounted the diving board. As he ran down the plank he stepped wrong, turned his ankle, and went off the side of the board at an odd angle.

"Really funny," Kenisha muttered sarcastically. She waited for him to surface. As she looked at the water, she thought she could see a dark shape near the bottom of the deepest part. "You idiot," she muttered. "Don't fool around with me." A moment later she said, "It's not funny at all." Then she screamed.

Nineteen-year-old Anthony Cross was in the lifeguard chair at the deep end of the pool. With the crowds, it was difficult to see where anyone was at any time, but, without conscious thought, Tony managed to keep track of the people going off the diving board. Something nagged at him for a moment, then he heard someone yell and he replayed the tape that his brain had been unconsciously keeping. A tall boy in a tiny black suit had gone off the board awkwardly. It all meshed.

He climbed down from his chair, blew his whistle three times, and hit the water in a shallow dive. As he treaded water, looking for the telltale shape, he heard the other guards echoing his emergency whistle and hustling everyone out of the pool.

He saw the shape almost immediately and dove. Two more guards hit the water to help him. He grasped the chest of the drowning boy, maneuvered him to the surface and onto his back. He immediately saw that the boy's chest was rising and falling. "He's breathing," Tony yelled. "Let's get the board in here. And call FVAC."

As they had in many drills, the lifeguards worked together efficiently. They all knew that diving accidents were a major cause of spinal-cord injury and that this boy needed especially careful handling. Although he'd never done anything like this on a real victim, Tony supported the boy's chin and pulled him toward the edge of the pool. A second guard got a cervical collar, jumped into the water, and fastened it around the boy's neck. Two other guards pushed a long backboard under the water and brought it up slowly under the unconscious boy, and the remaining on- and off-duty guards kept the crowd out of the way.

"Joey!" a voice screamed. "Oh, God, Joey." A guard let a short, shapely girl through the mob and she ran up, just as Tony and three other guards finished strapping the still-unconscious boy to the backboard and fastening head blocks to keep his neck from moving. With practiced motions, they lifted the boy-board combination onto the side of the pool.

"Is he with you?" Tony asked.

"That's my boyfriend, Joey," the girl said, sobbing. "I thought he was just fooling around. You know, trying to scare me. Is he okay?"

"The ambulance is on the way," Tony answered, "and they'll take Joey over to the hospital. What's your name?"

"Kenisha. Kenisha Weaver. Can I talk to him?"

"He's unconscious right now, but you can see whether you can wake him up." Tony and Kenisha crouched beside Joey's limp body as the other guards allowed people back into the shallow end of the pool. They would keep the deep-end empty until a full complement of guards was back on duty.

"Joey, baby," she said, her voice catching. "Can you hear me?"

Joey didn't respond.

It was over ninety degrees and the first due rig was out for a "woman with difficulty breathing" when the call for an unconscious male at the pool at Truman Park came in. On the third page, I responded and drove up the parkway, through the park entrance, and to the pool. I arrived at the same moment as the ambulance. "Heat exhaustion?" I asked Nick Abrams as he climbed out of the driver's seat.

"Don't know, Joan." He took the megaduffel, I grabbed the PCR forms, and, with Pam Kovacs who had been riding shotgun, we followed a park policeman through the back gate and into the pool area. I saw two lifeguards and a teenage girl bending over a shape on the ground. The guards waved us over. "Diving accident," Tony said.

"Yeah," another lifeguard said. "This guy brought him up from the bottom, breathing but totally out." He slammed Tony on the back. "Great job, man. Great job."

"Any sign of consciousness since then?"

"None," Tony said. "His name's Joey Porter and this is his girlfriend, Kenisha."

"Hi, Kenisha," I said, leaving Nick to do a primary survey. "Can you give me some information?"

"Yeah, sure. But he's so still. Is he going to be okay?"

I had no idea, but things didn't look too good. He'd been unconscious for about ten minutes, too long for just having his bell rung. And, with a diving accident, the danger of paralysis resulting from a neck or spine injury was great. More would be known when he regained consciousness and it was ascertained whether he had feeling in his extremities. "We'll take him over to the hospital and they'll examine him. Can you give me his full name?" I filled out my report with Joey's name, address, phone number, age, and birthdate. "Any illnesses?"

"Not that I know of. We're talking about getting married."

"Well, that's wonderful." I hoped that his injury wouldn't change that. "Is Joey allergic to anything you know about?"

"Yeah. He's allergic to strawberries." She smiled for the first time since I arrived. "He gets a rash all over."

"That's important to know," I said, writing down the information she was telling me.

By the time I had filled out most of the form, Nick, Pam, and Tony had dried Joey's body, lifted him, still tightly fastened to the board, onto the stretcher, and strapped him down. "Are you coming with us?" I asked the girl.

"I'll get his folks. They're having a picnic. We'll drive to the hospital."

I gave Kenisha directions to FGH and then we loaded Joey into the rig and drove, lights and siren, to the hospital. We transferred Joey to the gurney in the hospital, still unconscious. "His vitals are stable," Nick told Dr. Margolis. "Pupils equal and reactive. I found a lump on the side of his head behind his right ear and some possible deformity in his cervical spine." As Nick showed the doctor the location of the injuries, for the first time Joey groaned. "What's his name?" Dr. Margolis asked.

"Joey," I said. "Joey Porter."

"Joey," Dr. Margolis said, leaning close to the boy's ear, "can you hear me?"

"Yeah." The boy groaned.

"That's good. Can you wiggle your fingers for me?"

They wiggled.

"How about your toes?"

It was an anxious moment for all of us, then Joey's toes wiggled and his feet moved. "All right, Joey," I whispered. "All right."

As we were walking out, I heard Dr. Margolis sharing this good news with his family. "I think everything's okay, but we're waiting for X rays to be sure. But the best news is that all his extremities, hands and feet, move. That lessens the chance that there's a serious spinal injury."

"That's fine," I heard Kenisha say. "That's wonderful."

* * *

The park has been the scene of some tragic calls as well. One beautiful day early last spring, four boys from the local middle school skipped classes to hang out in the park. At about two o'clock, they swiped a rowboat from the storage area near the lake, jumped in, and rowed out to the middle of the water. They horsed around for half an hour, alternately smoking and reaching over the side of the boat, splashing each other with handfuls of cold water. Then one boy spotted a park policeman driving toward the boat dock on his usual patrol.

"Fuck," one boy said. "If he sees us, we're history."

"What can we do? We stick out like shit in the middle of this lake."

"We can go over the side and just hang on to the back of the boat. He might not notice the boat if we aren't in it."

"Oh yeah, sure," another said. "Brilliant."

The police car slowly approached the dock. "Got a better idea?"

Without too much thought the four boys jumped into the icy early-spring water and grabbed for the gunwale of the rowboat. As they went over the side, two of the boys easily grabbed the boat and held on. The two others, neither of whom could swim, thrashed for a moment, then slipped under the icy water.

"Oh shit," one of the two remaining boys said. "Help us," he yelled. "Help!" The park policeman heard their screams and radioed for additional manpower.

There's a saying in EMS that you're never dead until you're warm and dead. In very cold water, a body's need for oxygen diminishes and young, healthy people have been successfully revived after as much as an hour underwater.

The two boys held on to the boat until the park police pulled them from the water almost fifteen minutes later.

45–01 transported them, both suffering from mild hypothermia, to FGH for warming and psychological first aid.

The second rig, with me as part of the crew, stood by while the divers searched the bottom of the lake for the two boys who had disappeared. Hoping we might have the chance to save one of them, we kept our fingers crossed. We stayed until the search was suspended at dark. It was not until the search resumed the following morning that the two bodies were pulled from the water.

One episode in the park on a summer afternoon must be classified as a miracle.

Carla Wang needed some time to think. At twenty-six, her first serious relationship had just ended after almost five years. Mark had moved out the previous evening, telling her only that they had grown apart and that he no longer felt that there was any future for them. Carla suspected that there was another woman, someone younger and prettier and sexier. Pulling on a pair of shorts and a tank top, Carla walked to the park from her house only a few blocks away and wandered the tree-lined walks. It's all over for me, she thought. He was everything and now I have nothing. She walked for more than an hour, allowing her thoughts to wander down ugly, dark corridors.

She approached the boat-rental hut and, suddenly craving the solitude of the center of the water, she rented a boat and rowed to the middle of the half-mile-diameter lake. She stowed the oars and let the boat drift on the mirror-still water. How can I go on? she asked herself. And why?

Lost in her ugly, almost self-destructive thoughts, she was unaware of the thunderheads building to the west. As it can in the summer in Fairfax, the sky darkened quickly and lightning could be seen in the distance. The first clap of thunder brought Carla back from her reverie. She became aware of several people standing on the boat dock, yelling to her and waving her to shore. The rain started and, with the next crack of almost-simultaneous lightning and thunder, Carla picked up the oars and began to row. She didn't really hear the next snap.

The people onshore saw the lightning fork toward the boat and its occupant, and someone ran to call 911. Several others, disregarding their own safety, jumped into boats and muscled toward the now-drifting rowboat with Carla lying in the bottom.

I was on duty that afternoon and, with Stephanie DiMartino and Tom Franks, drove into the park toward the lake. As the rig pulled to a stop near the boat dock, two rowboats pulled in, towing a third boat by a rope tied to the bow. As we got out of the ambulance into the pouring rain, I saw a man in the towed boat, bending over someone lying in the bottom.

"She got hit by the lightning," the man yelled to me. "I told her to lie still. Come see."

I looked quickly at the clouds and saw that the thunder and lightning seemed to have diminished and moved to the east. I ran over and climbed gingerly into the rowboat, rain running down my face and dripping from the ends of my hair. I looked at the woman and saw that she was conscious, looking back at me. "Hello, there," I said, trying the shield her face from the rain with my body. "Just lie still while I examine you."

"Okay," she said softly. "I'm a little scrambled."

"Tell me how you feel," I said, reaching for her wrist to check her pulse.

"My hands and feet tingle, but otherwise I think I'm okay."

"Your pulse is a little fast, but that's understandable under the circumstances. What's your name?"

"Carla Wang."

I looked her over and found no obvious injury. "Well, Carla, it looks like you were amazingly fortunate. Does anything hurt you?"

She pondered, gathering her thoughts. "Just my neck," she said.

Fearing neck injury from the sudden jolt, I looked at her chest, above her top. The gold chain she wore around her neck had burned its impression into her skin. Carefully avoiding the burned area, I palpated her cervical spine. "Does any of this hurt?"

"No."

"Wiggle your fingers and toes for me, Carla."

She did, then reached up and gingerly touched the burn. "It's just the skin. Here. What happened?"

"It looks like your chain burned into your neck," I said. I did a full primary and secondary survey and, miraculously, found no injury besides her neck.

As the rain subsided, Carla struggled to sit up. "You should hold still," I said. "Let us immobilize you and take you over to Fairfax General."

"No. I don't need anything. Except for my neck I'm really okay. Help me up."

"Not a good idea," I said. Although it did look like there was nothing wrong with her other than her burn, our protocols required us to protect our patient and care for the worst possible case.

"It's okay," Carla said, struggling to a sitting position in the bottom of the boat. "Really. I'm fine. Just a little tingling still in my hands and feet. Let me get up and walk around a bit." She flashed me a wide smile. "Please."

As EMTs we can't force our services on a conscious, mentally stable patient so, with little other choice, I helped Carla up and out of the boat.

"Hey, lady," a man said, "I watched you get hit by that lightning. How come you aren't dead?"

"I have no idea," Carla answered, walking around with no apparent damage. "But I'm sure glad to be alive."

"It's a miracle," another man said.

"Maybe," Carla said. "Maybe."

"You need to get that burn tended to," I said.

"I'll put some stuff on it when I get home," Carla said as the sun emerged from behind the clouds, heating our soaked clothing. Sounding a bit awestruck, she continued, "I'm really okay."

I filled out the PCR and asked her to sign the RMA statement on the back. She did, and walked away smiling.

Fairfax is usually referred to as a bedroom community. Most of our adult residents are middle- and upper-middle class and commute to the city, returning to Fairfax at the end of the day to sleep. They demand good schools for their children and safe neighborhoods. Conservative and quiet, our town is sheltered from the worst of the horrors that we usually associate with "The Big City."

Davenport, a neighboring small city, is quite the opposite. An old river town, Davenport is populated by blue-collar workers, many of whom are unemployed and barely scraping by. Teenage youngsters hang out on the streets in all but the worst weather, owing their allegiance more to their friends and fellow gang members than to their families. Davenport Volunteer Ambulance members respond to calls that we in Fairfax seldom see: calls caused by violence.

In Davenport, like all cities and towns in the United States, as people arrived from different areas of the world, ethnic groups began to gather in their own ghettos in the city. Blacks, Hispanics, Asians—each new family moved where it would be surrounded by people with similar habits, foods, religion, and general way of life. The young people clubbed together, making friends with "their own kind." Each group of young people became a gang, each with its own turf, its own uniform, and its own insignia. Its enemies were everyone with a different turf, a different uniform, a different insignia.

In one area of the city two gangs predominated: the

Hawks, a group made up mainly of blacks of Caribbean origin, and the Cobras, mainly Hispanics. These groups were involved in the fun and games that usually occupy such gangs: drugs, gambling, sex, and frequent violence, usually directed against each other.

For several weeks, there had been a truce in that part of the city, but the fragile peace had fallen apart the previous evening when a member of the Hawks accosted the girlfriend of one of the Cobras' leaders. Now, the Cobras were out for blood. When Walter Ortiz—a popular local high school shop teacher and peacemaker—called both Hector Washington, the leader of the Hawks, and Juan Sebastian, the Cobra leader, and asked for a meeting to try to correct any "misunderstanding" about the events of the previous day, Juan readily agreed. He quickly decided that the time had come to kill several birds with one stone, literally.

The meeting was set for three o'clock one afternoon and was to be held in Walter's tenth-floor apartment. Although the Ortiz apartment was neutral territory and everyone had agreed to that in advance, the building wasn't and Juan had a plan. Had Walter known what was going to happen he would have tried to stop it. Unfortunately for the Hawks, Juan never informed him.

At five minutes to three, Hector and four of his lieutenants, all about sixteen years old, entered the building and pushed the elevator button. Each young man wore an identical denim jacket with the sleeves cut off. On the back of each jacket was a drawing, in full color, of a hawk that had just caught a small animal in its talons and was about to fly away. The five were not nervous exactly, but wary, wondering whether this meeting would do anything at all. They had, after all, agreed to it only at Walter's urging.

"What good's this going to do, man?" one of the lieutenants asked.

"Walter said he'd talk to us," Hector said.

As they got on the elevator and pressed the 10 button, they were joined by a young mother with a toddler by the hand and an older couple. The mother and child got off at four and the couple at seven. Finally, the five Hawks were the only ones left in the car.

When the elevator slowed at the eighth floor the five young men groaned. "Seems we're on a local, man," one of them said. "And elevators give me the creeps."

"We should be glad this one's working. Walking's a bitch," another said.

"Yeah, but it stinks of piss and puke," a third added. The car shuddered to a stop and, as the heavy door opened, all they could see were the muzzles of two automatic weapons. It was estimated later that more than twenty-five rounds were fired.

Davenport, like Fairfax, has an active ambulance corps and usually has little difficulty covering emergency calls. Occasionally, they get more calls simultaneously than they can handle. Then they utilize the county-wide mutual-aid system and request a rig from a neighboring corps to assist.

"Fairfax Police to the ambulance corps. All Davenport's rigs are out at a factory fire so they are requesting mutual aid to cover a call."

"Damn," Marge Talbot and I muttered simultaneously. We knew that a call that took us into Davenport would be lengthy.

"Go ahead," Steve Nesbitt said into the mike.

"They need a unit to respond to a report of multiple gunshots—Washington Towers, 1257 West Thirty-Fifth. Officers dispatched." Officers dispatched meant that we would wait in the lobby until the police told us the scene was safe. "Do you need assistance in finding the location?" Often, we would need a Davenport police car to lead us to the scene, but we all knew where Washington Towers was. And we didn't like the idea of going there for a report of shots fired. But we didn't have a choice.

"Negative," Steve said. "We are familiar with the location. 45–01 is responding. Tone out and see whether you can get a standby crew for the building. We may be out of the district for quite a while." The Davenport city line was a ten-minute drive up Route 10 and Washington Towers was ten minutes from there.

"10–4."

Steve drove, Marge rode shotgun, and I rode in the back. "Fairfax Police to the rig responding to Washington Towers."

Marge pulled the mike from its holder. "45–01 on."

"Be advised police at the scene request that you wait in the lobby until they secure the scene."

"10–4." Marge replaced the mike. "Can we wait in Fairfax?"

"I'm afraid not," Steve said.

When we arrived at Washington Towers, we parked behind three Davenport police cars and an emergency services unit. Two dozen spectators, of all ages, were milling around in front of the building so, after we unloaded our equipment, we secured the rig, locking the doors against the curious and/or reckless. We stacked the megaduffel and an extra oxygen tank, a longboard and the Reeves stretcher, a bag of assorted collars, straps and tape, and an extra trauma bag in the lobby, and stood reading the graffiti on the walls of the downstairs hallway, waiting for the police to call us.

The radio on Steve's belt squawked. "Davenport Police to Fairfax crew."

"We're in the lobby," Steve answered.

"It's all clear up here. We're on eight, in the elevator. There are two DOA and three others down, all multiples. And the elevator's out of commission."

"10–4," Steve answered.

The voice on the radio continued. "We've also got one Davenport rig that has cleared the fire scene en route here. Its ETA is about five minutes." Will we be happy to see them, I thought. Three victims, each with multiple gunshot wounds. "We've also got two units of auxiliary police," the voice said, "and whatever firemen they can spare from the fire scene on the way to help lift and carry."

Steve stared at the closed elevator doors. "I assume this is the only elevator."

"I'm afraid so," Marge said. "I've been here a few times before."

"Then I guess we walk," he grumbled. There weren't a lot of buildings in this neighborhood with working elevators, so when there was one, it was disappointing not to be able to use it.

In EMS, medics and EMTs tease about "the rule of threes." The rule states that if the patient weighs more than three hundred pounds, or if it's after three in the morning, or there are more than three flights of stairs to climb, the patient is going to die. The rule, of course, is a joke. We prepared to climb seven flights of stairs.

As we climbed, our arms filled with equipment, I thought, we'll have to carry our patient back down, too. That is, of course, if there is a viable patient. Shit. Shit. Shit. I hate this stuff. I shifted the trauma bag and longboard I was carrying to a more comfortable position, but that didn't make climbing any easier. Marge carried the megaduffel with its heavy oxygen tank, trauma supplies, and oxygen masks in one arm and the collar bag in the other and Steve struggled with the Reeves and a second oxygen cylinder.

As we passed the fourth floor, I was puffing and walking much more slowly. We rested for a moment on five, then continued upward.

We exited the stairwell on the eighth floor panting, my thighs screaming at the unfamiliar exertion. The sight that greeted our eyes made us forget our exhaustion. The walls of the hallway around the elevator were spattered with blood and there were young people's bodies draped everywhere. "What have we got?" I asked a Davenport cop.

He pointed to two bodies off to one side. "Those two are gone. The head of one is blown away and the other's got no chest left." I closed my eyes and swallowed hard. "Sorry," the cop said, "I forget you're not used to this."

"You are?"

"It happens too often here." He waved his arm at the carnage. "This was supposed to be a peace conference." He took a deep breath. "There's one in the back of the elevator with one wound in the belly and one in the thigh. Another in the elevator doorway who's got one in the neck but the bleeding's not too bad. The shot seems to have missed everything vital." He pointed to a boy lying in the middle of the hallway. There was a smear of blood leading from the elevator to the spot where he lay. "He's got a chest wound."

"Davenport Unit 3 on location, Washington Towers," the officer's radio squawked. Never was I so glad to hear another rig.

"What shall I tell them you need?" the officer asked.

Steve was already kneeling beside the belly wound so I answered, "One more longboard or Reeves to carry a victim, oxygen, and trauma supplies."

The cop relayed to the Davenport ambulance crew, who responded affirmatively. "We're on our way up."

Marge was examining the boy with the neck wound so I crouched beside the unconscious boy in the hallway with the gunshot wound to the chest. His lips were light bluish, his forehead was damp with sweat, and he was struggling to breathe. I pulled on my gloves and went to work. I checked his airway, then cut up the front of his shirt and exposed his chest. There was a two-inch diameter hole below his right nipple from which pinkish froth gurgled. More froth drizzled from his mouth.

I placed my palm against the wound, sealing the chest and preventing any more air from entering his chest cavity. Exit wound, I told myself. "I need to check his back," I said to one of the cops. "Can you help me with him? I've only got one hand." I couldn't release the pressure on the hole in his chest.

"Let him fuckin' bleed to death," a man in a plaid flannel shirt said from an open doorway. "Let 'em all fuckin' rot."

"Sir," one of the officers said, "please go into your apartment and close the door."

"Fuckin' scum. Used to be a nice neighborhood. Drugged-out little shits!" He spat onto the tile floor.

As the officer knelt beside the boy he said to the man in the doorway, "Sir, I asked you to go into your apartment." He reached out and I handed him a pair of latex gloves.

The man spat again, muttered, "Fuckin' goddamn scum," then withdrew and slammed his apartment door.

"What do you need me to do?" the cop asked me.

Three officers "escorted" two handcuffed teenage boys past me toward the stairs. "Found them on the roof," one cop said.

One of the boys looked down at the boy on the floor. "Spic bastard."

"I need to check the boy's back," I said to the officer next to me. He lifted the boy's shoulder slightly so I could reach my free hand underneath and palpate his back. No wound that I could feel and, as I pulled my hand back out, my glove had no additional blood on it. I ran my hands under the boy's buttocks and upper thighs, but found no exit wound for the bullet. "See anything?" I asked the officer.

"No. Not a thing," he answered.

I unwrapped a large trauma dressing and said, "See if you can clean him off so I can try to seal that wound." Any time I released the pressure, I could hear the sucking sound of air entering the boy's chest cavity. And he was having increasing trouble breathing. As the officer wiped the blood and froth from the boy's chest, I yelled, "Can someone get me an oxygen tank? Do we have one that's not in use?"

"No," Steve yelled back. "I need this one and Marge's got the other. Both patients are critical."

"Okay." Using my teeth and my free hand, I ripped the plastic packaging from another trauma dressing and folded the plastic envelope into a three-inch square. I lifted my palm from the wound and placed the plastic against the boy's chest, covering the hole. "Duct tape, anyone?" I yelled.

"Here," Marge called back and a policeman passed me the thick silver roll.

"Anyone not gloved?" It's very difficult to pull off hunks of tape with gloved fingers.

"Me. Can I help?" This officer looked about fourteen, but he seemed anxious to assist.

"Yeah," I said. "Pull off strips just longer than this plastic patch and hand them to me carefully, by the end. I don't want to get my gloves all stuck to the tape. There are scissors on the floor here." I motioned with my head.

The officer cut a first piece of tape and I took it and sealed the plastic to the boy's chest. As I taped two more sides, the officer with the trauma dressing wiped the boy's skin to make a drier, better-sticking surface. The young officer handed me a fourth piece of tape, and I taped the last side of the airtight dressing.

"You missed a corner," one officer said.

"I know. It'll act like a flutter valve. As he inhales, it'll seal so no air will get in. As he breathes out, air will escape from his chest cavity and help him breathe." The most immediately life-threatening injury had been taken care of for the moment and his breathing became a bit easier.

I next checked the boy's level of consciousness. "Can you hear me?" I yelled into his ear. Getting no response, I used my knuckle and rubbed his sternum, the heavy breastbone. He groaned but didn't move. He's a "P" on the AVPU scale, I told myself.

The AVPU scale is used to evaluate a patient's level

of consciousness. "A" means the patient is alert. He responds to his name and can answer questions. "V" means that he only responds to loud, verbal stimulus and only remains responsive for a moment. A patient who gets a "V" on the AVPU scale will wake briefly when yelled at, then lapse back into unconsciousness.

My patient was a "P." He responded to painful stimulus, like the sternal rub I gave him, but didn't respond to a voice command. A patient who doesn't respond at all is given a "U" for unresponsive.

I reached for the boy's wrist and felt a weak, thready pulse, beating too quickly to count. I estimated his rapid, shallow respirations at thirty at least.

"What's the situation?" a loud voice said. I turned and saw three Davenport EMTs emerge from the stairway.

"I need oxygen for this boy, stat," I said loudly.

An older Davenport member dropped to a crouch beside me and unzipped his oxygen duffel. "I'm Chuck. What's the story with him?" he asked, attaching the tubing from a non-rebreather mask to the cylinder's regulator.

"I sealed a sucking chest wound. No exit wound that I could find. No other serious injuries but I haven't done a full secondary yet. Pulse too fast to count, resps too fast and shallow but better than they were, BP probably about 90. He's got a weak, thready pulse."

"Bag him?"

"Don't know. We've got to get him down all those stairs. What do you think?"

"I think I want to use the elevator," Chuck said with a weak grin. He placed the oxygen mask over the boy's face. "How's his breathing now?"

I checked the boy's breathing again. "It's a bit better and his color has improved, too." The blue of his lips had turned slightly pink. "Got a board or a Reeves?"

As another Davenport member dropped to his knees beside me and started to unroll a Reeves stretcher I saw that the boy from the doorway of the elevator had been immobilized on a long backboard. The boy with the belly wound from the back of the elevator was being placed on a Reeves. "If we can wait for a moment," Chuck said, "I think we can use the elevator."

"Hallelujah," I whispered. By the time we had our patient on the Reeves, the elevator doors were closing with the first two victims inside.

"Hey, Chuck. Those two can go in the Fairfax rig," someone said. "We can take your guy in ours. The hospital's ready and they know you're coming in."

During the ten-minute drive to FGH in Davenport's ambulance, I was happy to see that, while the boy's condition didn't improve, it didn't deteriorate any further. We cut off all his clothes and found two other gunshot wounds, one to his lower leg and one to his hand, both minor. There was also a grazing wound to his scalp. We bandaged all his injuries.

When we arrived, the Fairfax ER was organized chaos. One doctor took charge of triaging the patients, deciding which one would receive what type of care first.

While we transferred our patient to the hospital gurney, we watched the boy with the belly wound being wheeled to the OR. While my patient waited for a second surgery team to assemble, a nurse started a line in each arm and an X-ray technician took pictures of his chest and abdomen so the doctors could locate the bullet, still inside his body.

Frequently, a bullet will bounce around inside a victim, and cause additional damage. Occasionally it will end up far from the entrance wound. There is a documented case of a bullet that entered the patient's chest, ricocheted, and exited through his knee.

By the time we left the ER my patient had been wheeled into the elevator on his way to the OR. The third boy was in stable condition and could wait.

Steve, Marge, and I, together with three Davenport

EMTs, stood outside the ER door to catch our breath. "Holy shit," Steve said. "You don't get them like that often in Davenport, do you?"

"Thankfully, not multiple victims like that. But gunshot wounds aren't unusual, I'm sorry to say."

"I think we'll just get back into our little ambulance and mosey back to Fairfax," Marge said.

"Good idea," Steve said. "Good idea."

We do, occasionally, get a gunshot wound. And sometimes we get a call during which we treat the patient and find out what happened later. And sometimes we just wonder.

"Fairfax Police to GKL–642."

"Ambulance on," I said into the mike.

"We have a report from the state police of a shooting in a car on the northbound parkway, just north of the park entrance."

"10–4," I said, "45–01 is responding to the northbound parkway, just north of the park entrance."

"A what?" Dave Hancock said as he pulled on his shoes. "Did he say a shooting?"

"That's what I heard."

In Fairfax, shootings are rare. We probably average one a year and those are usually suicide attempts. I followed Dave and shouted to Linda Potemski, who was in the bedroom taking a nap.

"Coming," Linda yelled. I drove and Dave rode shotgun. As the rig cleared the garage doors, Linda arrived, pressed the button to lower the door, and jumped into the back. "Did you say a shooting?" she shouted through the window to the driver's compartment.

"We'll know soon enough," Dave answered, shaking his head.

Since Truman Park is south of headquarters, we pulled onto the southbound parkway, took the Mill Street exit, drove around, and got onto the parkway northbound. As we approached the park entrance we saw the car almost immediately. A five-year-old black Chevy rested with its front end pressed against the guardrail. A police car was already at the scene and the officer was setting out flares. We left all the lights on the rig flashing to help warn drivers of the accident.

"Situation's safe," the state trooper yelled, so we approached the car. Four young men, all in their middle to late teens, sat in the car, two in front and two in the backseat. All four were big and rough-looking young Caucasian men with assorted tattoos, earrings shaped like skulls, and bandannas wrapped around their foreheads. "What happened?" Dave asked.

"Drive by," the driver said. "A big black car pulled alongside of our car and a guy just started shooting."

"Yeah," another said. "Big black car."

"Was anyone hurt?"

"Yeah," one of the backseat passengers said. "Paulie got hit." He indicated the man next to him.

I looked at Paulie, seated behind the driver. He was lying quite still, hands against his chest. A closer look showed blood seeping between his fingers onto his black polo shirt.

"Joan," Dave said, "you and Linda take care of him. I'll check out the rest of these guys." I silently thanked Dave for putting the women in charge of the injured man and taking the other three himself.

"Are you Paulie?" I asked, talking through the small opening in the boy's window. I didn't want to open the door until I knew the extent of the injuries and the harm that forcing him to change positions might do.

"Yeah," he said. Good, I thought. He's conscious.

As Dave started to check the other men in the car, Linda went around and, after the other backseat passenger climbed out, crawled in and questioned the injured man. "You got it in the chest. Anywhere else?"

"Yeah, lady. My leg." His voice was clear and his

words came out on one breath. His lungs were working fine and he was alert.

"Any pain in your neck or back? In your head?"

"Lady, I already said my chest and my leg. Motherfucker fired two or three shots right into the backseat."

"Your name?"

"Paulie Jensen."

"Okay, Paulie," Linda said. "How old are you?"

"Twenty-one." He looked about seventeen.

"Can I open this door?" I asked Linda.

"Yeah. He's out of the way."

I carefully opened the rear door and helped Linda continue a full survey of Paulie's body. His arms as well as one leg were uninjured.

As Linda cut up the front and sleeves of the man's shirt I saw a tattoo of a snarling wolf on his upper right arm and a full-masted ship on his chest. There was a hole in the hull and blood trickled into the tattooed water.

"Take a deep breath," I told the boy, holding a stethoscope against the sails of the ship. "Lung sounds good bilaterally," I said. "And good, equal expansion." I saw no evidence of serious injury to the rib cage.

"I think we can do without head stabilization," Linda said.

"Yeah, I agree," I said. "Chest wound's closed. The bullet must have ricocheted off a rib. Linda, can you check his leg?"

Linda cut the boy's pants and found an entrance wound on his thigh, midway between his hip and knee. "I've got an entrance wound," she said, palpating the rest of his leg, "but no exit. The bullet's probably still in there."

I bandaged the man's chest wound and Linda took care of the one in his leg. We completed a detailed survey and found no other injuries. "You seem to have gotten away lucky," I said as we transferred Paulie to a long backboard, and then to our stretcher.

"Yeah. Motherfucker. Must've fired at least ten shots."

It was three shots before, I thought. Dave reported that none of the others in the car had been injured by the "drive by" so we began our trip to FGH. We wrote our report on the way, then talked with the boy. "What did the guy who shot you look like?"

"How the hell should I know? Black. Yeah. He was black."

"In the front seat of the car or in the back?" Linda asked.

"In the backseat. There were four of them."

"Well," Linda said. "You were very lucky. Your friends, too."

"Yeah, lady," he said, rubbing his leg. "Real lucky."

We arrived at the hospital and transferred Paulie to a gurney. Linda got the paperwork signed, and Dave and I put clean linen on our stretcher. As we pushed the stretcher out through the sliding doors of the ambulance entrance, a state police car pulled up and a tall, slender officer got out. I recognized him as the one who had been setting out flares when we arrived at the shooting scene. "Hey, thanks, guys," he said. "You got there real fast. Did he tell you about the guys in the other car?"

"Yeah. He said four black men. The one in the rear passenger side shot him, he says," Linda said.

"Good story," the officer replied, "but not good enough."

"What do you mean?" I asked.

"Well, the driver of the car said there were four men, Hispanics, and one of the other passengers said there were two black guys. We searched their car and found a stash of cocaine and pot."

"I'm totally confused," I admitted.

"So were we until we found a .38 police special in the bushes about fifty yards from the car. We think these guys got into some kind of fight and someone in the car shot your victim."

"Oh," I said, shaking my head. "I'm glad that's for you to figure out."

He wrinkled his nose. "Thanks. Sometimes I do love my job." He walked into the hospital, and we got into the rig and returned to headquarters.

One of the things I most enjoy is teaching would-be EMTs the skills they will need to care for victims of all the various types of emergencies that he or she might encounter. We teach about auto accidents, heart attacks, childbirth, and so much more.

As EMTs we also must attend a refresher class every three years and, since we teach with, and are taught by, an assortment of instructors, we acquire new skills and techniques. We learn as much from each other as from books. Occasionally, however, we discover that what we've taught for many years in the classroom isn't true.

I was at headquarters helping Tim Babbett, one of our newer members, learn his way around the ambulance. Together we were prowling through the cabinets, drawers, and compartments of the rig, discussing each piece of equipment and what it was used for.

"There's so much, Joan," Tim said as I placed the megaduffel back onto its shelf and snapped it into place. "How am I going to remember everything?"

"You're going to be patient with yourself and ask a lot of questions. Then, maybe the third or fourth time you hear something, it'll begin to stick. And, most important, if someone asks you to get something at a scene, and you don't remember what it is, or where it is, ask. Don't run to the rig and hope that a magic voice will enlighten you. We all started as probationers."

The tones went off and Tim and I jumped. "Fairfax Police to the ambulance. We need at least one rig for a personal-injury accident on the southbound parkway, just south of the Route 10 entrance."

"10–4," I heard Heather Franks say from the kitchen.

She stuck her head out the door and looked questioningly at me. I nodded and turned to Tim. "Want to go along? Heather's on duty alone."

"Sure," he said. "As long as I don't have to know anything."

Heather and I both smiled. "You don't," we said in unison. We both knew that Tim had the makings of a fine EMT. He just needed experience. Heather returned to the mike. "We have a crew of three responding in 45–01. Please page out for one more member to meet us at the scene and a second crew to stand by at headquarters in case they're needed. We'll radio what we need when we get to the scene."

"10–4," police dispatcher Mark Thomas said.

Heather jumped into the driver's seat and pulled the rig out onto the apron. Telling Tim to get into the back, I closed the garage door behind the rig and, as Heather flipped on the lights and siren, I got into the passenger seat.

It took only about two minutes to arrive at the back end of the traffic jam that the accident had created. Despite the siren, it took almost three additional minutes to make our way through the pack of cars. As we listened to the police tone out for additional personnel, I heard Jack McCaffrey say that he was responding to the scene and several more people were en route to headquarters for a second crew.

Finally, we arrived at the two still-steaming vehicles, nose to nose, spread across the left and center lanes. Several people were out of their cars, blocking traffic and creating additional chaos. I saw the flashing lights of a state trooper car as it pulled onto the grassy median from the northbound lane. An officer got out with several flares in his hands.

Heather pulled up just behind the two smashed vehicles, using the flashing lights from the rig to warn traffic of the accident. She jumped out of the driver's seat and started toward the car in the left lane, a large dark blue station wagon facing the wrong way. We left Tim to gather equipment. Pulling on gloves, I ran toward the car in the center lane, a south-facing small black Toyota.

I leaned into the driver's window and saw Bruce and Mary Dolan, the two EMT instructors who had taught my most recent refresher class. Mary, in the passenger seat, had an oxygen mask already in place and was taking shallow breaths. Bruce, in the driver's seat, was holding his left arm.

"Oh, Joan," Bruce said. "I'm so glad to see your face."

You never know how even the best-trained people are going to react when they are themselves injured so I asked my first question, unsure of how professional the response would be. "How are you and how's Mary?" I needn't have worried.

"Mary's having difficulty breathing," Bruce said. "Her respirations are 24 and shallow. I suspect broken ribs and internal injuries. I had an oxygen cylinder in my trunk so I put her on a non-rebreather. Her door won't open."

"You've been out of the car?" I said.

"I had to get her on oxygen," Bruce said. "We were both belted, but that guy crossed the divider and hit us real hard." He stared at the station wagon, then looked back at me. "Just take care of Mary and get her out of here, quick."

"I will. How are you?"

"My left arm's broken, an open radius-ulna, but it's not serious. It gave me some trouble when I tried to lift the oxygen, but I managed. Take care of Mary first. I'll be all right."

"Any other cars involved that you know about?"

"I don't think so, but the accident's a bit of a blur."

"Okay, Bruce. Just sit tight." As I rounded the front

of the car, I waved at Heather, who was trotting back toward the rig. Since, except for Bruce and Mary, we were the only trained EMTs around, we had to coordinate and work where we were most needed. "What have you got?" I asked.

"The driver of the wagon is okay. She's complaining of neck and back pain and I need to do a full immobilization. She was belted, and I think it's really All-State-itis. What about you?"

"It's Bruce and Mary Dolan. They're pretty banged up."

Heather looked shocked. Like most of the members of our corps and all the surrounding corps and rescue squads, she had been a student of theirs. "Oh shit, is it serious?"

"Bruce gave me a complete report. Mary's having trouble breathing and he has an open left radius-ulna fracture. I haven't done much of a survey myself yet."

"I'll have Tim stay with the station wagon lady and we can work on Bruce and Mary." She called Tim over. "Tim," she said calmly, "stay with the driver of the station wagon and try to keep her from moving around. Just keep her calm while we tend to the people in the other car. You don't have to do anything else."

Tim was a bit wide-eyed, but he was a sensible young man. He nodded and walked toward the wagon.

"It looks like we'll need to do full immobilizations times three," I said. Three fully immobilized patients meant we would need at least one more rig. "Call for 45–02," I told Heather, "then bring an oxygen cylinder for Bruce. I'll do a complete survey and see what else we'll need."

As Heather trotted toward the ambulance to radio for more help, I saw Jack McCaffrey pull his car onto the median and run over. "Where do you need me?" he asked.

"It's Bruce and Mary Dolan," I said. "You take her."

Not understanding, Jack said, "If Bruce and Mary are here, what do you want me to do?"

"Bruce and Mary are the victims," I said, and saw his surprised expression. "In that car." I pointed.

"Damn," Jack said under his breath.

"Yeah, damn. Take Mary. She's on the passenger side. Bruce says the door's jammed. She's having difficulty breathing, with possible broken ribs. She's on Bruce's O_2. See whether you think we should do a rapid extrication or a full immobilization." If Jack decided Mary's condition was serious, we would forgo the KED and just collar her and carefully transfer her directly to a long backboard.

Jack rounded the car and leaned into the passenger window. Knowing Mary was in capable hands, I returned to Bruce.

I carefully opened the door and said, "Just sit tight, Bruce, and let me do a full assessment." I grinned. "Just like you teach it in class."

"But Mary . . ."

"Jack's taking care of your wife," I told him. "Let me do my job the way you would do it if it were someone else sitting here."

Reluctantly Bruce agreed. Heather returned and put the megaduffel on the ground beside me, handed an MCI bag to Jack, and took another MCI bag to the station wagon. For a multiple casualty incident, an accident in which there are many patients, the rig carries a number of small crash kits, containing trauma supplies, BP cuff, stethoscope, scissors, and other items that might be needed. The megaduffel I was using contained all that an MCI bag had, and additional supplies and oxygen equipment.

I heard a voice behind me. "Joan," Sam Middleton said, "what can I do?"

"Hook up a non-rebreather for Bruce." I watched Sam's face as he realized who our patients were. Other

EMTs arrived, and I watched Fred Stevens climb into the backseat and hold Bruce's head. Someone was getting the immobilization equipment from the rig's side compartment. "Bruce," I said, "we're going to do a full immobilization on you and take you out first. Since Mary's door won't open, we'll wait, then take her out your door after you're out of the way."

"But I've been out, walking around. I'm fine." He started to get out of the car.

"Stop and think, Bruce. Mary's stable and in good shape. Would you let someone in your condition get out and walk around? What would you do if you were me?"

Bruce's shoulders slumped. "What are Mary's vitals?"

"Jack?"

"BP's 135 over 85, her pulse is 80, and her resps are 26 and shallow," Jack reported. "I'm about to expose her chest and check her ribs."

"Okay, Bruce?" I said. "Her vitals are good. Let us do our job."

"You're right, of course," Bruce said.

"Someone get a short splint so we can take care of this open fracture," I said, using my shears to cut Bruce's jacket.

"Joan." I heard a small voice from the passenger seat. I glanced over at Mary. "Could you come around and stay with me? You can let Jack take care of Bruce."

Unsure why, but certainly willing to help, I switched places with Jack. While he splinted Bruce's arm, I looked at Mary. "Is there a problem?" I asked softly.

"You know," she said, around the oxygen mask, "we teach that there's no sex in first aid. I just discovered that that's bull. When you're in the middle of the parkway, about to have your clothes cut off by EMTs who were your students, there most certainly is sex in first aid."

We laughed together, glad to lighten the scene. It took only a few minutes for Jack and his crew to immobilize Bruce. Once he was out, I rechecked Mary's vitals and found them unchanged. As Bruce was lifted into the rig with the driver of the other car, we immobilized Mary. When she was ready, we moved her to the second ambulance and sped to the trauma center.

Bruce remained in the hospital for several days, after surgery to repair his broken arm. Mary was hospitalized longer, with three broken ribs and internal injuries. I'm happy to report, though, that they are now both teaching again. Mary and I, however, are a bit more careful when we teach that there's no sex in first aid.

In the story about the gang war, you learned one of the tongue-in-cheek rules that EMTs have developed over the years, "the rule of threes." Every profession has them, the sillinesses like Murphy's Law that usually appear on everyone's desk or in everyone's mailbox. No one will ever take credit for making the copies. Everyone laughs at them, but in most cases they contain a grain of truth or a slice of wishful thinking.

Here are some of the RULES OF EMS.

THE FIRST LAW OF EMS

All emergency calls will wait until the crew begins to eat, regardless of the time.

CONCLUSION #1—Fewer accidents would occur if EMTs didn't eat.

CONCLUSION #2—Always order food to go.

COROLLARY TO THE FIRST LAW

If you've finished eating and go to the bathroom, the tones *will* go off just as you sit down.

THE LAW OF LATE-NIGHT RUNS

If you respond to a personal-injury accident and you don't find a drunk, keep looking. You probably missed a patient.

THE LAWS OF MEDICAL EQUIPMENT

1. Interchangeable parts aren't.
2. Leakproof seals will.
3. Self-starters won't.

THE BASIC RULE OF PATIENTS

The more the patient yells, the less serious the injury.

THE BASIC TENETS OF EMS

1. If it hurts when you do this, don't do this.
2. If it ain't broke, don't fix it.
3. Air goes in and out, blood goes round and round, and if either of these stops, the patient is in deep trouble.

THE RULE OF HEROISM

Everyone's a hero until someone vomits.

THE PRINCIPLE OF MOTORCYCLE HELMETS

The proper term for a helmetless motorcyclist is an organ donor.

THE LAWS OF EMS PHYSICS

LIGHT: As the seriousness of any injury increases, the availability of light to examine the wound decreases.

SPACE: As the amount of space to work on the patient decreases the amount needed increases. Since the bathroom is always the smallest room in any house, guess where you'll find the patient.

RELATIVITY: The number of hysterical and uncooperative relatives increases with the seriousness of the patient's condition.

WEIGHT: The heavier the patient, the smaller your partner.

WEIGHT PART 2: The weight of the patient increases as the number of stairs you have to carry him down increases.

COROLLARY 1—Very heavy patients seem to gravitate upward, and toward the end of winding hallways.

COROLLARY 2—If the patient is exceptionally heavy, the elevator will not operate and the lights on the stairway will be broken.

This "Law of Weight" leads to the "Rule of Threes," which you learned earlier.

THE RULE OF LIGHTS AND SIRENS

Any emergency vehicle with lights flashing and siren wailing, whether responding to a call or traveling to the hospital, will be totally ignored by all drivers, pedestrians, and small and large animals within a three-block radius.

COROLLARY 1—Ambulance lights cause total, acute blindness. This condition is temporary.

COROLLARY 2—Ambulance sirens cause total, acute deafness. This condition is also temporary.

THE ULTIMATE RULE

Once a rule of EMS is accepted as absolute, an exception will be found.

And lastly, this quote:

We EMTs are a committed bunch of people. Not just involved but committed to everything we do.

Do you know the difference between involved and committed? In a bacon-and-egg breakfast, the chicken's involved, but the pig's committed.

Chapter 7

Every ambulance corps and rescue squad has to deal with them. They are called "regulars" or "frequent fliers." They are usually old and lonely and frightened. In the early morning hours, when the world is dark and silent and they are unable to sleep, the only way for them to get the human contact that they desperately need is to call for an ambulance, whether or not they have any medical problem. And when they call, we respond, sometimes furious inside at "these people who abuse our service," but we try to act as courteously as we do with any other patient.

I bolted upright in bed as the telephone rang. "Oh shit," I hissed, my usual expletive upon hearing the ring of the phone in the middle of the night when Joan and I are on duty with FVAC. I started to throw on my clothes as Joan got the information from Fairfax Police.

Joan hung up the phone. "Relax, Ed," she said. "It's Benny DiAngelo again. Bob Fiorella will bring the rig and meet us at his apartment."

As Joan put on her uniform, I fell back on the bed, desperately wanting to climb back under the blanket. It was January and cold outside. "Why does he always call when *we're* on duty?" I moaned.

"I guess he likes us," Joan replied. "And, if truth be told, it's not just us, it's every crew. He's called three times this week already."

"He's ours tonight, lucky us. Well, tonight I'm gonna

tell him off. There's never anything really wrong with him. He has no right to tie up an ambulance with his bullshit. What if someone really needs us and we're busy with one of Benny's bullshit calls? We ought to have him arrested for filing false reports. It's against the law to call an ambulance when you don't need one. . . ."

I was still railing about Benny's lack of consideration as we rushed out into the winter night. A light snow was just beginning to whiten the road. "Oh, great," I complained. "We'll probably get killed driving on these roads because of Benny."

Joan ignored my verbal tirade as I carefully drove the few miles to Benny's apartment. Fairfax Police Officer Eileen Flynn was already at the scene by the time we arrived, seated on the sofa next to Benny, talking to him and taking notes for her report. "Benny has been feeling dizzy," she told us.

As soon as I saw him my anger evaporated. Benny is seventy-eight, withered and stooped, with a turned-down mouth and deep wrinkles all over his face. "Hi, Benny," I said. "What seems to be the problem tonight?"

"I'm dizzy."

"How long have you been feeling dizzy, Benny?" Eileen got up and I sat beside Benny on the sofa.

"Oh, for a few days."

"Well, why did you call us tonight?"

"You know, my son-in-law is a doctor and he thinks I have something wrong with me."

"When did you see your son-in-law?"

"Oh, a couple of weeks ago." I knew that his daughter and son-in-law rarely visited him. Most of the time he was alone.

For many years after the death of his wife, Benny lived by himself in Hillcrest, a senior residence, and he did well. He walked into town and had lunch at the diner. He bought his few necessities at the various stores around Fairfax, then walked back home. He sat in the lobby and chatted with the other elderly residents.

Then one day Benny watched the police break into the apartment next door. Someone had alerted them that his neighbor at Hillcrest hadn't been seen recently and, when they finally entered the apartment, the woman's body was found, lying in the middle of the kitchen floor. She had been dead for three days. Benny became terrified that, like her, he would die alone, and he started to call 911 as often as five or six times a week.

There were weeks when he felt calmer and didn't call at all, but then his panic would begin again and he would start calling. Some of the Fairfax Police and FVAC members would take time to visit him when they were off duty. It seemed to help a bit.

"Isn't your son a veterinarian?"

"Yes, but he knows all about my problems."

"Benny, why did you call us tonight?"

"I have sixteen grandchildren, you know. And two great-grandchildren. They visit me all the time."

"Benny, why did you call us tonight?"

"I'm dizzy."

"But you said that you've been dizzy for a few days, Benny. Why did you call us *tonight*?"

"I can't breathe."

"Does it hurt when you breathe?"

"No, but my nose is stuffed up."

"Benny, you don't need an ambulance for a stuffed nose." I was torn between sadness for his situation and anger at being called to his apartment at three in the morning.

"But I feel kind of light-headed."

"Okay, Benny, why don't we check you out."

I examined Benny and found that his blood pressure, pulse and respiration, lung sounds, and neurological functions were all normal. "You seem to be okay, Benny. We'll take you to the hospital if you want, but it's awfully cold outside."

"Well, I do feel a little better now. Have you seen the pictures of my grandchildren? This one is Louisa." He pulled a wrinkled photo out of a drawer next to the sofa and held it out to us. "She's in high school now."

After we spent a while talking to Benny, he signed an RMA, refusing medical attention. "Would you feed my cat?" Benny asked.

"I already did, Benny," Joan said from the kitchen door. "Mazie is doing just fine." She handed Benny a cup. "Tea?"

"Thank you very much."

We left a few minutes later. We will undoubtedly see Benny again soon, we thought, and next time he will probably insist, as he usually does, on being transported to the hospital where he will be fed and there will be lots of people to talk to.

On the way home, Joan reminded me of the time that a new FVAC member was the first one to arrive at Benny's house. "He was taking vitals and writing down Benny's medical history. Remember his shock when you and I went directly into the kitchen without even saying hello to Benny? You fed the cat while I brewed Benny a cup of tea."

"Oh Lord, I'd almost forgotten. No one had told him about Benny. He thought we were nuts."

"You know, if we'd stop being nice to him he'd stop calling us."

"Would he?"

It was almost 4:00 A.M. when we got back into bed. "By the way, Ed," Joan teased, "I like the way you finally told him off."

"Shut up, wise ass," I grunted as I snuggled against her and fell asleep.

Recently Benny died. Alone.

It was a warm summer afternoon and Martin Ryan had taken his five-year-old daughter, Patti, with him when he had left the house so that his wife could have some time to herself. When Patti traveled with her mom, she always had to sit in the backseat, but Martin allowed her to sit in the front seat next to him.

They were on their way back home after picking up some equipment that they would need for their camping trip the following week and Martin was carefully negotiating the narrow road that wound along the shore of Fairfax reservoir. Martin loved spending time with his pretty, bright daughter, but sometimes he would become impatient with her. Patti asked so many questions, and he often didn't know the answers.

"Daddy," Patti asked, "why does Mommy make me sit in the back?"

"Oh, she just worries a lot, pumpkin," he answered. "She thinks you're safer in the back."

"Am I?"

"Well, I guess so. But I drive carefully and we're not going far."

"I like riding in the front." Patti beamed. "I like to pretend that I'm driving. Claire's mom and dad always make her sit in the back and wear a seat belt. When Claire's mom drives me home from school she won't even move the car before I have my seat belt on."

"Claire's mom worries too much," Martin snapped. It's the damn government, he thought. Always making new regulations. Always trying to scare people and interfere with their personal lives. They're probably in cahoots with the seat-belt manufacturers. Yeah. What the hell do they care if someone burns to death in a car because they can't get out of their seat belt?

Patti stared at her father, surprised by his sudden irritability.

Martin had just rounded the last curve before coming out onto Route 10 when a doe dashed out of the woods to his left. He slammed on his brakes and instinctively pulled the steering wheel to the right. Because he had not been driving very fast, the car had almost come to a stop when it bounced hard into a small drainage ditch that ran along the roadway.

* * *

I was making up a new batch of sugar solution for the hummingbirds that had been visiting my feeder. Both a male and a female had been coming to the feeder, though never together. That morning, two new hummingbirds had arrived together, fed together, and had then flown off together. They were probably young birds, I thought. Adult ruby-throated hummingbirds are solitary and never do anything together except mate. The two birds had probably been immature males. They had dark green feathers on their backs, like males, but they did not yet have the adult's brilliant red throat feathers.

I added a cup of sugar to four cups of water that I had brought to boiling on the stove, then dribbled in a few drops of red food coloring and mixed the solution. I was suddenly interrupted by the beeping of my Prescott Rescue Squad pager.

" . . . to the rescue squad. A full crew is needed for a PIAA on Lake Road just south of Route 10. Please call in."

I turned off the burner, removed the pot of red sugar water, placed it on one of the cold burners, and covered it. The hummingbirds would have to wait. I grabbed the phone and pushed the rescue squad speed-dial button.

"Prescott Fire Department, dispatcher McCann speaking."

"Hi, Ted, it's Ed Herman. I'll come to the firehouse as the EMT."

"Okay, Ed."

As I got into my car and switched on the blue light, I heard the pager again.

"Prescott Dispatch to the rescue squad. An attendant is still needed for a PIAA on Lake Road. Will an attendant please call in."

Since only an attendant was now needed, a driver must have called in, I thought, as I wheeled toward the Prescott firehouse.

Then, "Prescott Dispatch to the rescue squad. Be advised the call on Lake Road is covered."

Good, we had a full crew.

I pulled into the firehouse parking lot just ahead of Max Taylor, our driver. We got into the ambulance and rolled it out onto the apron. Less than a minute later Brenda Frost arrived and, with siren wailing, we headed toward Lake Road.

Officer Stan Garth met me as I stepped out of the ambulance. "There's only one patient," he told me. "It's a five-year-old girl. She has a gash on her forehead but seems to be okay. Her father was the only other person in the car and he's already signed an RMA for himself."

As I walked over to the almost-undamaged car that rested, nose down, in a drainage ditch, Prescott officer Mike Gold was kneeling at the passenger-side door and next to him was a man who appeared to be in his middle twenties. Mike was holding a gauze dressing over a little girl's forehead.

"What have you got, Mike?" I asked.

Mike looked up at me. "Hi, Ed. This is Patti and that's her dad," he said, nodding toward the man next to him. "Patti has a cut on her head. It was bleeding pretty badly when I arrived but it's stopped now. Do you want to see it?"

"No," I replied. "I'll just bandage it as it is. Why don't you just maintain head stabilization?"

Although I would have preferred to see how severe the cut was, removing the dressing might have started it bleeding again. Patti was sitting upright on the front seat, facing me. I knelt so that my head was level with hers. "Hi, Patti," I said. "My name is Ed. Does anything hurt you besides your head?"

"No," Patti replied, sizing me up.

"Patti, Mike is going to hold your head still while I put a bandage on your head. Is that all right?"

Patti began to sniffle. "Will it hurt?"

"No. I'm just going to wrap this roll of gauze around your head so that it doesn't start bleeding again."

"Okay," Patti replied tentatively.

"Were you wearing your seat belt?"

"My daddy said I didn't have to."

"Oh." I said nothing else. It wasn't her fault that her father was an idiot. "Will you do something for me from now on?"

"What?"

"I want you to always buckle up. That way, if you're ever in an accident again, and I hope you're not, you won't be hurt like this."

Patti considered, then said softly, "I promise."

After I finished bandaging Patti's head, I said to her, "Patti, I'm going to tell you everything that I'm going to do now. First, I'm going to put a collar around your neck to keep your head from moving too much. Then I'm going to lay you down on a board and carry you to the ambulance."

I turned to Brenda, who was behind me. "Brenda, why don't you get a pede c-collar and the pede board?"

Patti started to whimper. "No, I don't want a collar. It's going to hurt."

Brenda quietly said to me, "Ed, it took me a while to calm her down. Can't we just skip the collar and board?"

I nodded toward the star-shaped crack in the windshield above the front passenger seat. "She was unrestrained and we have to assume that she broke the windshield with her head," I answered. "I don't want to take any chances."

As Brenda went back to the rig to get the equipment, I turned back to Patti. "I'm not going to do anything that's going to hurt you, Patti. I promise. And I never lie to my patients. You can ask me anything you want and I will always tell you the truth. Now I need to ask you a few things."

While waiting for Brenda to return with the immobilization equipment, I examined Patti further and asked her a number of questions to determine whether she had any other injuries. She appeared to be uninjured other than the head laceration.

"I'm sorry about the seat belt," she said. "But my daddy doesn't . . ."

Patti was interrupted by her father, who had just returned from a conversation with a police officer. "Of course she was wearing a seat belt," he yelled.

I turned toward him.

"She always wears a seat belt. We make sure that she does," he loudly asserted, glancing at the officer standing a few feet away. The officer looked at me and momentarily rolled his eyes skyward.

What a lying sack of shit, I thought.

Brenda returned from the ambulance with a pediatric cervical collar and the pediatric immobilization board. I showed Patti how I was going to use the Velcro to secure the plastic collar around her neck, then applied the collar with no resistance. I showed her the pediatric board that she would lie on, then placed it behind her on the driver's seat. We turned her body and lowered her onto the board, secured her to the board with the attached Velcro straps, placed her on the stretcher, and carried her to the ambulance with only token protests. Realizing that Patti's father was contributing to Patti's uneasiness, I asked him to ride in the front with Max.

In the ambulance I showed Patti the pediatric blood pressure cuff. "I'm going to use this to take your blood pressure," I said.

"Will it hurt?" she asked warily.

"No. It will squeeze your arm a little."

"How will it do that?" she asked, now seeming more interested than fearful.

"I'm going to wrap it around your arm and then squeeze this bulb." I showed her how squeezing the bulb inflated the bladder of the BP cuff.

"How will it feel?" she asked.

"You will just feel some pressure on your arm."

"No. Don't tell me. Show me how it will feel," she demanded.

I grasped her upper right arm and applied some pressure. "About like that," I said.

"Okay," Patti said, and allowed me to take her blood pressure with no further protest.

After completing my assessment of Patti's vital signs, listening to her lung sounds, and checking neurological functions, I signaled the driver that we were ready to leave. "Take it code 2, Max," I said. "Nice and easy."

As we began to roll toward Fairfax General, Patti said, "This collar is uncomfortable. How long will I have to wear it?"

"At the hospital, they will probably want you to wear it until they take an X-ray picture of your neck," I replied.

"Will that hurt?" she asked.

"No. It's just a picture that they take with a big camera."

"Just a picture. Like my daddy takes with his camera?"

"It's a picture of your insides. Maybe, if you ask, they will show it to you."

"Okay," Patti said, now obviously at ease.

I pulled a blue latex examination glove out of the glove box and dangled it in front of Patti. "I'll bet you don't know what this is," I said.

"Yes I do. It's a glove, silly."

"No, it isn't," I teased.

"It is, too."

I held the base of the glove against my mouth and blew into it. The glove inflated until the fingers looked like the crest of some strange bird. I tied it off at the base then took a felt-tip marker out of my pocket and drew a face on the glove.

"It's a balloon," Patti yelled gleefully. "It's a chicken."

"Would you like to have it?" I asked.

"Yes." She laughed, reaching for the inflated glove.

Patti was now completely at ease and talked to me continuously during the ten-minute ride to the hospital.

Shortly after our arrival at the ER, Patti was examined by a doctor. I watched as he removed the bandage and dressing, exposing a wide-open, two-inch, vertical laceration. The doctor said nothing to Patti, but turned to her father.

"She's going to need several stitches and it's going to leave a scar because the cut's vertical," he said in a cold, businesslike voice. "If you want, we can call in a plastic surgeon." The doctor then turned and, without a word to Patti, walked out of the room.

When I went over to Patti to say good-bye, she was crying and too frightened and upset to respond to me. As I left I could hear her asking her father, "Is it going to hurt?" and her father telling her that the stitches "would not hurt a bit." She obviously didn't believe him and continued crying. On the way back to headquarters, I kept hoping that Patti would remember the EMT who didn't lie to her.

As emergency medical responders, we enter people's homes unexpectedly, and what we find is not always pleasant. Although our purpose in being there, and our primary obligation, is to deal with a medical emergency, it is sometimes difficult to deal with what we see, hear, and occasionally smell.

At times what we do or say can profoundly change the lives of other people. A call can be an opportunity to help people who are desperately in need of outside assistance, but it is also an awesome responsibility. It's often hard to decide whether to ignore what we observe or to contact authorities. And sometimes there is really nothing we can do.

On one occasion I was called to the home of an old man having difficulty breathing. When I entered the room it was evident that he had been lying in his own urine for a long period of time. He was filthy, dehydrated, and obviously suffering from malnutrition. He told us that he lived in the house with his son, daughter-in-law, and grandchildren, a family that appeared healthy and friendly, right out of a Norman Rockwell painting.

When I discussed the situation with hospital personnel, they told me that they would talk to the family, but that there was little else that could be done about neglect of an elderly person.

Nor can I forget the pretty little six-year-old girl who had broken her arm "again" by "falling off the swings." She would not answer any of our questions without looking at her father's face to make sure that her answer was okay. Unfortunately, even when we suspect child abuse, usually neither the police nor the hospital are willing to make accusations without some clear evidence.

I was at the Prescott firehouse, replacing first-aid supplies in the trauma kit that I keep in the trunk of my car and talking with Max Taylor, when the Klaxon sounded. Max and I walked over to our dispatcher, who was taking notes as he held the phone to his ear. He hung up the phone and handed us the information. "Infant having a seizure," he told us. "1430 Oliver Street. It's in the new Prescott Acres development."

Febrile seizures in an infant are not uncommon. Brought on by a high fever the seizure causes the child to suddenly become rigid, convulse, and even turn blue. Although it is extremely frightening to the parent, it's usually not a serious problem. By the time the ambulance gets there, the seizure is usually over and the child is breathing normally. Occasionally, however, a child does not start breathing again after a seizure and we have to begin resuscitation. That's why it's important for us to respond as quickly as possible.

Since Max was a driver and willing to go, all we needed was an attendant to complete our crew. "Page out for an attendant to meet us at the scene," I said.

Max and I climbed into the ambulance. Max started the engine, turned on the emergency lights, and pulled out of the firehouse.

"Where's the medic?" Max asked as I switched on the siren.

"I just heard him call back in service from that last call," I answered, shouting over the wail. "He's probably about three minutes behind us."

"Prescott dispatch to Rescue 1," the dispatcher's voice said. "Be advised that EMT Walsh will meet you at the scene."

"10–4," Max said into the mike.

Prescott Acres had been built only three years earlier. The small split-level houses were moderately priced and looked pretty now that the landscaping had started to fill in. We rolled to a stop in front of 1430 Oliver Street. As I strode toward the front door, Max went to the back of the rig to grab a crash kit and an oxygen tank. Prescott Police Officer Roy Zimmerman, who had pulled up just behind the ambulance, followed me up the walk.

As I entered the house, I was totally unprepared for the instant assault on my senses. Although it was a bright sunny day all of the shades and blinds were drawn so that the interior of the house resembled the inside of a cave. The smell of feces and urine assaulted me. As we crossed the entryway, passing two scruffy-looking black-and-tan cats, the soles of our shoes stuck to the floor.

With Roy and Max falling further and further behind me, I walked into the living room. I made my way around a dog and two more cats, toward a woman who appeared to be in her sixties. She sat on a sofa, holding a listless baby who wore only a diaper. Another cat lay draped over the far end of the sofa. None of the animals appeared to have any tags or collars and most were scratching incessantly.

I took a deep breath in through my mouth. "What happened?" I asked the woman.

"The baby's had a cold for a couple of days. I was trying to feed her, but she wouldn't eat. Then her eyes rolled back and she started shaking and choking. She's okay now."

I touched the child's forehead. She was burning up with fever, but she seemed to be breathing normally. "Can we get some light in here?" I asked.

Roy reached over and switched on a floor lamp next to the sofa. As I glanced around I couldn't help but wonder how it was possible to get a new house so filthy in so short a time.

"What's the baby's name?" I asked.

"Ashley Cole. I'm Martha Harris, the baby's grandmother."

"How old is the baby?"

"She's nine months, almost ten."

Trying to touch nothing but my equipment and the child, I took the stethoscope out of the trauma kit and pressed the end against her chest as she lay sleepily in the woman's arms. The baby's lungs sounded normal so I concluded that, fortunately, she hadn't aspirated any food during the seizure. But as I checked further, I found that her breathing and pulse were both rapid. In the light I could see that her body was covered with what appeared to be flea bites. My ankles started to itch and I desperately wanted to get out of that house.

Throughout the exam, the baby gazed at me quietly. "Let's get her into the ambulance so we'll be ready to roll by the time the medic gets here," I suggested.

"I don't think she needs to go to the hospital," the woman said.

"Ma'am, this child is very sick. Her fever's still very high and she may have more seizures. Has she been seen by a doctor?"

"Her parents don't like doctors. They charge too much."

"Where are her parents?" Roy asked.

"They both work. I take care of Ashley during the day."

"Have you called the baby's parents?" Roy continued.

"Yeah. But they can't get away from work."

I heard the sound of an approaching siren as the paramedic fly-car pulled up to the house. Paramedic Amy Chen came in and I briefed her on the baby's condition. Maybe, as a paramedic, she'd carry more weight and be able to convince the grandmother that the baby should be seen at the hospital.

Amy touched the tiny girl's forehead. "Ma'am, this baby has a high fever and really has to go to the hospital," Amy said, catching on to the situation immediately. "As a paramedic I can only reinforce what I'm sure Ed has already told you."

"Can't you just give her some medicine?" the child's grandmother asked.

"I can't give her anything unless you allow us to transport her to the hospital," Amy replied.

"Well, I guess I'll have to wait until her mom and dad come home this evening. They'll kill me if I let you take her to the hospital. Hospitals are so expensive."

"I'm sure they have insurance," Amy said. "And you want your granddaughter to have the best of care, don't you?"

The woman sat, cradling the baby, who had drifted into a light sleep. "My daughter will take Ashley to the doctor when she comes home from work," she insisted.

Roy stepped in. "That's enough of this nonsense," he exclaimed in his most authoritative cop voice. "Let these people take the baby to the hospital and stop giving them a hard time. They're just trying to help your grandchild."

"No." The woman stiffened. "Her mother will take

her to the doctor when she comes home from work and that's that. I'm in change of her and you can't take her without my permission."

We continued to argue with the woman, but could not convince her to allow us to take the baby to the hospital.

Roy walked out of the room, beckoning Amy and me to follow, while Max and Sally Walsh, our attendant who had just arrived, continued to talk to the woman.

"Is this a life-threatening situation?" Roy asked.

"Not right now," Amy replied, "but it could easily become one if the baby seizes again. It's very possible with that fever."

"Then the woman is right, I'm afraid," Roy said. "I can't force her to let you take the child."

I closed my eyes and sighed. "Well, I guess we've done all we can," I said reluctantly. Then I reached down and scratched my ankle. "Let's get her to sign an RMA and get the hell out of here. Maybe when she realizes we're leaving she'll change her mind."

She didn't. She signed the form refusing medical attention and transport and we left the house. After Amy drove away in the fly-car, I went over to the patrol car where Roy was writing his report.

"Roy, don't you think that child protective services should be advised of the situation? I've never seen such filth."

"Oh, I don't know, Ed. It certainly was disgusting but if someone barged into my house before my wife had time to clean up, they might think the same thing." Roy went back to his report.

I was unable to get the house and the baby out of my mind all night so the next morning I decided to call Amy Chen.

"Amy, about that call yesterday; the infant seizure."

"Yeah, Ed. I know. No kid should be raised in such filth. I've written a report to child protective services, but I'm still debating with myself whether or not to send it. You know, once they get involved with a family they're pretty hard to get rid of."

"I'd feel terrible if we did nothing. Why don't you file your report and I'll back you and file one myself. All we have to do is write what we saw and heard and smelled. The rest is up to the county."

Amy and I filed our reports, and we know that the family was visited by child protective services. We don't know whether the baby was ever taken to a doctor or what action child protective services took, but we were not called again. I assume that the child recovered and I hope that the conditions under which she was being brought up improved. We regret any inconvenience that our report may have caused, but so be it.

Emotionally disturbed persons—EDPs—give us some of our most difficult calls. Often, with psych emergencies, the ambulance corps receives the call from the police by phone since they don't like to put any details out over the radio.

I was on duty with Joan one afternoon, picking up some extra hours. We were deep into a game of Boggle when the phone rang. "Sorry, guys," Mark Thomas, the police dispatcher said. "I've got an emergency transport to the county psych ER for you. The guy's getting violent and the psychiatrist from crisis intervention thinks we better get him down there fast." He gave us the address. "And no lights or sirens. Just get the guy out of there."

"We're responding," I said as Dave Hancock, our third EMT, got into the driver's seat and Joan climbed into the back of the ambulance.

When we arrived in the driveway, an officer met us. "Joan, you'd better stay in the rig, out of sight. He's a nutcase and totally off on women. Let Ed and Dave run things. When we transport they can stay in the back, and you can drive." Joan nodded. I was sure that driving was fine with her. We all find that being in the back of the rig with someone who's not reacting rationally is very nerve-wracking. You don't know what will trigger a reaction or what that reaction might be.

It took about fifteen minutes to get the man loaded into the rig. When they were settled, Dave called to Joan through the window between the box and the cab. "Okay, Jo . . . Okay, Joe," he said. "Our patient seems to have settled down and we have an officer with us. Take us to the psych ER and you can take it as a transport."

No lights and sirens, Dave meant, so Joan proceeded at normal speed toward the parkway.

I sat on the crew bench and watched the patient, who was completely unaware of my presence. "Goddamn broads!" the man said loudly. "Think they own the world. They don't own me. I don't have to do what any of them say." Then he followed with a string of colorful expressions about the nature of women, spiced with four-letter words and phrases that left little to the imagination. About halfway to the hospital, he began to outline exactly what sexual things he was going to do to the next woman he saw. About five minutes from the hospital, he focused on my face and said, "Hey, guys, I gotta pee."

"We're almost at the hospital," I said, with no intention of stopping the rig or letting him out of the seat belts that were holding him against the stretcher. "You can go there."

"Yeah, but I gotta pee, bad."

"I'm sorry, sir," I said. "Try not to think about it. It'll be just a few moments."

"Try not to think about it? I gotta pee."

"The only other thing I can do," I said, "is to give you a urinal and you can use it while we drive."

He considered, then said, "I'll wait, I guess. Goddamn broads. Make you wait. Can't even let you pee."

Since he was unaware that we had a female driving, I wasn't sure what women had to do with our not letting him pee. But at least he had finally realized that we weren't going to make a rest stop for him.

When we arrived at St. Luke's, Dave and I lifted the patient, stretcher and all, from the ambulance and wheeled him into the ER. St. Luke's Trauma Center is a huge facility. In addition to being a level-one trauma center, its huge psychiatric facility has its own rapid admissions area, referred to as the psych ER. As usual, the large, comfortably furnished room was almost empty, with only a few visitors waiting for permission to see friends and family on the upper floors. There were several nurses and two or three burly orderlies waiting for the next adventure.

"I gotta pee," our patient shouted, gaining the attention of everyone in the ER.

"Of course, sir," a female nurse said, unaware of our patient's difficulty with women. "Is he in restraints?" she asked me.

The doctor from crisis control who had signed the patient over to us at his home hadn't ordered any restraints. "No. But he's a bit agitated."

"Oh, that's all right. I'll take him to the bathroom." She unsnapped the stretcher seat belts and helped the man to his feet. "Can you walk, sir?" she asked, taking his arm.

"Keep your fuckin' hands offa me," he shouted, yanking his arm from her grasp. "Just show me the john."

"Just follow me," the nurse said in a syrupy voice.

As the man disappeared down the hall with the nurse and a security guard trailing behind, Joan walked in. "Where is our patient?" she asked.

"He said that he had to pee so a nurse and a security guard took him to the bathroom." I shrugged, waving the papers with the admitting nurse's signature at the bottom. "Not my job now."

As I finished the state paperwork, I heard a commotion coming from the hallway outside the hospital bathroom. "Mr. Lansing, you have to come out now." After a whispered conversation with the guard, the nurse came bustling back toward us.

"Goddamn broads!" The man's voice carried easily through the bathroom door. "Get them away from me."

"It's all right, Mr. Lansing," the security guard said. "I sent the nurse away. There are no women out here right now."

"There better not be," Mr. Lansing yelled, "because if there are . . ."

Suddenly I heard the bathroom door crash open. Down the hall I could just make out the furious Mr. Lansing, naked as the day he was born. "Mr. Lansing," the guard cried, "you can't run around like that. You have to put some clothes on."

"Goddamn broads! I don't have to wear clothes just for them. Goddamn broads!"

As we burst out laughing, we turned our backs and all but ran back to the rig. Fortunately, he was no longer our problem. I just wondered what he might have done if we had stopped on the trip down county to let him pee.

Joan and I were riding our usual Saturday overnight shift. The phone rang at about 3:00 A.M. "Got a call for you," Mark Thomas said. "A woman who attempted suicide. She says she took seventy Valium and some other stuff. We called Bob Fiorella first and he's getting the rig. He suggested you go directly to the scene."

"We're on the way," I said. "Ask the officer at the scene to call poison control and have them on the line for us. If there are any prescription bottles from what she took, have the officer read information to the folks at poison control so they can be ready for us. We'll talk with them about treatment when we get to the scene."

On the way, Joan and I discussed the things we might have to do. Syrup of ipecac to make her vomit, activated charcoal to absorb substances in her stomach. We considered that our patient might be unconscious, in which case we could give nothing by mouth. She might also have stopped breathing.

Since Bob was picking up the rig, Joan and I drove directly to the scene, a small house at the far edge of town. We found our patient, a plain-looking woman in her late forties, fully conscious, sitting in her downstairs hall, dressed in an old chenille bathrobe, socks, and sneakers. While Joan started the paperwork, I began to interview the woman. "What's your name, ma'am?"

"Ann Martinson."

"Ann, do you know what you took?"

Calmly she explained, "I took seventy Valium about half an hour ago. This is my first suicide attempt in thirteen years, you know."

"How do you feel right now?" I asked.

"Not too bad."

While I took the woman's vitals, Joan went into the kitchen to talk to poison control. While she was gone, I got more information from Will McAndrews, the police officer who had been first at the scene. "Her husband called us," he explained, "after she woke him to tell him what she had done." He motioned toward a heavyset man in his early fifties, seated on a lower step just gazing at his wife. The officer pulled some small bits of paper from his pocket. "We didn't find the pill bottle but these are her suicide notes. After her husband called us, he says that he found them all over the house. I'll keep one for my report, but I don't know what to do with the rest."

"I'll take them. We'll give them to someone at the hospital. Maybe some counselor there will be able to use them."

I heard the ambulance arrive and, a moment later, I heard Joan coming back from the kitchen. "I'll get the ipecac from the rig, Ed. And the stretcher."

"Ipecac to make me throw up. I suspected as much," the woman said matter-of-factly. She turned to her husband. "Brad, get something for me to throw up in. A wastebasket with a plastic bag inside. They'll want my stomach contents at the hospital. And bring a glass of water for the ipecac." Slowly, her husband rose and climbed the stairs toward the kitchen.

I shook my head, took a set of vitals, and found them within normal range. Joan and Bob returned from the rig with the ipecac and the stretcher. I mixed the prescribed amount of the liquid into the glass of water her husband had brought and the woman drank it. "The ipecac will take fifteen or twenty minutes to work," I told her as her husband disappeared back upstairs. "We'll get going to the hospital and let it do its job on the way."

The woman's husband returned from upstairs with a small white wastebasket, which he handed to the woman. "Call me later, when you need a ride home," he said softly, then sat back down on the stairs.

"Of course, Brad," she said.

Holding the wastebasket, the woman calmly got up and sat down on the stretcher. "Where's the seat belt?" she asked. "I need a seat belt for this thing."

As we strapped her in, I kept trying to reconcile a woman who was afraid to let the stretcher move without a seat belt with a woman who supposedly wanted to kill herself.

On the trip to the hospital, Mrs. Martinson chatted with us, very matter-of-factly about the suicide attempt. She didn't discuss the reasons, just the details of what she took. All the details, over and over again. "Seventy Valium isn't really enough to kill me, you know," she said.

I allowed Joan to talk with the woman. I was angry. Just plain angry. I clenched my teeth and dug my fingernails into my palms.

About halfway to the hospital, Mrs. Martinson pulled the prescription bottle from the pocket of her robe. "There were a few more Valium left," she said, "but I didn't take them. I know Valium and I didn't take enough to kill me, really."

Suddenly, I snapped. "I had a cousin who thought the same thing. On his third attempt, though, he succeeded. We never knew whether he meant it or not but it no longer mattered. He was just as dead either way." The woman stared at me, then became very silent.

About five minutes from the hospital, the syrup of ipecac began to do its work and the woman deftly handled the garbage can as she vomited.

We delivered Mrs. Martinson to the ER, finished the paperwork, and completed changing the stretcher linen. I didn't want to talk to anyone for a while, even Joan, so I asked if I could ride alone in the back of the rig. As we drove back to the scene to pick up my car I sat, silently, in the dark.

I was silent until Joan and I arrived home. As Joan undressed she asked, "Do you want to talk?"

I nodded, then said, "It's just such a manipulation. I think that kind of thing is the ultimate manipulation. I thought so when my cousin did it and I think so now. Greg kept everyone in the family hopping with his talk of suicide and his two unsuccessful attempts. Everyone was so solicitous, but eventually it wore very thin." I sighed and sat on the edge of the bed, still in my uniform. "I want to be sympathetic toward my patients, but sometimes they just make me furious. And some trigger old hurts and angers . . . and guilts, I suppose. I'll be okay. It's something I'll just have to deal with."

Almost an hour later, we finally climbed into bed and talked and cuddled, both realizing how wonderful it is that we have each other. Finally we fell asleep.

Having grown up on city streets, I have always wanted to own a house deep in the woods. For practical and financial reasons, however, I ended up with a typical suburban house on a typical suburban street, on a quarter-acre plot of land. There were some trees behind my house when I moved in and, since then, I've allowed the entire property to go wild. In the twenty years that I have lived in the house the hedges and trees in the back and the ones that form the border of my front and side yards have grown, and I only cut them enough to provide walkways and to rescue the trees and shrubs from the wild vines that threaten to strangle them.

A few years ago, I had to have my front lawn dug up to replace my fifty-year-old septic fields. When the work was done, instead of replanting that bit of lawn with grass, which requires mowing and cannot be used for fear of the deer ticks that carry Lyme disease, I replanted the entire lawn with snapdragons, portulaca, and wildflowers, all of which reseed themselves each year.

The result of all my efforts is that from within, my house appears to be surrounded by forest and meadows. I often see deer, raccoons, and other forest animals in my backyard, and my front yard is filled with butterflies. Hummingbirds are constant visitors, and mockingbirds, sparrows, and purple finches nest in my vine- and berry-covered shrubs. My neighbors, however, see my property as an unkempt eyesore.

It was late afternoon on a hot, steamy day in late July, the time of year when shrubs grow faster than it seems possible for a plant to grow and the tendrils of vines threaten to reach out and grab you if you walk too slowly. Whether it was on his own initiative or upon the suggestion of one of my neighbors, a middle-aged man walked up my driveway and rang the bell at my front door.

"Hi, my name is Joe Walsh," he said as I opened the door. "I've been doing tree work for some of your neighbors. Your hedges look like they could use some trimming. Would you be interested in an estimate on what it would cost you to get them fixed up?"

"No, thank you. I like them just as they are," I said. Then I thought of the large branches that hung over the back of my house, threatening damage to my roof. "I might have some work for you at the back of the house, though."

After walking around the building, Joe offered me a reasonable price for the work that I wanted done and we agreed that he would do it the next day. "What time will you be here?" I asked.

"Around nine o'clock," he replied. "Will you be home all day?"

"Yeah, I work out of my house, but I often have to leave suddenly to respond to ambulance calls. You can start the work if I'm not here when you arrive."

Joe nodded toward my car in the driveway. "I saw the blue-and-green lights on your car. Are you with the Prescott Rescue Squad?"

"I'm with both the Fairfax Ambulance Corps and the Prescott Rescue Squad."

Joe's face broke into a big grin. "I thought I recognized you," he said, "but I didn't know from where. You got me out of my car two years ago after I had driven into a tree. You probably don't remember me, but I remember you very well."

I studied Joe's face but didn't recognize him. "I responded to well over two hundred Prescott calls that year, and almost one hundred for Fairfax. It's hard to remember all of them, especially the ones that were not serious," I replied, looking at this obviously strong and healthy man who earned his living by doing hard physical work.

"Well, it didn't look very serious," Joe said, "but it was very serious for me. I want you to know that the only reason I'm able to walk today is because of the way you took care of me after that accident. You had me all splinted and tied up so that I couldn't move, and it's a good thing you did."

"Where did it happen?" I asked, searching my memory.

"In Fairfax, on Hunter's Hill Road, just over the crest. Some jerk pulled out of his driveway, blocking the whole road. The road was wet and there was no place to go. I skidded off the road, up an embankment, and into a tree. It was in October."

As I thought back, I began to recall the accident.

We were in the ambulance, returning from the second of two back-to-back, early morning calls, the second coming in as we were returning from the first. Jack McCaffrey was driving, I was riding shotgun, and Marge Talbot was in the back. I thought of the remains of my breakfast waiting almost two hours for me at home. The coffee would be cold and the shredded wheat a soggy mass by the time I got to it, but I was almost hungry enough to eat it that way.

"GKL–642 to 45–01."

Jack picked up the microphone. "01 on."

"Are you available to respond to a call?"

No I'm not, I thought to myself.

"That's affirmative, 642," Jack replied.

"Respond to Hunter's Hill Road, just over the crest of the hill. Report of a car into a tree."

"10–4. 45–01 is responding to Hunter's Hill Road."

"Your time is 10:48."

Jack pressed the master switch turning on our emergency lights then turned the siren knob on the control panel as I pulled a new sheet out of the PCR box and noted our time of dispatch. Two calls, back-to-back, was unusual. This was crazy. First a difficulty breathing, then a minor personal-injury accident, now this.

Officer Stan Poritsky had already set out flares and approached us as we pulled up to the scene. "The driver was wearing a seat belt and doesn't seem to be badly injured," he reported.

"Any other patients?" I asked.

"No. Just the driver. There were no other cars involved in the actual crash."

As we climbed the embankment, I could see that the front end of the car had absorbed most of the impact.

The windshield was broken but had remained in its frame. The man in the driver's seat appeared conscious and alert as I spoke to him. Marge opened the rear door and went into the car to hold head stabilization.

"Please try not to move, sir," I said, through the driver's window. "That's Marge behind you. She is going to hold your head. My name is Ed. What's your name?"

"Joe. Joe Walsh."

I quickly surveyed the inside of the vehicle, noting that Joe was still wearing his seat belt, neither the steering wheel nor the dashboard were bent, and there was no invasion of the passenger compartment. It looked like the injuries would be minor. Maybe we wouldn't even need to do a full extrication.

"Where are you hurt, Joe?" I asked.

"My back hurts a lot," Joe replied.

Oh well, I thought, we'll have to fully immobilize him. I was hungry and tired and really didn't want to do a complete vehicle extrication, which would add ten or fifteen minutes to the length of the call. So many people complain of back pain after an accident because they anticipate a lucrative lawsuit, and Joe didn't seem to be badly injured. But with a complaint of back pain I had no choice.

"Are you hurt anywhere else?" I asked.

"Yeah, my knees hurt."

"Can you move your hands?"

Joe raised his arms and wiggled his fingers.

"How about your feet?" I asked, leaning into the window to see.

Joe's feet moved.

"Okay, Joe," I said, opening the door carefully. "I'm going to examine you. Please don't move."

While Jack got into the passenger side of the car and began checking Joe's vital signs, I did a head-to-toe body survey. As I slid my hands along his neck and back, I could feel no deformity or swelling and he did not complain of any point tenderness when I touched him. Everything seemed to be all right until I touched his knees.

"Ow," he complained. "That hurts."

"I'm going to have to cut your pants, Joe."

"If you have to." Joe didn't sound too happy about losing a good pair of jeans.

Joe's knees were red and slightly swollen but there was no deformity and they didn't seem to be broken. All in all, Joe appeared to be okay.

"Joe, you seem to be in good shape, but because you have some back pain, we're going to have to do a full spinal immobilization. That means that, even though it's still a month from Thanksgiving, we're going to truss you up like a turkey, then tie you to a board before we transport you to the hospital."

"Naw," Joe said. "It just feels like muscle pains in my back. I'll get out of the car myself." He started to move.

I reached out and held him in place.

"Look, Joe. If you want us to take care of you, you've got to let us do it our way. If your back hurts, we have to take certain precautions to protect you before we can transport you. Why don't you just relax and let us do our job?"

"Okay," Joe reluctantly agreed.

Holding three fingers between Joe's jaw and shoulder to measure his size for a cervical collar, I turned to Jack, who had completed obtaining Joe's blood pressure, pulse, respiration, and pupil response to light. "Jack, we'll need a regular size c-collar, KED, longboard, spiders, and head blocks."

When Jack returned with the equipment, he and I worked together on either side of Joe, putting the cervical collar around his neck, then immobilizing his spine with the Kendrick Extrication Device, while Marge continued to hold Joe's head. When Joe was completely immobilized, we rotated his body so that we could free his legs from under the dashboard. Before any additional movement, we splinted both knees, just as a precaution, even though they didn't seem to be badly injured. We then slid him out of the vehicle onto a wooden longboard and packaged him for the trip to Fairfax General Hospital.

We stood in my driveway as I learned the outcome of that accident. "You were right that there were no fractures," Joe told me, "but I had serious ligament damage to both knees and I did have a spinal injury. I had numbness and tingling in both of my hands for over a year and it took a long time until I could walk well. It's only been the last six months that I've been able to climb trees again. When I told my orthopedic doctor that you had splinted and immobilized me so that I couldn't move an inch, he told me that I had been very lucky. He said that, if you hadn't, I might never have walked again."

Joe and I talked for a while, and the next morning he came and trimmed the tree branches that were threatening to fall on my roof. Watching him climb the tree with his chain saw was one of the most rewarding moments of my career as an emergency medical technician.

Joan and I have been collecting stories since our first book came out, and we've heard many that, well, make you just shrug your shoulders and smile.

The ambulance crew arrived at an auto accident in which a car with two women in their early twenties had driven into a fire hydrant. The crew chief opened the driver's-side door and, as he leaned in to check out the driver, he was assaulted by the overwhelming stench of alcohol.

"Has either one of you two been drinking?" he asked.

"Of course not," the passenger said, holding a handkerchief against a bleeding laceration on her forehead. "We're on our way to an Alcoholics Anonymous meeting."

Another crew arrived at a minor auto accident and found a very inebriated older man leaning against the fender of his crunched pickup truck. "You've had a few drinks, I assume," the crew chief said.

"Just a few beers," the injured man answered. "I got an advance on my new job and went out to celebrate."

"And what time was that?" the EMT asked, glancing at his watch, which indicated it was after four in the morning.

"About six. On Friday nights they have some wings and stuff until seven."

"Sir," the EMT said, "it's four in the morning. And," he said, hesitating a short while, "it's Wednesday morning."

"Oh shit," the man muttered. "And I was supposed to start my new job on Monday." He smiled an ingenuous, uneven smile. "I guess I missed it, huh."

A crew was called to the scene of a man with a shoulder injury. The EMTs arrived and found a man in his early twenties lying in the middle of the living room floor, dressed in only a pair of white cotton underpants. The crew chief checked the man out and found a badly dislocated shoulder.

"How did this happen, sir?" the EMT asked.

The young man looked up at the woman sitting in the corner of the room. "My mom gives a great massage. I had a lousy day and she offered to rub me down. I guess she pulled the wrong way."

A crew was called for a "man down" in the middle of the sidewalk in a run-down area of town. They arrived and found the man, writhing and screaming on the sidewalk. "Sir," the crew chief said, squeezing his shoulder in a gesture of support, "can you hear me?"

"I need something for the pain." He moaned.

"Where does it hurt?"

"Everywhere. Just give me something for the pain." The man's respirations were rapid and he was covered with sweat.

"We can't give you anything," the EMT said, "but we'll take you to the hospital and let them check you out. They'll decide what will help you."

"Nothing for the pain?" the man said plaintively.

"I'm sorry, sir."

The man took a deep breath and sat up. No longer moaning, he said, "What the fuck good are you? I'm okay. I don't need you guys. Buzz off." He dragged himself to his feet.

"But sir, we need to check out your pain."

"No you don't. I'm fine. I just need a drink." He signed the "Refused Medical Assistance" statement and disappeared.

It is usually a simple matter to call the hospital to alert them to the arrival of the patient. You tell them the age and sex of the patient, the presenting problem, along with vital signs and other relevant facts. Occasionally, however, things get a bit complicated.

"Medic one to the trauma center."

"Go ahead, medic one."

A slightly breathless voice responded. "We are en route to your location with a twenty-one-year-old male, the victim of a gunshot wound. Patient is conscious but disoriented. He has a blood pressure of 90 by palp, pulse of 120, and respirations of 36. We have the MAST inflated and are currently bagging the patient with one-hundred percent oxygen. Our ETA is five minutes."

"Where was the patient shot?" the trauma nurse asked.

"At the intersection of Elm and 14th."

* * *

Or the call to the hospital from the crew who had picked up a man who had been thrown from his car. "The patient was ejaculated from the vehicle," the EMT explained over the radio.

Another crew was transporting a man in severe cardiac distress. While watching the monitor carefully, the EMTs saw his condition deteriorate. Suddenly, the man's heart rhythm changed from normal sinus to ventricular fibrillation, a disorganized rhythm incapable of supporting life. "Pull over," the EMT yelled to the driver. "We'll have to shock him."

The driver turned to try to figure out the nature of the problem. "What did you say?" As he turned, the ambulance bounced hard off the curb, causing the patient's rhythm to convert back from v-fib to a normal sinus rhythm.

"Never mind," the EMT in the back said.

Chapter 8

We in EMS like to think that nothing can surprise us. The good, the bad, and the ugly—we've seen it all. Well . . .

"Hi, honey," the girl at the door said. She had waist-length black hair and black eyes with an exotic slant. Her lips were painted bright red and contrasted vividly with her soft, white skin.

"Hello, there," the man said. "My name is Victor. Victor Harper."

"You can call me Amy," the girl said. "May I come in?"

"Of course," Victor said, backing away from the door of his motel room.

Amy walked into the room and slowly removed her trench coat. Beneath, she wore a bright red teddy, long red stockings, and red patent-leather shoes with amazingly high heels. "We've never met before, have we," she said. It was a statement, not a question. "I would have remembered someone as nice-looking as you."

Victor knew it was all part of the line. He was sixty-one, a bit paunchy, with thick glasses and a balding pate. He ran his fingers through the drifts of graying hair behind his ears. "That's a lovely thought, but no, we've never met before."

"But Maria tells me that you've dealt with the escort service before. Since you're a regular, you can pay me later, honey."

"No problem." He started to unbutton his shirt, but Amy pushed his hands aside. "Let me do that," she said, purring. As she slowly pushed the buttons out of their holes, she asked, "Do you have something you particularly like to do?"

An hour later, the two were lying on the bed, relaxing after a strenuous and delightfully athletic evening. "That was wonderful," Amy said.

When Victor was silent, she said, "Did you enjoy it?" She heard Victor's heavy breathing and propped herself on one elbow. "Are you asleep?" She looked down at his ashen face and watched a rivulet of sweat wend its way from his temple into his ear. His eyes were open, but seemed unfocused. "Victor? Are you okay? Victor?"

"Fairfax Police to the ambulance. The rig is needed at the Parkway Motor Inn for an unconscious man."

"10–4, 45–01 is responding." I was filling in for Jill Tremonte who had had a family emergency.

"I'll ride in back, Joan," Fred Stevens, the crew chief said to me, so I climbed into the passenger seat and Pete Williamson took his place as driver. It was unusual for the crew chief to ride in the back, but Fred preferred it that way. As we drove to the inn, Fred checked the contents of the megaduffel to be sure everything was in its place. As we arrived at the motel someone waved us around to the back. We saw a police car in front of Room 106.

Fred jumped out of the back and charged into the room with Pete and me right behind him. "What happened?" Fred asked, putting down the duffel and kneeling on the gold, industrial carpeting. In the center of the double bed lay a naked man, extremely pale and sweaty, eyes closed, breathing heavily.

Officer Eileen Flynn stood beside the bed fastening an oxygen mask over the man's face. A spectacularly beautiful girl dressed in a trench coat and high-heeled shoes sat in a chair in the corner of the room.

"What happened?" Fred asked.

"We," the girl said, "well, we spent the evening together and afterward, well, he was like that." Fred looked at me and rolled his eyes. "I didn't know what to do," the girl continued, "so I dialed 911."

"When I arrived," Eileen said, "he was breathing, but unresponsive, as you see him now."

"Not a bad fuckin' way to go," Fred muttered. Efficiently, he examined the deeply unconscious man while Pete took a quick set of vitals. "Blood pressure 175 over 120," he said, "pulse 80 and bounding, resps at 24."

I had the PCR box in my hand and tried to get some information for our report. "Ma'am," I said to the woman, "can you tell me his name?"

"Victor," she said, clearly flustered. "That's all I remember. Just Victor." She thrust a slip of paper at me with the motel's name and a room number on it. "This is all I have."

"Okay. We'll get the rest at the hospital." The staff would go through the man's wallet to ascertain his name, address, and date of birth.

Unable to rouse the naked man, we used the sheet underneath him to transfer him to the stretcher. Fred bundled the man's clothes and tucked them under his feet to assist his circulation. As Fred and Pete wheeled the man toward the ambulance I picked up the mega-duffel and started toward the door.

"Miss," the woman said to me, "can you help me?"

"If I can. What do you need?"

"Well, this is a bit embarrassing."

"I guess it is. What can I do to help?"

"My money. I haven't been paid. I didn't think of it until now, but I really need my money."

You've got to be kidding, I thought. "I'm sorry. I don't think I can help you."

"In his pants pocket. Can you get his wallet and pay me?"

"I'm sorry, miss. I really can't go through his wallet." I motioned to Officer Eileen Flynn, now standing behind the ambulance. "Maybe Officer Flynn can do it for you."

The girl stood up, flipped her long hair over her shoulder, and stalked out the door. "Never mind," she said over her shoulder. "Just never mind."

We drove the man to the hospital, code 3, and left him in the care of the ER staff. I never did learn how he made out.

Children are amazing creatures and you can never predict how they will react in an emergency. Some scream and yell during the smallest incident. "Mommy, he's touching me." "Daddy, he took my Power Ranger." "She's on my side of the car." Some are amazingly calm despite everything going on around them.

Melissa Rappaport was four when I first met her. The call came in for a child choking in the A&P. We have a saying about a choking call. When you get there it's either RMA or DOA, meaning that either the situation has resolved itself and the patient will refuse medical attention, or, if there's no one at the scene who can help, the patient will be dead on our arrival. And this call was for a child.

I was around the corner at the post office so, although there was a full crew responding, I drove to the A&P, pulled up in front, and ran inside.

"What happened?" I puffed as a red-jacketed young man led the way to the manager's cubicle at the far end of the store.

"A little girl's got something stuck, I think."

As we arrived at the cubicle, I saw a girl of about four standing, mouth open, looking mildly distressed. False alarm, I said to myself. Something had probably irritated her throat and now she's enjoying the attention.

"She's choking!" the woman standing next to her screamed. "Help her! Do something!"

I knew that the crew would be breaking all landspeed records to arrive quickly so I keyed the mike on my portable. "45–24 to rig responding to the A&P. Be advised the patient is conscious and alert."

"10–4, 45–24." I could hear a sigh.

I knelt beside the child, placed a hand on her back under her long dark brown hair, and stroked her cheek with the other. Ignoring the woman for the moment I asked the little girl, "Are you okay, sweetheart?"

Her enormous brown eyes locked with mine and she pointed to her throat. Saliva was running down her chin and her breathing was deep and slow. "Just relax, honey." I turned to the woman. "Are you with her?" In a similar situation years ago I would have asked whether the woman was her mother. Since then, I've learned never to assume anything.

"She's my daughter," the woman said. She was a short, thin woman, but the number of decibels she could produce belied her size. "She's choking! Help her!"

"Ma'am," I said, "she's breathing fine and her color's good. Can you tell me what happened?"

The woman took two or three deep breaths. "She swallowed a Jolly Rancher. You know, those candies you suck on?" Her voice level rose. "How do you know she's breathing all right? How can you be so sure? Oh, God," she screamed. "She's going to die!" The girl reached over and patted her mother's hand.

"Ma'am, calm down. Look at her. She's doing fine. I don't know whether the candy is in her windpipe or not, but I need you to try to relax. What's her name?"

"Melissa. Melissa Rappaport. I'm her mother. Are you sure she's okay?" The woman's shoulders shook with silent sobs.

"She's breathing, but she's obviously not totally okay," I said gently. "Something's caught somewhere." I remembered a story I tell whenever I teach CPR of a child who inhaled a coin, which lodged in his windpipe, acting like a valve. When the coin was crosswise, it closed the windpipe and the child couldn't breathe. When it was vertical, air passed without obstruction. I wondered whether this was a similar situation. "Let's take her over to the hospital and let them examine her."

"Are you sure she's not going to die?"

"She's not going to die. Just calm down." I turned to the little girl. "Melissa, I don't want you to talk or move your head. Just tell me with your eyes. Besides your throat, how are you feeling?"

She softened her eyes and smiled.

"That's great. You scared your mom a lot, you know."

Melissa looked at her mother, gazed heavenward, then shrugged.

"I was terrified," Mrs. Rappaport said, pulling a cigarette from her purse. "I'm so glad you came. You saved her life." Her hands shaking, the woman dropped the cigarette back into her purse and began to weep.

"I did no such thing," I said, handing Mrs. Rappaport a tissue. "I was glad that I was just around the corner and that I could help, but she was just fine long before I got here."

"Will you go with us to the hospital?" she asked.

When I felt Melissa's hand slip into mine, I agreed.

While we waited for the ambulance, I counted the little girl's pulse and breathing and found them to be normal. When the ambulance crew arrived I offered to go to the hospital and so Melissa, her mother, and I, along with the EMT and attendant on duty, all crowded into the back of the rig. On the way to Fairfax General I held Melissa's hand and managed to keep Mrs. Rappaport calm.

When we arrived at the emergency room, I filled Dr. Margolis in on what I knew as he examined the little girl. "Lots of drool?" he asked.

"Yeah," I said.

"Sounds like the candy is lodged in her esophagus, keeping her from swallowing. Nothing serious. We'll do a quick X ray, then remove the object." He turned to Melissa. "You have to be careful with candies like that. Maybe from now on you should stick to lollipops. With flexible sticks. Okay?"

"Oh she will, Doctor," Mrs. Rappaport chimed in. "Won't you, Melissa?"

Melissa just nodded slowly.

A year later, I was at the cleaners when the pager tones went off. "Fairfax Police to all home units. A full crew is needed for a child with a possible broken arm in the A&P. Any available units please call in."

"45–24 to the police."

"Police on, 24."

"I'm in town and responding as an EMT."

"10–4, Joan."

Again I arrived at the A&P and a middle-aged female employee led me to the deli counter. There, standing with her left arm supported on a pile of loaves of packaged rye bread was Melissa, calm and dry-eyed. I knelt down beside her. "What happened?"

"I remember you," Mrs. Rappaport said. "You were here when she swallowed the Jolly Rancher. You saved her life. You're always here when we need you. I'm Linda Rappaport." She patted her daughter on the head. "And you remember Melissa."

"I certainly do," I said. "What happened this time?"

"Well this time she was climbing out of the shopping cart and got her arm caught right here." She motioned to the wide space between the kiddie seat and the body of the cart. "I heard the snap and I'm sure it's broken."

I remembered Melissa as being a stoic child, but if her arm were truly broken it would hurt a great deal. Sure that her mother was just making another fuss, I said to the child, "Melissa, do you remember me? We met right here about a year ago."

"I remember," she said softly.

"Does your arm hurt a lot?"

She nodded.

"May I touch it?" I asked.

She nodded again.

Sure that nothing too serious was wrong, I palpated her left humerus, watching her face for signs of pain. I was amazed to find a fifteen-degree bend midway between her shoulder and elbow. When I touched it, however, her expression didn't change. "Does that hurt when I touch it?" I asked her.

She nodded. "Yeah. A little."

"Well, I think we'll have to get you over to the hospital and let them do an X ray to see what's up in there."

"It's broken, isn't it?" Mrs. Rappaport said. "Oh, God, I'm sure it's broken."

Sure that it was, in fact, broken, I gave the standard answer. "I don't have X-ray eyes, ma'am. Let's get her comfortable and take her over to Fairfax General."

"I'm sure it's broken. Oh Melissa, what am I ever going to do with you? You know I have three other children and they never get into anything. But Melissa . . ."

"45–01 is on location," my radio squawked. "45–01 to 45–24."

I keyed the microphone of my radio. "24 on."

"What do you need in there?" Phil Ortiz was on duty.

"Just a short splint and cravats. And the stretcher, Phil."

"10–4, Joan." Phil arrived moments later with the equipment and the stretcher. "What have we here?"

"This is Melissa's mother. Why don't you get some information for the report while I take care of Melissa."

As Phil led Mrs. Rappaport a little ways away, Heather Franks walked over. "Can I help?"

I pointed to the exact location of the break. "Sure, Heather. This is Melissa. She's banged up her left humerus and we're going to splint it."

Heather looked at me, aware from my expression of what I'd found, and just as amazed at Melissa's calm as I was. I nodded slightly at her questioning expression, then said, "Heather, will you stabilize the arm for me, please?"

As Heather placed one hand on each side of the fracture, I said, "Melissa, will you tell me, or tell Heather if we hurt you?"

"Okay," Melissa said.

I placed two of my fingers in the girl's left hand. "Can you squeeze my fingers?" Her grip was strong. "That's great." She beamed. "Do you go to George Washington School?" I asked

"Yes," Melissa said.

I checked the pulse in her left wrist and found it easily. "You know Heather works at your school," I said, placing the short splint against her upper left arm.

"At my school?" she said.

"I sure do. I work in the cafeteria."

"Wow. I'm in kindergarten so I don't go to the cafeteria yet."

"Well you'll see me next year then." Heather looked at the splint I was holding. It was longer than Melissa's entire arm. "You know, Joan, that's really overkill. How about just a sling and swathe? Use her body as a splint."

"Good idea," I said. "You know, Melissa," I continued, putting the splint on the stretcher out of the way. "Heather's right. That thing was just too big." I fastened one triangular bandage over her arm and around her neck as a sling, then folded a triangular muslin bandage into a wide strip and placed it over the girl's entire upper arm. I brought the ends around her body and tied the swathe tightly on her chest just forward of her right arm. "How does that feel?"

"Tight," she said.

"It needs to be tight to keep your arm from moving. Is it too tight? Does it hurt a lot?"

"It's okay."

"Will you sit on the stretcher for me?" I asked.

"Would you carry me instead?" she asked in a tiny voice.

"But if I carry you, it might hurt your arm."

"No it won't. Please carry me."

I picked the little girl up gingerly, carefully avoiding her immobilized left arm, and balanced her on my left hip. With Mrs. Rappaport following behind, we walked to the rig. Melissa sat on the stretcher for the entire ride to the hospital, contorting her body so she could hold my hand with her uninjured hand.

At the Fairfax General ER, Dr. Margolis took my report as Melissa sat quietly on the hospital gurney. "Severe deformity in the left humerus," I told him. He raised an eyebrow as he looked at the tearless girl. I was sure he didn't believe my report.

"All right, Melissa, let's unwrap all this stuff," he said, quickly untying my careful splinting job. "We'll just check this and get you out of here." As he touched Melissa's arm, I smiled silently. I could tell from the sudden change in his facial expression that he had altered his opinion of the seriousness of Melissa's injury. "Rosemary," he said to Mrs. Harper, an ER nurse, "let's prepare for an X ray and we'll need orthopedics, too."

I was finishing my paperwork as Melissa was wheeled toward the X-ray department down the hall. Dr. Margolis walked over to me. "Joan, I'm sorry. I was sure that you were wrong about her arm. She was so calm and that must hurt like hell."

"I know. I had the same problem when I arrived at the scene." I reminded him of the little girl's previous visit.

"Oh, right. I remember," he said. "I remarked at that time how calm she was. Never cried." Over the hospital background noises we could hear Mrs. Rappaport loudly admonishing an orderly to wheel the little girl carefully through the halls. "That's good, though. Her mother makes enough noise for both of them."

Twenty-nine-year-old Alice Considine had been confined to a wheelchair since childhood. With a motorized, specially equipped chair and a seven-year-old golden retriever service dog named Priceless, she was a familiar figure around Fairfax. With Priceless at her side to fetch things for her, she shopped at the supermarket, visited the local Caldor's, and had lunch at the diner. She and Priceless gave presentations at the local schools demonstrating all the things Alice and Priceless were capable of doing together. Her smile was radiant and her life was good.

She lived in a small apartment in Hillcrest, an apartment complex that had made special arrangements for the elderly and the physically challenged, including ramps and handrails. Alice's only additional assistance was her roommate, a brawny young man named Billy whom she had found through a local agency. In return for a bed on the fold-out couch in the living room and the meals he cooked, he helped her bathe and dress, get into and out of bed, and tend to the chores she couldn't manage.

One late spring evening, Alice returned from the lounge area and settled into her favorite spot to watch TV with Billy. Since it was particularly warm, Billy had opened the windows to "get some air through the joint." Priceless stretched out on the bathroom floor where it was cooler and quieter.

"I don't feel so well," Billy said. "I'm dizzy and my head is splitting."

"You look lousy," Alice said, reaching over to touch his forehead. "You're very sweaty, and your skin is cold."

Billy lifted his hands and held them, palms down, out from his body. "My hands are shaking. Lord, I feel awful. I gotta go to the john."

"Maybe you should just sit still for a moment, until you feel a little stronger."

"I know," he said, stretching his large body out on the couch. "You certainly can't pick me up if I fall." After a minute, Billy sat up and said, "I gotta get to the bathroom." Billy heaved his huge frame off the sofa and stood up on wobbly legs. As Alice watched, Billy's eyes closed and he collapsed, falling against the wheels of Alice's wheelchair.

"Oh shit," Alice hissed. She stared at Billy's chest but could see no signs that he was breathing. She grabbed the wheels of her chair and tried to maneuver around her aide's inert body but it was no use. Her chair was caught between Billy and the sofa. She couldn't reach the phone to call for help. Alice took a deep breath to calm herself, then called, "Priceless, come."

Wagging his tail, ready to work, Priceless trotted beside Alice's chair. "Priceless, phone. Get the phone." It had been five years since Priceless had been trained to understand the word *phone*, and Alice had never had to use this command before. She crossed her fingers and said again, "Priceless, get the phone." She pointed to the cordless telephone and watched Priceless walk to it. He worked his lips and teeth until he could lift the receiver, but dropped it onto the floor. "Good dog, Priceless. Now bring it here." Again Priceless worked at the heavy receiver, finally lifting it with his mouth and dropping it into Alice's lap. "Good baby," Alice said, quickly dialing 911.

When my crew and I arrived in Alice's room, we rolled Billy onto his back, allowing Alice to move her chair. His shirt was soaked with sweat. As I felt for breathing and a pulse I asked, "What happened?"

"Billy looked awful, pale and sweaty. His hands shook. He said he was sick and had to go to the bathroom. Then he stood up, and dropped like that. I couldn't help him so I called you."

I felt a rapid pulse, but he wasn't breathing. Jill Tremonte had already hooked the oxygen to the bag-valve mask and I fitted the mask over Billy's face as Jill squeezed the bag to force pure oxygen into Billy's lungs. "Anything unusual before this happened?" I asked.

"He's been, well, off his feed. Not eating much."

"He's usually a big eater?" I asked.

"He usually eats enough for three normal people."

I felt Billy take a deep breath. I waited and he took another. "He's breathing," I said. I looked at my watch as he breathed two more times. "His respirations are about 20. Let's get him on a non-rebreather." Jill switched the oxygen cylinder to a non-rebreather face mask and she fitted it over Billy's face.

"Ma'am, does Billy have any medical history?"

"No. He's always been healthy as a horse."

"What's your name?" I asked.

"I'm Alice," she said. I looked at the gorgeous dog, now lying at her feet. "And this is Priceless," she said, patting the dog's back.

Billy groaned softly and moved his head. "He's coming around," Jill said. "How about sugar if he regains consciousness?"

I nodded and Jill got the tube of glucose, pure sugar in its most digestible form, from our megaduffel. "Has he ever had any problems with his sugar?" I asked Alice.

"Not that I know of."

"Okay." I bent close to Billy's ear. "Billy? Can you hear me?"

Billy puffed, then said, "Yeah."

"Billy, do you know what happened?"

"I fainted, I guess. I feel awful."

Jill took the top off of the tube of glucose. "We're going to squeeze some sugar into your mouth. It's very sweet but swallow as much as you can. It will help you feel better." I didn't know whether it would help or not, but the power of suggestion wasn't to be overlooked. Jill raised Billy's head, placed the opening of the toothpaste-shaped tube into Billy's mouth, and squeezed. He licked his lips and swallowed.

As Jill squeezed the rest of the glucose into his mouth I checked Billy's vital signs. His blood pressure was 110 over 85, his respirations were full and deep, and his pulse was bounding at over 120. As we waited to see whether the sugar would have any effect, I looked around. Officer Merve Berkowitz was getting information from Alice, and Jack McCaffrey was standing outside the apartment door with the stretcher.

I caught Jill's eye and from her expression I knew she was asking herself the same question I was. How the hell were we going to get Billy, who probably weighed over three hundred and fifty pounds from the cramped space in the crowded apartment onto the stretcher? "Let's hope it's his sugar," I whispered to Jill, "and that he comes around enough to help us."

Jill tossed the empty tube into the garbage can under the coffee table. "Feeling any better?" she asked Billy.

"Yeah, I think I am."

I breathed a silent thanks. After a few minutes, Billy felt well enough to work with us. With Merve holding him under one arm and Jack under the other, he stood and moved so we could roll the stretcher underneath him. When he dropped onto it, his body hanging off of both sides, I remembered reading that the stretcher had a weight limit of three hundred pounds but I decided to ignore it. I had no idea what we'd do if we couldn't use the stretcher. Not trusting the slender aluminum tubing that held the wheels, I suggested that we leave it in its fully lowered position.

As Jill, Jack, and Merve wheeled Billy into the hall, I asked Alice, "Billy had you pretty well blocked in. How did you get the phone?"

She patted Priceless's head, now resting in her lap. "Priceless got the phone for me. He's really a human being in fur." She scratched Priceless behind his ears. "I never knew I'd need that command, and he hadn't heard it for years. But he knew." She bent down. "Didn't you, baby."

Billy was diagnosed as having a sugar disorder, but with diet, he keeps his condition under control. Alice is still an active member of the Fairfax community, as is Priceless.

"Fairfax Police to the ambulance corps."

I got up from the kitchen table and keyed the mike. "Ambulance on. Go ahead."

"The ambulance is needed for a hand injury—a lawn-mower accident at 12 Whitehouse Street."

I wrinkled my face. Every summer we get several mower accidents. In some, feet get badly mangled when the person mowing slips and the mower runs over his or her foot. Despite all the warnings about wearing heavy shoes, our victim is usually wearing sandals or sneakers.

Hand injuries are equally common. Grass clippings and debris begin to build up under the housing of a power mower. When the clog becomes big enough, the blade jams and stops. People don't realize that although the blade has stopped turning, unless they physically turn off the motor, it may continue to run. Without thinking, someone tips the mower over, reaches underneath to remove the junk, and then the blade is suddenly released and resumes turning. Fingers or entire hands are the immediate casualty.

Yes, I thought, I've had a few messy lawn-mower calls, but thank heavens I'm not on duty.

"10–4, Fairfax Police. 45–01 will be responding."

"Joan," Pam Kovacs said, "I have a dentist appointment. I can probably get back in time, but would you take this one for me?"

Pam is a delightful woman and has taken a few calls for me, so, reluctantly, I agreed. "Sure," I said, heading for the door with Sam Middleton ahead of me and probationary member Tim Babbett on my heels.

Sam drove, lights and siren, toward Whitehouse Street, usually referred to as the "high-rent district." An area of four-acres-and-up homes, many with tennis courts, pools, and enough acreage for horses, Whitehouse Street is about five minutes from headquarters.

As we rounded a bend, we saw a boy in his early teens, sitting on an off-road vehicle in the middle of the road, waving his arms. "That must be the house," Sam said.

Obviously panicked, the boy careened up the driveway with us following. As we pulled to a stop in front of a four-car garage, we looked around. It was magnificent, a huge rolling lawn with white split-rail fences dividing it into large pastures in which several horses grazed quietly. There were several cars parked around the garage, a BMW, a Mercedes, and an old Nissan. "Must belong to the servants," Sam muttered.

"It's my dad," the boy said, puffing. "Hurry, hurry."

"Just try to calm down," I said. "We're right behind you."

Tim hefted the megaduffel as we followed the boy, almost running to keep up. "Hurry," the kid called behind him. "He's bleeding bad."

Oh shit, I thought, expecting to find a man unconscious on the floor. I entered the large wood-paneled dining room and saw a middle-aged man holding a great wad of paper towels against his left hand. There were spatters of blood on the floor, but it didn't seem to be a great quantity. "I am the dumbest creature on the planet," he said. "Dumb, dumb, dumb. And I thought about it when I did it."

Sam, as crew chief, took control. "How bad is it?" he asked. "May I look?"

"Don't bother," the man said, holding pressure on the hand. "I've almost severed one finger and maybe a second. Dumb, dumb."

"How did this happen?"

"The usual. The riding mower conked out and I reached under to release some grass."

"I've told you you should hire a service," a young man of about seventeen said from the corner. He was on the phone, obviously on hold.

"I know, but I enjoy doing it."

"Can I take a set of vitals?" Sam asked.

"No need," the man said. "My pulse is a bit rapid at about 100, resps are 20 and fine. I took my own BP and it's 140 over 85. The systolic's a bit high, but I'm sure that it's the excitement."

As Sam wrote the information down on the PCR, I said, "You sound very knowledgeable. Are you in EMS?"

A tiny smile tipped the corners of his mouth and he gazed at me ruefully. "I'm chief of thoracic surgery at St. Luke's."

"Oh shit," I muttered.

"Yeah, 'oh shit' is right," he said. "My son's on the phone to the chief of plastic surgery. They're assembling a microsurgery team even as we speak. Dr. Goldfarb will meet me in the ER and he'll take care of everything."

There was little we could do. We left the paper towels in place to prevent any reopening of the wound, swathed his hand in gauze, then splinted it to his body to prevent any additional movement. We walked the doctor to the ambulance and drove him to the trauma center, where we were met by several obviously high-ranking doctors. As we left him in their care, I finally asked the question I hadn't dared ask. "Are you right-handed?"

"Thank God, yes," he answered.

As we drove toward headquarters, Sam said, "Poor guy. What a loss if he loses function in that hand."

What a loss.

* * *

The call came in for an unknown medical problem at The Pines, a senior citizens' residence about a half mile from the center of Fairfax. Since the first rig was at the park for a heat-related problem, the police toned out for a second crew. I responded to the scene.

When I arrived, I pulled my crash kit and a BVM from my trunk and rushed inside, a bit surprised that no one was in front of the building to guide me. At the front desk, a woman showed me into a small office. Inside sat a woman I recognized as being a member of the staff of The Pines. Behind the desk sat a middle-aged woman in her early forties with a platinum crew cut.

"How do you do," the woman with the crew cut said. "I'm Dr. Cardone and I work for crisis intervention out of Oakside Psychiatric."

"Nice to see you again," I said, recalling the hair-raising calls I had shared with her previously. I still wondered how she had ever gotten her job at Oakside. The few times I had encountered her in the past, she had behaved as if she should have been on the inside, looking out. I had been appalled at her seeming lack of concern for her patient.

"We need you to transport a seriously combative eighty-four-year-old man."

"We no longer handle nonmedical transports," I explained. Our corps policy had changed recently, so I assumed she was unaware of the new directives. "You should call a paid service to do this."

"We asked the police to dispatch you. The man will be going to Oakside."

"We don't transport to Oakside anymore," I explained further. "It's now outside our area of response."

"I know that," she continued. "He will be going to Fairfax General for the medical evaluation he needs before he's admitted to Oakside." Dr. Cardone signed a small paper in front of her and stood up. "This is an order for transport, and for the use of restraint as necessary. He's suffering from severe senile dementia and has been abusive to the staff. This lunchtime, he began to throw things around the dining room."

Damn, I thought. After this many years of riding with Fairfax, I've finally encountered a situation I don't know how to handle. In our EMT courses we used to teach simple ways to restrain a combative patient. We showed how to use cravats to softly tie hands together without causing injury. It never worked. We also demonstrated how to roll someone in the Reeves stretcher, facedown, and tie the device tightly around the patient. It always looked cruel to me, and fortunately in my career with Fairfax I've never had to do it.

We no longer teach the use of restraints. In Fairfax, as in many other areas, unless a patient is in police custody, or we have a direct, signed order from a physician, or we deem our patient to be a danger to himself or others, we do not have the right to use restraints. In addition, one of the first things we teach in EMT classes is that the safety of the rescuer is of primary importance. We are not to put ourselves in danger by battling with a hostile patient. Period.

In cases of drug or alcohol impairment a policeman will usually have already handcuffed the patient and will ride along with us as we transport. Although we are concerned about restraints that might inflict soft-tissue damage, once the police have the subject in handcuffs, we transport that way.

In Fairfax, a physician may order restraints for a patient. Dr. Cardone had written such an order. *Restrain PRN* (restrain as necessary), the paper she handed me said. "You'll probably need the police," she continued. "Mr. O'Hara is in the dining room and he won't want to go with you. He'll put up quite a fight."

I'm in way over my head, I said to myself.

"45–01 is on location." Fred Stevens arrived with the ambulance. A longtime Fairfax volunteer, I hoped that he could help me to figure this situation out. "24, what do you need?"

"Nothing right now. Just meet me in the office."

When Fred arrived, I explained the situation to him. "Do we have to take this call?" I whispered.

"We were dispatched and, unfortunately, it was for an unknown medical emergency, not a psych call. I think we're stuck."

"Anyone else coming?" I asked.

"Yeah. Pete's on the way. He can't transport, but when he heard the call he said he would help out at the scene."

I heaved a sigh of relief. Pete Williamson is a professional paramedic in the city and has seen it all. He was the perfect person to handle this. "That's great," I said.

Dr. Cardone, the woman from The Pines staff, Fred, and I walked out the front door and stood under the overhang. "Have you called the police?" the doctor asked. "We're going to need their help."

"Not yet. You called them to dispatch us, didn't you?"

"Of course."

"Well, I assume they have someone on the way."

Pete pulled up in his Bronco and parked in front of the building. "Dr. Cardone, this is Pete Williamson. He's a professional paramedic and should be able to help us."

Quickly, Dr. Cardone outlined the situation to Pete. When she was done, she pointed to a well-dressed man standing in front of the building. "That's Mr. O'Hara. He just walked out here."

"What do you think, Pete?" I asked.

"Most of the time the patient can be convinced to take a nice quiet ride in the ambulance. If it's handled right."

Yeah, I thought. Handled right. That describes Dr. Cardone all right.

"Let me try to talk to him," Pete said.

I didn't hear Pete's end of the conversation, but I heard Mr. O'Hara threaten to hit him, to sue, and to call the newspapers. He glared at his daughter, who had joined us under the overhang. "I'll never forgive you for this," he shrieked, waving his finger at the poor woman. I watched a tear trickle down the daughter's face.

Finally, after about five minutes, Mr. O'Hara started walking toward the back of the rig, where Fred had put the stretcher. "We won't hurt you, Mr. O'Hara," I heard Pete say. "Just a nice ride to Fairfax General where they can check your blood." I hate the idea of lying to a patient, but if it made the trip easier, it had to be done, I guess.

"I don't have to go," Mr. O'Hara said. "I know my rights. I don't have to go."

"Yes, you do," Dr. Cardone said. "I'm your doctor and I say you have to go."

"You're not my doctor," Mr. O'Hara said, becoming agitated. "I know you're not my doctor."

"Dad," his daughter said. "I asked this nice doctor to help you. Let her do what she thinks is best."

"You're doing this to me," Mr. O'Hara said. "I'll never forgive you. Never."

He sat on the stretcher and Pete fastened the three seat belts across his body. "Just seat belts," Pete told him. "And not too tight." We lifted the stretcher into the rig and Dr. Cardone, the man's daughter, and I climbed in behind. Fred got into the driver's seat and we started toward Fairfax General.

As we drove, I wondered: What happens if he changes his mind and starts swinging in here. I looked at the portable oxygen cylinders, formidable weapons in the hands of someone not in possession of all of his faculties, and shook my head. How had I let myself get into this? My safety was compromised, as was that of Dr. Cardone and the man's daughter.

We chatted about the unusually hot weather and, when the conversation waned, I enjoyed the silence. Nothing to set Mr. O'Hara off. Then Dr. Cardone began to discuss Oakside Psychiatric with the man's daughter. "He'll be comfortable there," she said. "It's a secure facility and it's the best place for your father."

"Dr. Cardone," I said softly, worrying about getting Mr. O'Hara agitated. "I'm sure our patient is aware of what you're saying. Mightn't it be better to leave things unsaid for the moment?"

Dr. Cardone reached over and patted Mr. O'Hara on the shoulder. "Of course he hears everything we're saying. He knows we're doing everything for his own good." Pat. Pat.

I gritted my teeth. If there's one phrase that makes me furious it's, "We're doing this for your own good." All I could think of was the poor people being sent to Bedlam, the old English asylum, and being told it was "for their own good."

I believed the doctor and the staff of The Pines when they said that Mr. O'Hara had been combative in the dining room. I remember my grandmother who lived with my mother and me during my teenage years. Beginning at the age of seventy, she deteriorated slowly due to senility, as it was called at the time. During one particularly bad period in the course of her slide, I recall my mother being awakened almost every night by slippers being hurled onto her bed. My grandmother was in one of her rages again. I would hear my mother get up, calm my grandmother, and help her back to bed. Fortunately, in my grandmother's case, this period was blessedly short. After a few months, she retreated further into the silent world in which she spent the rest of her life, smiling and seemingly happy.

Hopefully this phase of Mr. O'Hara's illness would pass quickly. Whether he would ever emerge from Oakside Psychiatric was another matter and not my concern.

"I'll never forget this," Mr. O'Hara said, glaring at his daughter.

"Of course you will," Dr. Cardone said. Pat. Pat. "You

forget everything. I hope you'll remember that we're doing what's best for you." Pat. Pat.

I worried about Mr. O'Hara's reaction when we reached Fairfax General, but he was docile and, when we wheeled our stretcher beside the hospital gurney, he climbed across easily.

That call has bothered me ever since. I allowed myself to be bullied into taking a combative, unstable, nonmedical patient in the ambulance and I placed myself in a potentially dangerous situation. I've given it a lot of thought. Put in a similar position again, I will refuse to transport. If the rest of the crew wants to do it, fine. If Dr. Cardone needs to call a paid service or must drive the patient in her own car, so be it. I will not do anything like that again. Period. I'll probably be suspended from FVAC, too.

Some First-Aid Hints

You've been reading about EMTs and the way we do our job. What is also important to us is how you do yours—you who could be the first one on the scene of a sudden illness or accident. Ed and I would like to give you some tips on what to do till the ambulance comes. Remember, there's usually something you can do to help.

First: Try to stay calm. Take several deep breaths, if necessary, and keep your wits about you. In a crisis adrenaline pumps through your body, giving you the extra burst of energy you need to fight or run away. This adrenaline causes your heartbeat to speed up, your breathing to become faster, and your hands to shake. The emergency causes your brain to race and your thoughts to become jumbled. That is counterproductive. Take a moment and tell yourself to keep cool.

Second: Check the area around your patient for hazards. Your safety is most important. I don't want to arrive in the ambulance and find that, instead of a patient and a rescuer, I have to care for two patients. Check for the following:

Electrical hazards. Take care that power is turned off before you step into the puddle of water with an electrocuted patient. Don't overlook broken power poles with dangling wires. On one occasion I arrived at a scene in my car, parked, and began to care for my patient. It was fifteen minutes before one of the police officers pointed out the broken electrical pole and the wire hanging only inches from my vehicle.

Animals. A barking dog does bite, as do rabid animals, snakes, and other creatures. If it just bit your patient, it might just bite you, too.

Fire hazards. Don't climb into a burning car or building to rescue people. I know that sounds harsh, and I guess it is. On those rescue TV shows, we see the valiant and successful efforts of those who brave serious injury and rescue the entrapped victim. I applaud them and appreciate their bravery. What you don't see on those shows, however, are the dozens of heroic people who, under similar circumstances, braved smoke and flames and were overcome and seriously injured or killed. Let the professionals do what they are trained and equipped to do.

Automobile-accident hazards. Take care with cars that are not firmly anchored. When the car goes over the cliff, don't be in it. Enough said.

Third: Look around for information. What happened? How many victims are there? Are there others who can help? If you're on a roadway, be sure you know where you are. Look for street signs and/or mile markers.

Fourth: Check the victim. Is the victim unconscious? If so and if you know how to do this, see if he/she is breathing and has a pulse. Is there any severe, spurting bleeding that you can control with direct pressure (discussed below)?

Fifth: Dial 911 or your local emergency number. Tell them your exact location and the kind of help you need, your name and the number from which you are calling, the number and approximate seriousness of the injuries, and whether anyone is giving care. Don't hang up until the dispatcher hangs up. He or she may be able to give you information about what care to give or may have additional questions.

After you call for help, there are several things you can do to care for a victim of illness or accident. But here's a big no-no. Don't move anyone unless you absolutely have to. Do not "make him more comfortable" by helping him out of the car or putting a pillow under his head.

You absolutely have to move someone if he's in a dangerous situation: fire, flood, explosion, cave-in, or the like. In that case, if you are already beside him or her, move the victim carefully, helping him walk, carrying him or dragging him by the shoulders along the long axis of his body. Try never to move anyone sideways.

A few specific ways you can help a victim.

1. If the person has no pulse and/or isn't breathing and you know what to do, start CPR, do rescue breathing, or initiate the Heimlich maneuver.

2. Care for serious bleeding. First, put something between your hands and the patient's blood: latex gloves, plastic wrap, a sandwich bag, or whatever else you can find. Next, place the cleanest thing you can find against the wound: a sterile dressing or clean cloth. Then apply direct pressure to the wound with your hand, elevating it above the level of the heart if possible. Keep the pressure on until the bleeding slows down.

3. Keep a sick person from moving. That might involve sitting with a conscious patient until help arrives, or it might mean holding the head of a groggy victim to prevent movement.

4. If the person is walking around, help him to sit or lie down. If he seems chilly or his skin is cold or sweaty, cover him with a blanket or whatever you can find. Keep the patient calm by reassuring him or her and remaining calm yourself.

5. Don't give anyone anything to eat or drink. The only exception is a diabetic who specifically tells you he needs sugar. In that case, and that case only, you may give a fully conscious person a drink of juice or soda. I was at a nature camp with a group of eighth graders a number of years ago and I was called to the side of a young man in insulin shock. He had taken his shot that morning and had then exercised heavily without eating. Some bystander, trying to be helpful, was giving him Diet Pepsi. I quickly substituted a nondiet soda, explaining that the boy needed sugar and diet soda has none.

6. Cool a burn with lots of cold, running water for several minutes until the victim says it feels better. Then, if the ambulance is still far away, cover the burn loosely with something sterile and dry. Do not put on burn cream if the burn might require medical attention! It only gets in the way. Do not clean the burn in any way or break blisters. Keep the victim warm and calm and wait for the ambulance.

7. If you think someone has been poisoned, call for emergency medical assistance, then call your local poison control center. The phone number should be in the front of your phone book. Tell poison control everything you know about what the patient might have swallowed, or breathed, or gotten on his skin. Inform the poison control operator that an ambulance is responding and, if you know, how long it will take to reach the scene. Answer any questions the operator might have and act accordingly. If you can and the ambulance isn't too far away, keep poison control on the line until the ambulance arrives so the EMTs can confer with the operator.

This information is, of course, no substitute for training. The American Heart Association and the American Red Cross offer courses in adult, child, and infant CPR, and the Red Cross also has an excellent standard first-aid course that includes adult CPR. If you're interested, contact your local chapter of one of these organizations, or your local ambulance corps or rescue squad for more information.

There are also many excellent books on emergency medicine written for any level of interest and training.

The most important thing is to be mentally prepared to check the scene, call the emergency medical services, and care for the patient.

Chapter 9

When we teach CPR, chest compressions and rescue breathing are performed on nice, clean mannequins. We tell students how many lives have been saved because bystanders began CPR immediately. We don't discuss the fact that CPR is rarely successful in cardiac arrest due to trauma.

Many CPR instructors have never performed CPR on a real person, and they themselves don't understand that it's a messy procedure—ribs break when you do chest compressions and patients vomit while you are doing mouth-to-mouth. When you are unprepared for the reality of CPR, the experience can be shattering.

I had been a member of FVAC for two years, and had myself become a CPR instructor before I ever had to deal with a code—a cardiac arrest—and, like everyone else, had demonstrated all the techniques on Annie, my mannequin. My first experience with CPR on a real person occurred, not on an ambulance call, but on my way home from work. Whereas today I carry first-aid equipment, including protective CPR masks, and a disposable BVM in my car, twenty years ago, when this accident happened, I had nothing with me other than my hands and my mouth. And AIDS hadn't been invented yet.

Evening rush-hour traffic was heavy but moving at the speed limit as I turned onto the parkway and headed north. A fire engine had gotten onto the parkway just ahead of me with its siren wailing and I vaguely wondered where it was going. As I drove, traffic parted and the engine disappeared from view.

Coming around a curve after cresting the first hill, I could see that the engine had pulled over onto the shoulder of the road about a thousand feet ahead of me. I slowed down and, as I approached, I could see a car that had driven into a tree. I pulled over in front of the fire engine, eager to be of help.

The first thing I heard as I stepped out of the car was the shrieking of a teenage girl who was lying on the grass about thirty feet from me. I ran over to her and quickly determined that, although she was obviously badly hurt and in extreme pain, she did not appear to have any immediate life-threatening injury. Glancing up toward the almost-demolished car, I saw a woman slumped forward over the steering wheel and a fireman pulling the driver's-side door open. I ran over. "My name's Ed and I'm an EMT," I said.

"I don't think she's breathing," the fireman said to me. "Do you want to check?"

"Of course," I said with the confidence of my EMT skills behind me.

The fireman stepped aside and allowed me to get to the woman. The windshield was shattered and her head was covered with blood and broken glass. She didn't appear to be breathing and, pressing my finger against the side of her neck, I could find no carotid pulse. "I think she's in full arrest," I said. "Let's get her out fast."

The fireman and I quickly dragged the woman, who appeared to be in her forties, out of the car and placed her, faceup, on the ground. I placed my ear next to her nose and mouth and looked at her chest, while palpating her neck for a carotid pulse. She was not breathing and had no pulse. I looked at the fireman. "Do you know CPR?" I asked.

"Yeah. I'll do compressions."

I looked down at the woman's lifeless face. It was covered with blood and broken glass, some of which was imbedded in her skin. While the fireman got into position to begin chest compression, I brushed away as much of the glass as I could and began blowing into her mouth, just like I had done in CPR class a hundred times. As the fireman began to compress the woman's chest, I heard the snapping of ribs. I looked at his hand position and it looked all right so we continued.

At that time CPR was performed a bit differently than it is now. I had to fit my breaths between his compressions so I had to concentrate to establish the correct rhythm. I remember it so well. At that time the rhythm was one one-thousand, two one-thousand, three one-thousand, four one-thousand, five breathe.

After several minutes I was getting tired. "Wanna switch?" I asked.

"Sorry, but I won't do mouth-to-mouth."

Okay, I thought. We'll continue this way.

It seemed like we had been doing CPR for hours when we heard the siren of an approaching ambulance. At last we would be relieved. As the siren grew louder the woman's stomach contents began to come up. I cleaned her face and continued breathing into her mouth.

Out of the corner of my eye I watched the ambulance crew tend to the screaming, injured girl and load her into the ambulance. The fireman and I continued doing CPR as the ambulance rolled away, leaving us doing CPR without any help. "Hey," I yelled between breaths. "What about us?"

I knew that we were legally obligated to continue until we were physically unable to do so, and I had always assumed that physically unable to continue meant too exhausted to do any more chest compressions. Now, however, I found it increasingly difficult to continue to do rescue breathing. Between breaths, I looked down at the woman's face, covered with blood, glass, and stomach contents. Every time I attempted to breathe into the woman's mouth, my throat muscles went into spasm, and, finally, I was unable to continue. "I can't do any more," I gasped, gagging.

The fireman stood up. "Yeah," he said, "me, too. It's no use anyway. She's dead." He turned and walked away.

I continued to kneel at the side of the lifeless body for a few more seconds, then, realizing that there was nothing more I could do, I too stood and walked back toward my car.

I have done CPR many times since that automobile accident. I have even had a few saves over the years, including a traumatic arrest save, but I have never again been able to do mouth-to-mouth rescue breathing. I carry a BVM in my car and, at any call in which there might be a need for rescue breathing, it's the first thing I pull out of my trunk.

My reputation is that of an overtreater—an EMT who often takes unnecessary precautions. The characterization is probably justified, but I would rather fully immobilize a hundred automobile-accident victims who don't have a spinal injury than fail to immobilize one who does and possibly produce a paraplegic. Of course, the immobilization is uncomfortable for the patient and time-consuming for the crew.

Despite the great cost I would rather call a helicopter to transport a questionably critical patient than have a patient die in the ambulance en route to the hospital, or arrive too late to be saved. But sometimes those decisions can be embarrassing.

I listened to my scanner as the Davenport dispatcher toned out for the second time. "Police to the Davenport Ambulance Corps. A full crew is needed for a rollover on Ash Road near Winston Court. Please call in."

No one had responded to the first page, and I doubted

that Davenport would be able to raise a crew. Davenport is a two-hundred-year-old river city to the north of Fairfax. Its ambulance corps, like many other volunteer ambulance corps and rescue squads, is often unable to raise a crew during the day on weekdays, and this was a second-rig call. They had needed to page out five times to cover the first call: a woman in labor.

The intersection of Ash and Winston is over the town line, but only a few minutes from my house, and I knew that, if they could not raise a crew, Davenport would call Fairfax for mutual aid. That would take another five minutes, and by that time I could be at the scene. I saved the material on my computer screen, grabbed my coat and pager, and dashed out of the house as Davenport toned out for the third time. I would probably be the first EMT at the scene. If Davenport raised a crew I would assist them. If they called Fairfax for mutual aid I would work with the responding crew.

Ash Road winds through a narrow ravine that connects Fairfax with Davenport. As I rounded a particularly sharp bend, I saw the car, which lay on its side across the center of the road surrounded by Davenport firefighters. As I approached, I identified myself. "I'm Ed Herman, an EMT with Fairfax Ambulance. Can I help?"

A Davenport firefighter whom I knew turned to me. "Oh, hi, Ed," he said. "We couldn't raise a crew so we called you guys. They're toning out now."

"Yeah, I've already radioed in. All they'll need now is a driver and an attendant. What have we got?"

"Talk to Chet."

As the firefighters parted to allow me to get close to the car, I gasped. It seemed unlikely anyone could live through an accident that caused that much damage. The car lay on the driver's side, the front end pushed in like the face of a pug dog. Pebbles of safety glass from the demolished windows lay mixed with white and red glass from the lights. Even the up-facing passenger side was crushed, indicating that the vehicle had rolled at least once.

I looked down through the passenger-window space and saw a teenage girl lying faceup draped across the driver's-side door, her head on the pavement through the missing window and her feet out through the opening where the windshield had been. I saw no blood or obvious sign of injury. The girl's eyes were closed and she was silent. I assumed the firefighter leaning in through the windshield opening was Chet. "How is she?" I asked, kneeling beside him.

"I can't find any injuries," he responded, pulling out of the vehicle and shaking his head. "I think she's just scared. We're going to pull her out, feet first, through the windshield."

"Hold up until I check her out," I said. "Can you guys get the passenger door open so that I can get to her head?"

Within a minute, the passenger-side door, now the top of the car, was open and a group of firefighters lifted me and dropped me in. I knelt and placed my hands on both sides of the girl's head.

"My name is Ed," I said. "I'm an EMT with the Fairfax Ambulance. What's your name?"

Although her chest was rising and falling, the unconscious girl did not reply. I noticed that she was a pretty girl with unmarked ivory skin and long red hair. I could see no obvious sign of injury. "Where are you hurt?" I asked.

No response.

"Does anyone know her name?" I asked the firefighters through the missing windshield.

"It's Eva," one of them answered.

"Eva. Can you hear me?" I asked.

Eva lay silent.

I pinched her skin. "Eva, can you feel that?" I asked.

No response.

I looked at Eva's face. Her eyes had opened, but they

were glazed and staring. Without warning Eva began to shriek and flail her arms and legs, but strangely her head remained still, pressed between my hands and resting against the door.

"It's all right, Eva. We're taking good care of you. Try to relax and tell me what hurts."

Eva did not look at me or seem aware that she wasn't alone. As she continued struggling and yelling at the top of her lungs I tried to slide one hand further under Eva's head to check for a head injury. I was unable to do so. My gloved fingers wouldn't slide between her scalp and the pavement. What the hell is going on? I wondered.

Suddenly, I realized that several thick locks of her long red hair were caught under the roof of the car, pinning her head to the road surface through the shattered side window. The back of her head had obviously hit the pavement hard when the body of the car had rolled and trapped her. Her combative behavior was a good indication of a severe head injury.

"Get the chopper here ASAP," I yelled through the windshield and I watched one of the firefighters sprint to the radio in the engine. My priority now was to free my patient. "I need some muscle," I yelled. "This girl may have a critical head injury and her hair is caught under the car. Can you guys roll the vehicle just a fraction of an inch so that I can get her loose? Do it real easy and try to protect her neck."

Three burly firefighters pressed their gloved hands against the roof of the car and pushed. As soon as the car had moved enough to free Eva's hair, she tried to sit up, continuing to shriek and flail her arms and legs. "Eva, try to relax. Try to calm down. My name is Ed and I'll stay with you. Easy." I fought to hold her head stable and keep her supine. Suddenly, Eva stopped shrieking, and her body became limp. Her eyes closed and she was again silent and unresponsive. I felt the back of her head but could find no blood or swelling.

By now the Fairfax Ambulance had arrived and Fred Stevens was kneeling at Eva's feet. "What do you need, Ed?" he asked.

"Get me a penlight, Fred," I said. "And get a c-collar, backboard, and head blocks over here stat. Let's get her immobilized while she's quiet."

"What size collar do you need?" Fred asked, handing me a penlight from the megaduffel.

Because of her unconsciousness, I was momentarily able to release her head. I placed my fingers in the space between Eva's shoulder and the bottom of her jaw. Two fingers fit. "Looks like a short collar should be fine."

Fred went to get the equipment I had asked for. I knelt over Eva's face, gently pulled her left eyelid open, and directed the narrow beam of light onto the pupil of her eye. The pupil was open wide and, at first, did not react to the light. "Damn," I muttered, "her pupils are blown." Dilated and unresponsive pupils are another indication of severe injury to the brain. As I watched, slowly and weakly the pupil began to contract.

Fred returned from the rig and passed a cervical collar to me through the windshield opening. I quickly fastened it around Eva's neck while the ambulance crew placed the top of the longboard at Eva's feet. "We'll pull her right onto the board, feet first," Fred directed.

"Okay," I replied. "I'll keep holding her head."

The crew got into position to move Eva, then Fred called to me. "We're ready. On your count, Ed."

"Okay. One, two, three." As the crew slid Eva out of the car, I held her head as still as I could. After her head had passed through the windshield, another crew member took over while I climbed out of the car. We had just gotten Eva into position on the backboard and were about to strap her down when her eyes flew open and she began to shriek and fight us again.

"It's okay, Eva," Fred said, trying to calm her. "We're here to help you."

Eva continued to scream and fight our efforts to strap her to the longboard. Oxygen is our first line of defense against the damage done by a head injury but, when I tried to put an oxygen mask over her face, she grabbed at it and pushed it away.

"Eva," Fred shouted into the girl's ear, "this oxygen will help you."

"I don't think she can hear you, Fred," I said as we struggled to hold her still and immobilize her. Eva's continued combative behavior assured me that I had been right in calling for the helicopter.

We managed to get her strapped down and, in order to keep her on oxygen, we tied her wrists to the handholds of the long spineboard. At least now we could keep the mask over her nose and mouth. As we transported her in the ambulance a half mile to the high school parking lot that had been designated as the helicopter landing zone, I checked the girl's body, looking for signs of other injury. I found no broken bones, no signs of internal injuries. That's good, I told myself. Maybe the head trauma isn't complicated by anything else.

I heaved a sigh of relief when, within a few minutes, Eva was aboard the helicopter and en route to St. Luke's Trauma Center. As I watched the "bird" disappear, I thought to myself, thank God for the helicopter. I was not sure that Eva would have survived without it. As a matter of fact, I was not sure that the girl would survive anyway, and, as often happens after a bad call, I was afraid to call the hospital for fear of learning that my patient had died.

Two days later, I was summoned to ambulance headquarters by Pam Kovacs, the corps' first lieutenant and hospital liaison. "Ed," she said to me. "Do you know how much a helicopter flight costs?"

"No," I replied. "I guess I've never thought about it, Pam. Why?"

"Well, it costs close to $2,000 for a single flight and insurance doesn't even cover half of that. The hospital wanted me to discuss the cost with you with regard to that rollover the other day."

I could feel my face redden. "We needed that helicopter. That girl had serious head trauma," I replied, feeling confused and growing angry.

"Why did you decide that? The hospital apparently found nothing wrong with her. They kept her overnight for observation and released her the next day."

I felt the flush in my face deepen, with embarrassment now. Had I gone off half-cocked and grossly exaggerated the situation? A car on its side, flashing emergency lights, screaming . . . It was easy to get carried away. But I hadn't.

"Listen, Pam," I said, "here's what happened." I related to her point by point what I had found and what I had done. As I went over the call I realized that calling for the helicopter had been absolutely appropriate according to the mechanism of injury and what I had observed at the scene of the accident.

When I ended my account of the call, Pam said, "I would have done the same, Ed. I'm really sorry I mentioned it." Still, there was no way to squelch the talk around headquarters, that I had insisted on calling the helicopter for an uninjured patient.

I never learned the reason for Eva's bizarre behavior but I've discussed the call with many other EMTs since. "Drugs," some suggested. "Alcohol, maybe." "Maybe a concussion that scrambled her brain for a while." "You know, I never will understand teenagers," an old-timer said. "Maybe she was just hysterical."

Oh well. I'll continue to sin on the side of caution. Although I'm still a bit embarrassed about that call, at least no patient in a similar situation has come to harm through my inaction.

* * *

911 is a lifesaver. Literally. Not only is there one, simple number to remember, but with the enhanced system we have in our county, the caller's phone number and the address from which the call was placed appear on a computer screen. In that way, a lot of confusion is eliminated. Unfortunately, on some calls, even 911 can't help.

The wail of our siren wound down as we turned into the quiet, residential street and rolled to a stop in front of 1505 Blackberry Hill. Bob Fiorella was going to meet us at the scene. Our crew chief, Stephanie DiMartino, riding shotgun, picked up the microphone from the control panel. "45–01 to GKL–642 Fairfax Ambulance base," she called.

"Base on," our dispatcher Greg Horvath replied.

"Be advised 45–01 is on location."

"10–4, 45–01. You are on location at 15:32."

"What do you need, Steph?" I asked.

"I don't know, Ed," Stephanie replied. "The call came in as an unknown medical. Bring the oxygen and the crash kit and let's see what we have."

I went around and opened the side door, grabbed the red bag that contained the oxygen tank, airways, and trauma supplies in one hand, and the defibrillator in the other, and followed Stephanie up the path to the front door. Stephanie rang the doorbell then tried the door. It was locked. "Fairfax Ambulance," she shouted, then grabbed the metal knocker and rapped several times sharply on the door.

We could hear movement in the house and after a few seconds the door was opened by a woman who appeared to be in her late fifties. "Yes? Can I help you?" she asked, looking at the uniformed ambulance crew at her front door with a puzzled expression.

"Fairfax Ambulance."

"Yes?"

"Where's the patient?" Stephanie asked.

"What patient?" the woman replied.

"Didn't you call for an ambulance?"

"No. Nobody called for an ambulance here."

"Is this 1505 Blackberry Hill?" Stephanie asked.

"Yes it is, but no one needs an ambulance here. There's just me and my grown daughter. She's upstairs taking a nap. We're both fine. I don't know who called you, but we didn't."

"Your name, ma'am?"

"Mrs. Roy Arnold."

Stephanie held her portable radio to her mouth and keyed the microphone. "45–01 to GKL–642 Fairfax Ambulance base."

"Base on," our dispatcher replied.

"Can you verify the numerical on this call?"

"10–4. It's 1505 Blackberry Hill."

"We're at the location and the call appears to be unfounded. Do you have a callback number?" Stephanie asked.

"Negative. The caller was in the city, dialed the old police direct number, gave the Blackberry address, and hung up."

"Greg, contact FPD and see if they have any way to verify the numerical," Stephanie suggested. "We'll stand by here."

"10–4," Greg acknowledged.

"Have any of your neighbors been ill?" I asked the woman, while we waited. "Maybe the house number is wrong."

"No, not that I know of," the woman replied.

"Is there anybody who might want to play a practical joke on you?" I asked.

"No," she answered indignantly. "We get along fine with all of our neighbors."

Stephanie's portable barked. "GKL–642 to 45–01."

"45–01 on. Go ahead, 642." As Stephanie spoke, Bob Fiorella pulled up in his car, green light flashing.

"FPD doesn't have any more than we gave you. A

man called them and told them that he had been on the phone with his wife when she suddenly told him that she didn't feel well, and then the line went dead. He gave her address as 1505 Blackberry Hill, but hung up before they could get a callback number. FPD replayed the tape and they're pretty sure the numerical is 1505 although there was some static on the line."

"10–4, Greg. We're going to stand by here for a while. We'll let you know when we're back in service." Stephanie turned to me and Bob. "It's probably a false alarm but let's knock on some doors before we go 10–8. I'll get the houses to the left. Bob, you take the ones to the right. And, Ed, why don't you try the houses across the street."

Leaving all our equipment on the doorstep at 1505, we spread out and began knocking on doors. I walked up to the house directly across from 1505 and rang the bell. After a few seconds, the door flew open and a woman in her mid-twenties glared at me. "What the hell do you want?" she snarled.

"I'm sorry to disturb you, ma'am," I apologized, "but this is an emergency. Did anyone here call for an ambulance?"

"No," she snapped at me. "And who the hell do you think you are, coming here and making noise. You woke my baby up." She slammed the door in my face.

In contrast, the man in 1510 was courteous and concerned. "No, I didn't call for an ambulance," he said. "Is there anything I can do to help?"

Just then, I heard Mrs. Arnold's loud voice from across the street. "She's unconscious, she's unconscious. Help! Come back!" She now stood just inside her front door, waving her arms.

We sprinted back to the house. "Upstairs. Please hurry," Mrs. Arnold pleaded.

In a bedroom at the top of the stairs we found a woman of about twenty, fully dressed, lying faceup on a bed. She appeared to be unconscious. Her hand hung over the side of the bed and beneath her hand was a telephone receiver.

"After you left, I remembered that the phone rang about ten minutes before you got here, and that she must have picked it up. I came upstairs to check on her, just to be sure and I found her like this." The older woman had tears streaming down her face. "Her husband works in the city. He must have called the police when the phone fell out of her hand. I didn't know it was her. Is she dead? Oh, Jesus."

"What's her name?" Stephanie asked.

"Celia Wally. What's wrong with her? Oh, God, I should have checked on her when you first got here."

"Celia!" Stephanie shouted at the girl. "Can you hear me?"

"Unh," the girl replied, eyes still closed.

"She's not dead?"

"No, ma'am," Stephanie said.

"Look at her," the woman yelled. "She's all wet. What's wrong?"

As Stephanie touched the girl's forehead, I reached for her wrist. Her pulse was strong and a bit rapid. Her breathing was shallow and rapid and her body was drenched in sweat.

"Celia. Can you tell us what happened?" Stephanie asked.

Celia moaned and shook her head.

Stephanie turned to the girl's mother. "Has anything like this ever happened before?"

"This happened a month ago and she went to the doctor. She had lots of tests, but she doesn't tell me anything. I'm only her mother, after all."

"Did you see her this morning? Did she seem all right?"

"I saw her at breakfast. I ate, she drank coffee."

"Did she have lunch?"

"I haven't seen her all day. Just stays up here in her room and watches those TV talk shows."

As I reached into the trauma bag for a tube of glucose, I heard Sally Jessy Raphael in the background.

"Did the doctor say anything about her sugar?" Stephanie asked.

"She didn't tell me. She tells her husband, but not her mother."

Ruling nothing out, Stephanie asked, "Does your daughter take any medications on a regular basis?"

"If you mean does she do drugs, the answer is absolutely no." She glared at the two of us. "She's a good girl."

That hadn't been what Stephanie meant, but the woman protested almost too vigorously. The symptoms and her mother's mention of medical tests suggested insulin shock, a rapid reaction to too-little sugar in the blood. It was usually caused by a diabetic taking insulin and failing to eat properly. However, drugs couldn't be ruled out.

"Celia," Stephanie asked, "have you taken anything?"

Celia shook her head from side to side. She was responding to our questions, although she was very groggy.

"Ed, why don't you give her that glucose," Stephanie suggested. "She may be hypoglycemic even if she isn't a diabetic."

I pulled a plastic tube of insta-glucose out of the trauma bag, twisted off the top, and held the tip of the tube to Celia's mouth. "Celia, I'm going to put something in your mouth. It's very sweet and it doesn't taste very good, but it may help you. Can you open your mouth for me?"

The girl groggily opened her mouth and I squeezed some of the pasty glucose into her mouth. She spat most of it out, coating my hand with sticky, pink goo.

"Celia," her mother barked. "Don't do that!"

"She's not aware of what she's doing," I told her.

Slowly, with as much ending up on Stephanie and me

as in Celia, we emptied the entire tube of glucose. It didn't seem to have any effect.

"Celia, we're going to take you over to the hospital to find out what's wrong with you. Okay?" Stephanie asked.

"Unh." Celia nodded. We'd try to get another tube of glucose into her en route.

By the time we arrived at Fairfax General, Celia, Stephanie, and I, as well as the stretcher and much of the inside of the rig, were coated with insta-glucose. But Celia's condition had begun to improve. She was more alert and did tell us that the doctor had told her she had blood-sugar problems.

Celia's condition should be easily controllable with diet and medication. We haven't had to return to the house on Blackberry Hill.

We were on the way back to headquarters after transporting a very inebriated man to Fairfax General. I was driving and Steve Nesbitt was riding shotgun. "Ed, pull into the Parkway Motor Inn for a minute. Someone was supposed to leave something for me at the office there."

"OK, Steve," I replied.

"Oh and by the way. Don't drive under the overhang," he added, smiling.

"No, Steve." I grinned back. "I *never* drive under the overhang at the Parkway Motor Inn."

"Well, I'm just making sure," he said, loudly so that Tim Babbett, who was riding in back, could hear. "That drunk we just transported reminded me of the time long ago that I took a call here and bad things happened."

"What bad things?" Tim yelled through the window from the back of the rig.

I made the left turn into the long driveway to the motel. Ten or fifteen years ago, Steve's storytelling would have made me cringe, but now it was just a story, and a funny one at that.

"It had something to do with a drunk, didn't it, Ed?"

"Yeah, it did, Steve. But it was a long time ago." I gave him my best you're-not-going-to-tell-that-story-again look.

"I think I remember," Tim tried to contribute to the conversation. "Wasn't it about three years ago?"

Steve turned around in his seat. "Naw, you're too young to remember it, Tim." Then he turned back to me. "But Ed remembers it, don't you, Ed?"

I pulled up in front of the office and rolled my eyes. "Get the fuck out, you old fart, before I tell Tim about the time you locked yourself in the ambulance alone with that big toothless lady-psycho who was after your body. If I remember correctly, she almost had your pants off by the time we got the door open."

Steve roared with laughter as he opened the door and stepped out of the ambulance.

But I couldn't help remembering that night, almost twenty years ago.

Both of my children, three-year-old Davida and one-year-old Arielle, were miserable, with heavy colds, and had been up repeatedly during the night. It was after 3:00 A.M. and since they had finally both fallen asleep I rubbed my gritty eyes and staggered into the bedroom. Maybe I can get a few hours of sleep before I have to get up to go to work, I thought, climbing between the sheets. Suddenly the phone rang.

Shit, I thought, I'm on ambulance duty. I lunged for the phone so that it wouldn't wake the kids.

"Hello?"

"Hi, Ed. It's Mark Thomas at FPD. You've got a call. A drunk at the Parkway Motor Inn fell and cut his head. He's in Room 205, just above the office. The officer at the scene says to take it easy. The guy's not hurt bad, but he wants to go to the hospital. Steve Nesbitt and Linda Potemski will meet you at FVAC."

"Okay, Mark, I'll respond to headquarters." I threw on my uniform and staggered out into the night.

The ambulance was already on the apron and the garage doors were closed by the time I pulled into the FVAC parking lot. Steve, who was crew chief, was in the front and Linda was in back. I was scheduled to be the driver on this shift. I climbed behind the wheel, pushed the series of switches to turn on the emergency lights, and rolled out into the street. At this hour of the night, I would probably not need my siren and there was no reason to wake up the town. I flicked the *horn/ siren* switch to siren so that, if I needed to use the siren, all I had to do was press the horn on the steering wheel.

As we rolled down the motel driveway and approached the long, two-story building, I saw an FPD patrol car. It was parked in front of the office, under the overhang, which allowed people to enter the office from their cars without getting wet during bad weather. The overhang was too low for the ambulance to fit under. All of the members of FVAC were aware of that.

I pulled up close to the overhang, just behind the patrol car, assisted Linda in getting some equipment out of the rig, then followed Steve up the stairs.

Our patient was standing in the middle of a very messy room. Clothes were strewn everywhere and the bedspread and sheets were in a heap in the center of the floor. The man was in his mid-thirties, six feet tall, about two hundred and fifty pounds, red-eyed, and very, very drunk. His white T-shirt was covered with blood, but Police Officer Chuck Harding had already dressed and bandaged his head injury.

"He fell and hit his head against the corner of the desk," Chuck told us, "but the bleeding had stopped by the time I got here. His name is Sam. Sam Wagner."

"Who the fuck are they?" Sam glared at us.

"They're EMTs with the ambulance corps. Let them examine your head," Chuck ordered.

"I don't need no fuckin' EMTs. I need another drink.

Where's my Scotch?" He began lifting the mattress, as if the bottle might be underneath it.

"It's gone," Chuck replied. "You finished it."

Chuck showed Steve an empty bottle of a rather expensive Scotch whiskey. "This guy gets drunk on only the best," he said. There were also a number of bottles of imported German beer scattered around the room.

"Sam," Steve said, "let us examine you, then we'll take you over to Fairfax General."

"What for?" Sam asked.

"You fell and cut your head."

"I didn't fall and I ain't goin' to no fuckin' hospital."

"Sam," Chuck interrupted, "you asked us to call the ambulance. You got them up in the middle of the night. Now, why don't you just let them do their job."

Sam looked at Chuck then at Steve and me. "I got you fellas up in the middle of the night?" He paused, then tears formed in the corners of his eyes. "You were asleep? I'm awful sorry. Thanks. That's so great. Let me shake your hand." He held an unsteady hand out to Steve. Steve shook his hand then led him to a chair.

Oh well, I thought, better maudlin than belligerent.

"You guys are really great to do this," the man wailed. "Really great."

We examined Sam, obtained a quick set of vitals, and decided against any immobilization.

"Hey, guys, thanks for coming," the guy said again. "Really. Thanks."

With Chuck's help, we led Sam down the stairs to the waiting ambulance. In addition to being exhausted, my stomach was starting to rebel against the smell of the vomit-and-whiskey-soaked room that our patient had been in.

As I walked around to the driver's seat, I gulped a deep breath of night air. It helped, but not enough. I swallowed hard, then climbed behind the wheel and waited while Steve and Linda settled Sam on the stretcher and fastened the seat belts.

Chuck came over to my open window. "I'll follow you to the hospital, in case of any trouble," he said. He got into his patrol car and pulled forward just as Steve yelled to me, "We're all set, Ed. Take it code 2, nice and easy."

I picked up the microphone. "45–01 to all units. Be advised 45–01 is en route to Fairfax General with one male patient." Then I shifted to drive and slowly began to drive forward.

Suddenly I heard a grinding sound from the top of the cab and the ambulance lurched to a stop. What the hell is going on? I asked myself. Then, with a sickening feeling in my gut I realized that I had parked so close to the overhang that, in the dark, it was high enough to be out of my line of sight. In my exhausted state, I had simply forgotten that it was there and had attempted to follow the patrol car.

Shit, I've damaged the top of the rig, I thought. There'll be hell to pay. Damaging the ambulance is considered to be an almost-capital offense at FVAC. Well, I thought, I'll have to worry about it later. I have a patient in the back who needs to be transported to the hospital. I'll just back out and go around, like I should have done in the first place. I thought about our new captain, Mark Leary—a tough, no-nonsense postal worker who had just been elected. Damn, damn, damn, I thought.

I shifted into reverse and pressed lightly on the gas pedal. The engine whined, but the rig didn't move. Oh, great, I thought. It's stuck. Maybe just more gas will do it. I pressed a little harder on the gas pedal, and with a lurch, the ambulance moved back.

I remember the rest like a disjointed movie: The tons of concrete crashing down in front of me as the overhang collapsed, demolishing and partially burying the front of the ambulance. The cloud of steam rising from the wreckage. The sound of the approaching fire engines and police cars. The second rig arriving to pick up our patient. The photographer's flashbulbs. The questions. The attempt to explain what had happened in my written report. The next day's headlines. And the horrible feeling, "Oh, God, what have I done?"

I was suspended from riding the ambulance pending an investigation of the incident, and a hearing was held by FVAC's board of directors. I was charged with negligence. I was shocked to find that some FVAC members wanted to hang me over what I considered an accident; a serious accident, but an accident nonetheless. Others were supportive.

About three weeks after the accident, I received a phone call from the chairman of FVAC's board of directors. "Ed," he said, "the board has decided that what happened was an accident and that you should not be penalized. The insurance will, of course, pay for all the damage and many of us want to leave it at that." I could hear a heavy sigh. "We have a problem, however," he continued. "Captain Leary is furious about it and he feels that you were negligent."

I could picture Mark's face, with its usual scowl.

The chairman continued. "Evidently the chief of the fire department told him that he had hung the newspaper picture of the wrecked ambulance in the firehouse with the caption DON'T LET THIS HAPPEN TO YOU. Mark is embarrassed and feels that you've made him look bad. He told the board that, whatever we decide, he will not certify you to ride as long as he is captain."

"Can he do that?" I asked. "Even if the board exonerates me?"

"Yes, I'm afraid he can. He has the authority, and he doesn't even have to give a reason other than that he doesn't feel that you are competent to function on the ambulance.

"Also, Ed," he continued, "the corps is very divided. Some members want to throw you out and others are strongly defending you."

"Well, what can I do?" I asked.

"The board is unofficially asking you to take a leave of absence for a year. If you try to fight the captain, it will split the corps apart. And you won't win."

"Shit," I muttered.

"Mark is planning to move to Washington State next year when he retires, and obviously he won't run for captain again. So next year, with a new captain, you can return from leave and start riding again."

"I'll think about it," I said.

I thought about it for two days. Being an EMT was very important to me, and, despite lots of personal infighting and bickering, FVAC was, and still is, one of the finest volunteer ambulance corps in the area. I have always been willing to fight for what I want or believe in but two days later, I filed an official request for an indefinite leave of absence from FVAC. My request was immediately granted.

I spent the following year doing volunteer work in the emergency room of Fairfax General Hospital. In order to maintain my EMS skills, I became an American Red Cross CPR and Advanced First Aid Instructor and took a course in driving emergency vehicles.

One year later, three days after the new captain took office, I began riding with FVAC again as probably the most qualified EMT in the corps.

There are times when we conveniently develop *radio problems* during ambulance calls.

We had been dispatched to a collision between an automobile and a motorcycle on Ash Road, the winding road that leads from Davenport into Fairfax. We were responding with lights and siren. Car versus motorcycle accidents tend to be bad and we were concerned about the serious injuries we might have to deal with at the scene. We were about a half mile from the town line when the radio awoke. "Fairfax Police to 45–01."

I picked up the microphone. "45–01 on. Go ahead, Fairfax Police."

"We've been advised by a Davenport PD unit on the scene that the PIAA is over the town line. Davenport Ambulance is being dispatched. You can cancel your response."

I released the microphone key and looked at Pam Kovacs who was driving. "We're about one minute from the scene," I said to her. "Davenport will have to tone out for a crew."

Pam and I both knew that, if Davenport VAC could raise a crew on a Monday afternoon, it would take them at least ten minutes to respond from their headquarters. And it was also possible that they would page out unsuccessfully for three or four minutes, then end up calling on us to respond as mutual aid anyway.

"Davenport will be pissed if we buff the call," Pam responded, but did not slow down.

"Let them be pissed," I replied. "This could be a bad one. I'm not going to leave someone lying out on the road because he's twenty feet over the town line."

I keyed the mike. "45–01 to FPD. Would you repeat your message, please."

The Fairfax Police dispatcher repeated the message.

"45–01 to FPD, you're being stepped on." Our radio frequency is used by other agencies and frequently their transmissions, although not audible, will interfere with ours. "Say again."

The dispatcher repeated his message for the third time.

"We cannot read you. We'll try you again in a few minutes."

As we crossed the town line we could see the row of flares and the Davenport patrol car. A Davenport cop was kneeling over a supine body lying next to a badly mangled motorcycle.

As we rolled to a stop, I keyed the mike. "45–01 to FPD. We're out on location." I winked at Pam. "Be advised this PIAA is in Davenport. Please dispatch Davenport VAC and advise them that we will render assistance until they get here." If the injury were serious, I had no intention of waiting for Davenport to arrive. We would transport the victim and deal with intersquad bruised feelings later.

The officer kneeling over our patient was not concerned with who was responding, just with the fact that he was being relieved by an ambulance full of EMTs. "Thanks for coming, guys," he said. "I appreciate it."

The motorcyclist, a twenty-seven-year-old woman with a badly fractured leg, turned out to be the only person injured. By the time the Davenport ambulance arrived, we had splinted the leg and packaged the woman for transport. We assisted the Davenport crew in loading the patient into their ambulance, then made our way back to FVAC headquarters. We had no further radio problems that day.

We were surprised a few days later when, instead of the expected complaint for responding to a call in Davenport territory, we received a letter of thanks from the Davenport VAC captain for our assistance.

In my state, there are very specific protocols for administering oxygen to patients who need oxygen. These protocols sometimes differ from those in a hospital setting—and this difference sometimes leads to *radio problems*.

People with long-term breathing problems (like emphysema and chronic bronchitis) can be adversely affected by remaining on high concentrations of oxygen for long periods of time. In a hospital or nursing home setting, therefore, such COPD (chronic obstructive pulmonary disease) patients are usually administered low concentrations of oxygen by means of a nasal cannula.

Since we work in emergency situations, however, and treat our patients for relatively short periods of time, our protocols dictate that we always administer high-flow oxygen by means of a non-rebreather face mask for any patient who needs oxygen. In an emergency situation in which a patient needs oxygen, the danger of giving insufficient oxygen is much greater than any possible problems resulting from giving too much oxygen.

Our patient, Richard Ackerson, had the typical barrel chest of an emphysema patient. His forty years of cigarette smoking had all but destroyed his lungs and it was probably only a matter of time until a minor respiratory infection would kill him. He had an oxygen tank next to his bed, set up to deliver four liters of oxygen per minute through a nasal cannula, but when we arrived, it was obviously not enough. He was gasping for breath and his lips had a bluish tinge. We quickly replaced the nasal cannula with an oxygen mask delivering twelve liters of oxygen per minute and we could see an immediate improvement in the color of his lips. We decided to transport him as quickly as possible.

About four minutes from Fairfax General, our crew chief, Heather Franks, began her routine radio transmission. "Fairfax Ambulance 45–03 to Fairfax Emergency."

"This is Fairfax Emergency. Go ahead, 45–03."

"Good morning, Fairfax Emergency. Be advised we are en route to your location with a sixty-two-year-old male COPD patient complaining of severe breathing difficulty. His vitals are as follows: pulse 85, strong and regular; respiration 28 and shallow; BP 165 over 85. We currently have him on twelve liters of O_2 by non-rebreather. Our ETA is four minutes."

"10–4, 45–03. Room assignment on arrival. Please put your COPD patient on a nasal cannula at four liters."

Heather and I looked at each other, then she keyed the microphone. "Your oxygen order is contrary to our protocols, Fairfax Emergency. We will need the name of the physician who is assuming medical control for our patient."

"This is Ellen Harriman, and I'm an R.N. Please turn the oxygen down."

"Say again the name for our records, please," Heather said, winking at me.

"Ellen Harriman, R.N."

"Sorry, we're unable to copy you." The *radio static* was so bad that we never were able to hear the name of the person who would take responsibility for reducing the amount of oxygen to our patient. So we continued to give him high-flow oxygen.

It was early June and six-year-old Debbie Wise had gotten bored at her cousin Carol's birthday party. She had eaten too much and really didn't want any of the birthday cake. Besides, the boys were starting to get a little wild.

Debbie wandered off toward the corral where her favorite horse, Ranger, was munching on grass. Debbie loved visiting her cousin, whose mom and dad owned the Redtail Riding Academy. She could gaze at the horses for hours and knew the name of each of them. Sometimes her uncle Jed would even put her on a horse and lead the horse around the corral a few times. And he had promised that he would teach her to ride when she turned seven.

Debbie climbed the corral fence and waited for Ranger to come over to her, which he always did. The horse slowly walked over and nuzzled her as she patted his nose. Then, realizing that Debbie had no food for him, Ranger walked away and resumed munching the sparse clumps of grass.

Debbie climbed down from the fence and wandered over to the swimming pool. She loved the water and had been taking swimming lessons. During the last lesson, she had dog-paddled all the way across the pool with hardly any help from her instructor. She climbed the steps to the redwood deck that surrounded the four-foot-deep aboveground pool. She squatted at the edge and, gazing down, saw a ladybug that had flown into the water and was flailing its legs in a vain attempt to free itself. Debbie reached her hand toward the insect, but it was too far out. She edged closer and leaned out as far as she could, then lost her balance and fell head-first into the pool.

At first Debbie wasn't frightened. She had never been afraid of the water and now she thought she knew how to swim. So when she realized that the water was too deep for her to stand, she tried to dog-paddle, the way she had been taught. But as she worked her arms and legs, she was hampered by her new shoes and her party dress, now thoroughly waterlogged. She tried to keep her face above the surface, but began choking on the water that was entering her mouth. In panic she began flailing her arms and tried to scream for help, but the water closed in around her, and soon she was still.

Seven-year-old Sandy Freedman was also becoming bored with the party. She also wanted to get away from Chucky, the little boy with the red hair and freckly face, who had started teasing her and pulling her hair. She wished that boys didn't get invited to parties. They acted so nasty.

Sandy had seen Debbie leave and went out to find her. Looking out toward the swimming pool, she thought she saw Debbie on the deck near the edge of the pool, but now she was gone. Sandy trotted over to the steps and climbed up. She immediately saw Debbie thrashing in the water. At first she thought that Debbie was pretending. "Debbie," she called, but Debbie continued to thrash and began to sink into the water.

Suddenly, Sandy knew that Debbie was in trouble. I have to do something, she thought. Her first impulse was to run back to the house for help, but she thought that it might take too long. Debbie was now under the water and she wasn't moving anymore.

Then Sandy saw the telephone at the side of the pool.

Her first-grade class had had a visit from an ambulance corps lady in a fancy white shirt about a month earlier and Sandy had listened to the lesson intently. "Stay calm," she told herself, remembering the lesson. She took a deep breath. "Dial 911." She ran to the phone, picked up the receiver, and pressed the buttons.

"911. What is your emergency?" a voice answered.

"My friend is drowning in the pool," Sandy answered. "You gotta help her."

"Are you at the Redtail Riding Academy?" the dispatcher said, looking at her screen.

"Yes. In the back. And hurry."

"Stay on the line," the voice said. Don't hang up, she remembered the ambulance lady saying. She held the phone against her ear, listening to beeps and boops.

The 911 dispatcher had immediately realized that she was speaking to a child and, when she returned to that line, she spoke slowly and calmly. "All right, honey, help is on the way. Is the girl breathing?"

"I don't know. She was splashing, but she's down under the water now."

"What's your name?"

"Sandy Freedman."

"Sandy," she said. "I'm sending the police, an ambulance, and the fire department. Don't hang up the phone. Just put it down. I want you to run and find a grown-up. When someone gets the little girl out of the pool, I want them to pick up the phone, and I'll tell them what to do. Can you do that?"

"Okay," Debbie answered. She put the phone down and ran toward the house.

Gerry McCarthy had been an EMT and a volunteer with the Fairfax Fire Department for more than twenty years, but his current position as assistant chief of the department did not give him the opportunity to do much emergency medical work. A lot of the volunteer work that he did now was administrative, and he missed the hands-on experience. Still, he enjoyed being assistant chief and was looking forward to becoming chief in a few years. He had worked hard for a long time to rise to his current position and was respected and well liked in the department.

Gerry was beginning to sweat under the three-piece suit he was wearing. It was an unusually warm day for early June, and Gerry, his wife Martha, and his four-year-old son Mark were on their way home from Mark's preschool graduation ceremonies. Even though it was just nursery school, the parents had been expected to dress up for the occasion.

Gerry had just pulled his car over to the side of the road so that he could take off his jacket, vest, and tie when his pager began to beep. "GCC–905 Fairfax Fire Department to all units. Be advised engine 44–31 is responding with FPD and FVAC for a possible drowning at the Redtail Riding Academy."

Gerry turned to his wife. "That's just off the next intersection," he said. "We can be there in less than a minute."

Proud of everything that Gerry did for the emergency services in the town, Martha didn't hesitate. "Let's go."

Gerry flicked on the emergency light switches and turned on the siren of his assistant chief's vehicle, shifted into drive, and stepped on the gas. At the intersection he made a right turn, and then, immediately, another right turn onto the property of the riding academy. Since he had responded to a few riding accidents at Redtail, Gerry was familiar with the grounds and knew where the pool was located. Passing a group of people running across the lawn, he drove across the grass, up to the pool, leaped out of his car, and ran up the steps to the edge of the water.

In the pool, Gerry could see the body of a small child, facedown and not moving. Still in his three-piece suit, he jumped into the four-foot-deep water. Up to his chest in water, Gerry placed his right forearm and hand under the child's chest and face and placed his left forearm and hand over her back and head, then rotated her body so that her face came out of the water.

Immediately he saw that her lips were blue and she wasn't breathing. Still in the water, Gerry breathed two breaths into the child's mouth, then slid his fingers to the side of her neck. She had no pulse.

By now several people had arrived at the side of the pool and Gerry could hear the distant wail of emergency vehicles. But there was no time to wait. He handed the child to the people at the side of the pool and pulled himself out of the water. Someone laid the girl on the deck and Gerry immediately began CPR.

As he began to compress the child's chest, water gurgled out of her mouth, so Gerry turned her on her side to permit the water to escape. Then he rolled her back and continued CPR, alternately compressing her chest and breathing into her mouth. Suddenly the child began to cough and then breathe. She opened her eyes, saw Gerry, grabbed him with both of her hands, and began to cry.

I arrived in the ambulance and was glad to see that, other than transport the still-frightened girl to the hospital, we had little to do. When Gerry handed the girl to Marge Talbot, our crew chief that afternoon, he had to pry her hands from his dripping shirt. "It'll be all right, Debbie," he told the shaking girl softly. "This is Marge and she'll take good care of you."

Debbie was discharged from the hospital the following day. At a ceremony honoring Gerry as Fireman of the Year, he stressed the importance of Sandy's timely call to 911. "Her presence of mind and calm are a credit to her teachers."

"And what about you?" someone asked him. "You saved a life. Was there any lasting effect on you?"

"Well, the suit still fits, but the shoes are a little messed up."

* * *

It was 2:15 A.M. and we had been called to the scene of an MVA, a motor vehicle accident, car versus tree. From the skid marks it was obvious that a car had run off the parkway, down an embankment, across a stream, and into the tree. Fortunately, from what we could make out as we unloaded our equipment, it appeared that the car had lost most of its speed by the time it hit the tree and there seemed to be only moderate damage to the front end of the vehicle.

Despite the floodlights from the side of our rig, the car was in deep shadow, making it hard to see and, as I plowed through the underbrush, I was glad that, despite the warm summer night, I was wearing sneakers and heavy socks.

With Bob Fiorella and Pete Williamson behind me, arms filled with extrication equipment, I arrived at the vehicle and saw a state trooper shining a flashlight around the inside of the car. He was questioning a man of about thirty who sat in the right backseat of the car, shirtless and barefoot.

The trooper turned to us as we put down our mega-duffel, longboard, collar bag, and KED. "His name's Walter Perry. He says his foot hurts, but he doesn't want to go to the hospital."

I leaned into the car. The stench of alcohol was unmistakable. "Walter, we'd like to check you out," I said.

"Nah. Don't bother. I'm okay," he replied. "I just wanna get home."

As I looked him over, I saw a wide bruise striped from Walter's left shoulder diagonally down across his chest toward his right hip. Although it looked nasty, the typical seat-belt wound was probably minor and had undoubtedly saved him from serious injury.

"You were obviously wearing your seat belt."

"Huh?"

"Well, that's quite a bruise across your chest," I said, pulling the stethoscope out of the trauma bag. "Why don't you let me listen to your breathing to make sure there's no serious chest injury?"

"I'm fine. I can breathe all right. I just want to go home," the man replied.

The state trooper motioned me back and leaned into the vehicle. "Okay, Walter. Let me get this straight," he said. "Your girlfriend was driving and a buddy of yours was sitting next to her?"

"Yeah. That's right," the man answered.

"And you were sitting in the back, where you are now."

"Yeah. I didn't move after the accident."

"Well, where are your girlfriend and your buddy?"

"They took off after the accident."

"Took off? How?" the trooper asked.

"They just started walking down the road."

"They left you here?"

"Yeah. Some friends, huh. My foot hurt and I couldn't walk. I couldn't even get out of the car."

"Sir," the trooper asked, "where are your shoes?"

The man looked down. "They're on the floor somewhere."

"I'll tell you where they are," the trooper said. "Your sandals are on the floor under the gas pedal."

"Oh, yeah," the man replied cheerfully. "That's because I got thrown into the front by the impact when the car hit the tree."

"Then how did you get into the back?" the trooper asked. "I thought you told me that you didn't move after the accident."

"Gee, I dunno," the man replied, seeming to struggle to remember.

"And that seat-belt stripe across your chest," the trooper continued, "it would be going the other way if you had been sitting where you are now. But it's just where it would be if you had been driving."

I examined our patient and found that, aside from a seriously wrenched ankle, he was uninjured. Although he allowed us to splint his foot and lower leg, he loudly refused to let us immobilize his neck and back. He draped one arm around my neck and one around Pete's and we half carried him to the rig and he insisted on sitting on the crew seat as we transported him to FGH. After he failed the Breathalyzer test, his ankle was X-rayed and placed in a soft cast. Then he was placed under arrest for DWI and spent the rest of the night in jail.

Under stress, people say the most amazing things. . . .

An EMT was heard to refer to a patient in extremely serious condition as being C-R-O on the CROAK scale.

One ambulance was dispatched for heavy breeding after sex.

After a particularly bloody auto-accident call in which the crew had treated a serious open head injury, one EMT remarked, "Brains don't like fresh air."

One crew was transporting a thirty-three-year-old man who had suffered a late-night heart attack while having sex. The crew chief gave the following report to the doctor on duty. "The patient experienced sudden onset of substernal chest pain while doing exercise in bed."

Ninety-four-year-old man who fell off a ladder at 3:00 A.M. "Sir," one crew member asked, "what were you doing on a ladder at three in the morning?"

Looking at the EMT as though that was the dumbest question he had ever heard, he responded, "I was trying to kill a spider for my wife."

Thirty-two-year-old woman had swallowed one hundred twenty ten-milligram Valium capsules. As the crew placed her on the stretcher, she glared at her husband. "Now you don't have to worry about how much money I spend," she growled. "You can spend it all."

The crew responded to a late-night call for two people feeling weak and dizzy. Upon their arrival, a man and a woman were found, in bed, without clothes. "Have you any idea what could have caused this?" the EMT asked.

The woman reached into her bedside drawer and pulled out two tubes. "I think I might have used the nitroglycerin paste instead of contraceptive jelly."

One crew was dispatched for "a man who's probably having a possible heart attack."

The crew responded to a construction worker struck by a car. As they approached the injured woman, a man was standing over her, screaming at her.

"The guy doing all the yelling is the guy that hit her," a cop told the crew.

"You bastard," the driver screamed, waving his arms at the injured woman, lying on the ground. "You're making me late for work, you son of a bitch."

We arrived at the scene of a three-car accident. Officer Eileen Flynn was nose to nose with a very intoxicated woman.

"I'm a Hallahan," the woman shrieked, "and I don't take crap from anybody."

"Well I'm a Flynn," the officer retorted, "and I don't take crap from *you*."

Chapter 10

During the time that Ed and I have been writing these books, we've asked corps members, friends, and others directly or indirectly attached to the EMS community to share their stories with us. Some of those stories have been incorporated into our writing, and for simplicity, we have told the tales as though Ed and I were part of the action. In the following adventures, however, the characters tell their own stories. Like all the rest of the stories in this book, they've been fictionalized to conceal all identities.

My name is MaryAnn Hargrove and I've been a member of the corps since it was founded over twenty years ago. In all that time, one call stands out in my mind above all others. It was almost fifteen years ago. . . .

"Fairfax Police to Fairfax Ambulance. An ambulance is needed for a man stabbed in the neck at Redtail Riding Academy. Better expedite. The caller seemed very agitated and said there was lots of blood."

"10–4, we're rolling."

As I sprinted toward the rig, I remember thinking how unusual a stabbing was. In my years in the corps I'd never had any violence to deal with.

Hal Walzac jumped into the driver's seat and started the rig. About fifty, Hal was extremely overweight and he drove all of us crazy with his chain-smoking. I never liked to be in the front of the rig with him because his clothes always reeked of old tobacco.

Patty Lamont opened the garage doors and, when the rig was clear, closed them behind us and jumped into the back. Patty, on her first call as a probationary member, was only nineteen, cute and blond with a figure all of us envied.

"Patty," I yelled into the back over the sound of the siren's wail. "Stay in the back until we're sure the scene is safe." As crew chief, the safety of the crew was my responsibility and with a stabbing, we needed to know that the stabber was either under control or gone.

Looking totally overwhelmed, she nodded.

We drove through the whitewashed gates, and several people frantically waved us toward one of the outbuildings. As Hal pulled up next to a crowd of people I heard the sirens of the approaching police car. I jumped out, and as the crowd parted, I saw a man lying facedown on the ground, his face in a pool of blood. His breathing was rapid and shallow and he was moaning softly.

Wondering whether there was some knife-wielding weirdo still around, I asked, "What happened?"

"He was working in the barn and somehow fell and stuck himself with that pitchfork." The lethal-looking instrument lay a few feet away.

I heaved a sigh. No crazy stabber. "Patty," I yelled toward the ambulance, "bring the trauma kit and the oxygen bottle." Then I selected three strong men from the crowd. "Help me turn him over," I said. Three of the bystanders grabbed the man's clothes and, as I supported his head, we turned him over. I immediately saw the deep, three-inch gash across the side of his neck and watched dark blood flow freely from the wound, soaking his shirt. He probably severed his jugular vein, I told myself.

With an injury to the jugular vein, besides the blood loss, there is an additional danger. The pumping action of the heart creates strong suction that can pull air into the vein. Should that happen, the air bubble can completely block a vessel—a potentially fatal situation. I had to close the vein quickly.

While my crew was bringing bandages, I reached my gloved hand into the wound, found the ends of the severed vein, and squeezed them closed. "What's his name?" I said loudly.

"Chris Perez," someone said.

Patty arrived with the trauma bag. "Pull the packaging from a large dressing and fold the plastic into a pad about four inches square," I told Patty. "We'll use that as an occlusive dressing, and bandage over it." Without comment, Patty did what I told her to.

The bleeding slowed almost immediately and I began to try to talk to the patient who, fortunately, was conscious and alert. "What happened?" I asked.

The young man looked sheepish, then breathlessly told of a freak fall with the pitchfork in his hand. "So dumb," he said softly.

When Patty was ready with the dressing, I released my hold on the ends of the vein. When the bleeding didn't resume, I placed the occlusive dressing over the wound. "Patty, cut me four pieces of tape about six inches long." I would tape the occlusive dressing in place, then cover it with a bulky pad and tape.

I straightened my aching back, proud of the quick job I had done. All that was left was to finish the bandaging, place the patient on oxygen, take vitals, and transport the man to FGH. I noticed that our third crew member was missing. "Where's Hal?" I asked.

"I don't have any idea," Patty said, looking around. "He was right behind me with the oxygen."

I placed the patient's hand on the dressing so he could hold it in place, stood up, and looked around. No Hal. Leaving Patty cutting tape, I walked around the rig and saw him, kneeling on the ground, clutching his chest. "Hal," I said as I approached, "are you okay?" Suddenly, he keeled over, unconscious.

"You keep working on the bandage," I yelled to Patty. "Tape all four sides carefully." I called over a Fairfax policeman who had responded to the scene. "Get more manpower and another rig here stat," I told him, and he quickly radioed his dispatcher. Thank heaven Patty was sufficiently bright to understand how to tape the dressing without me.

I felt for a pulse in Hal's neck, and simultaneously checked his breathing. When I discovered that he had no pulse and was not breathing, I began CPR.

I tried not to think that I was working on a crew member, a man I didn't know well, but with whom I had ridden from time to time. I continued by rote, compressing Hal's chest and breathing air into his lungs as I heard help arrive. The rest was a blur. More members arrived, the crew relieved me, and, while continuing CPR, whisked Hal away toward Fairfax General, lights flashing and siren blaring.

In a daze, I returned to my original patient and found that Patty had done a fine job of bandaging. When the second rig arrived, we loaded the young man into it and followed the first rig to FGH.

Despite all my efforts and the efforts of all the people who arrived later, Hal didn't make it. So far, in my twenty years with the corps, that was the only time I've had to work on someone I knew.

We don't experience death the same way when we work on someone we have never known alive. There's no real emotion involved, just a feeling of sadness for the patient's family and friends. On this call I experienced the death of someone I knew, and it bothered me a lot for a long time.

I'm happy to say that our patient survived the severed neck vein.

* * *

In our state, a rescue squad differs from an ambulance corps in one important way. An ambulance corps is an independent corporation that makes its own rules and has its officers and chain of command. At the scene of an emergency, the crew chief is in control of the patient and the ambulance crew members. The highest-ranking line officer, usually the captain or first lieutenant, is in overall charge of a scene at which there are multiple ambulances and the fire department is in charge of any necessary extrication.

A rescue squad, in contrast, is an adjunct of the fire department and, as such, must fit its officers into the fire department hierarchy. At a scene, in many districts, the first or highest-ranking fire officer is in command, whether or not he has any EMS training. In most cases things run smoothly and officers defer, as necessary, to those with superior EMS knowledge and training. Occasionally, odd situations arise.

One of our members told the following story of the rescue squad he rode with upstate.

Chief Nichols was a bear to work with and a bit of a bully. He was elected chief primarily because he had been in the department for seventeen years and, to give credit where credit is due, at fire calls he was a wonderful commander and a fine firefighter. At rescue calls he didn't know his thingamabob from a whatchamacallit.

Helicopter service had recently been instituted and all of us in the rescue squad were glad that our twenty-minute transport time to the hospital would be significantly shortened. At first, Chief Nichols was reluctant to call for helicopters and, on occasion, canceled them when he believed that they weren't absolutely necessary. At a scene, he was frequently heard to say, "We got along without them all these years, let's not bother them with this."

One afternoon I was in the rescue bus returning from the hospital when we were dispatched for an MVA at a bad intersection. We flipped on our lights and siren and sped toward the scene with an ETA of seven minutes.

As we watched traffic pull over ahead of us, we heard Chief Nichols arrive at the accident and then, almost immediately, call for the helicopter. "Shit," my partner said, "the old man's mellowing."

"Guess so," I said.

A moment later I heard one of our members arrive at the scene and, after a brief silence, the radio said, "The injuries aren't very serious so all units can respond with caution. And someone call off the chopper."

We arrived at the scene and began to bandage the driver, who was suffering from a bloody, but not serious, scalp laceration. Suddenly, we heard the helicopter overhead. "I thought someone called them off," I said.

The first EMT at the scene looked chagrined. "Actually, no one had the nerve to tell Chief Nichols that we didn't need the bird so we let it come."

I could well understand that.

So the patient got the bird flight to the trauma center. I must say that the chief relaxed after that and the helicopter made more frequent, and usually necessary, trips to our district.

I've made several out-of-state friends through my membership in America Online. One of them, an EMT and vivid storyteller, sent me this tale. On this call she was riding with a crew of only two, herself and a driver.

I had been told that the psychiatric patient, a twentyish female, was quite calm and I didn't need to worry about restraints. My partner and I loaded her into our ambulance and positioned her on the gurney with the seat belts on, of course. I sat on the jumpseat behind her.

During the short ride to the receiving facility, she was telling me all about how her neighbors were trying to kill her and how she believed that there were cannibals in the United States. When my only comment was, "I really doubt it," she pulled the blanket over her head to take a nap and I stuck my nose in a paramedic manual.

She must have been dwelling on that thought because, in a few minutes, she came flying off the gurney (don't know how she got off so fast) and had me cornered, trying to bite me. I yelled at my partner to pull over and get the hell back there. At the time we were in the speed lane of the freeway so it would take a minute or two to maneuver the rig onto the shoulder.

I rapidly considered two things. First, I knew that I could easily upend her with my foot, but I also realized that she might fall back against an oxygen tank and regulator or the bar on the side door. Second, I didn't want to alarm the patient's mother, who was in a car behind us and could see the situation clearly. I decided to try and fend the young woman off until my partner could bring the rig to a stop and get into the back to help me.

I managed to do that, but not before she got a lip lock on my right thumb. The instant the rig stopped moving, Bill, my driver, charged into the back and we wrestled the woman down onto the bench seat. Then it was like she came out of a fog. She looked up at me, stared at my bleeding thumb, and said, "Gee, I'm sorry, but I thought you were a cannibal." I think she got it slightly backward.

The rest of the trip was uneventful and my thumb has long healed. Occasionally I still transport a patient without restraints, but only when I'm sure he or she doesn't bite.

I received this story from an EMT named Helena.

I had been an EMT for about three years and had just recently trained, with the other members of my corps, to be part of the newly instituted EMT-D program. All of us had learned how to use the defibrillator and, although no one wanted anyone to go into cardiac arrest, we were all anxious to try out the new equipment. Everyone wanted to be the one with the first EMT-D save.

We received a call from the local fleabag motel for a man down. As crew chief, I was riding shotgun next to the driver and there were two young EMTs in the back. I yelled through the window to the back to tell the two others, also both relatively new to EMS, to assemble oxygen, the BVM, the jump bag, and the defibrillator. "Ever done a CPR call before?" I screamed over the siren.

"Neither of us have," came the voice from the rear.

When we arrived at the scene, the motel manager was standing at the open door. With the rest of my crew in hot pursuit, I charged into the room. An elderly man lay in the middle of the floor, eyes closed, no one else around. Just me and the rookies.

Okay, I told myself. Airway. I tipped his head and checked for breathing. None. I inserted an oral-pharyngeal airway and one of the crew members knelt at my side, BVM in hand. Very good. He fitted the mask over the patient's face and I squeezed the bag. Airway clear. "Bag him at about three," I said, wanting to hyperventilate him. Between ventilations I checked the man's pulse. None. Another member started chest compressions while I unpacked the defibrillator. I was both nervous and elated. I was actually going to use the "jumper cables."

My crew of young, recently trained members continued to perform good CPR while I attached the shocking electrodes and hooked up the cables. My driver, not EMT trained, was outside, gathering what sparse information she could. I placed the electrodes in their proper position on the man's chest.

I pressed the *analyze* button and, while the machine charged, I checked for a pulse. None. "I'm clear, you're clear, we're all clear." And voilà. The screen showed course v-fib, a lethal, shockable rhythm. My hands were shaking and I had an advanced adrenaline rush. I looked around to be sure everyone was clear.

My finger was approaching the button that would deliver 200 joules of electricity to the man's heart when suddenly the patient sat up. He spit the airway out, gave three gasps, and dropped back to the floor.

Like any other good, experienced EMT would do at the time, I yelled, "What the fuck," and allowed the defibrillator to discharge. I looked around and my two crew members were backed up against the walls of the room, wide-eyed. I checked the patient for breathing and pulse and found none. "Begin CPR again, please." It took three requests before my startled, spooked crew members would return to the patient.

I analyzed again and found fine v-fib, a rhythm that the machine wouldn't shock, so we did CPR and transported, lights and siren, to our local hospital. When we arrived we watched the team work the code, shocking, doing CPR, and pushing drugs until finally the patient's condition stabilized.

As we watched, elated that, for some unknown reason the patient's condition was improving, my driver filled me in on the background. The man had been in jail for a year on a drug charge. He had been released the preceding day, scored, and had done an unknown amount of crack, some heroin, and five beers that afternoon.

According to one of the nurses at the hospital, what I had witnessed was some sort of cardiac seizure, and not uncommon under these conditions. A save? Maybe. But, for me, it will always be the CPR call that wouldn't die.

And here's one from an EMT who works in a rural setting.

* * *

It's a hot June evening in 1994, the first full day here for Cleaus, the fifteen-year-old Swedish hockey player we are hosting for a month (English is *not* his first language). We are eating dinner and all of a sudden two pagers and a monitor all go off at once! "The rescue truck and ambulance respond to—" and he gives an address in a farming area a few miles away "—for a man down in a field, unknown problem."

If only you could've seen Cleaus's face when his new "mom" jumped up from the table, grabbed a portable radio, flew out the door, jumped in the van, and turned on the blue light. Cleaus must have thought a bomb had dropped. My kids never missed a bite—Mom has to go on another call—*no big deal!*

I call that I am en route and dispatch has no further info. Well, with a dispatch like that, what's the first thing that comes to mind? Full arrest, right? I couldn't have been more wrong!

Picture this. I arrive on the scene and a family member advises me that the victim had been attacked by a bull. Okay, I think, safety first. Well, it's probably a cow with horns and we can deal with that.

Next picture. I am running a half mile up a rocky-bumpy field that only feet or a four-wheel drive can negotiate, portable radio in hand, when I encounter a flock of geese—who are in the mood to play tag—and I'm the target! Broken field running begins.

Next picture. Huffing and puffing, I arrive at the victim's side where Joe, a firefighter, had already arrived in his truck and established scene/patient safety to the best of his ability. Now, I know Joe wouldn't be there if the scene wasn't secure since, in addition to being a farmer himself, he is a past fire chief/EMT and knows his stuff.

First thing I notice is a "dingo" dog, one of those nasty little twenty-five-pound creatures you find on farms that chase everything from cows to humans just for kicks. The dog is snarling, barking, and dancing around. Oh boy. Another obstacle to deal with. Joe used to have one of these dogs so I asked him if the dog was going to create a safety hazard for us.

His reply? "If I were you I wouldn't be worrying about this dog—he's saving your butt right now. Turn around—*slowly.*"

What I saw when I turned made my blood run cold. The scene was safe for the moment but anytime now we were going to be play toys. The dog, five feet of field, and a piece of barbed wire separated me from a bull that weighed over one ton. The monster, complete with golden ring in the nose, stood grunting, stomping, slobbering, and mad as hell, looking me straight in the eye. Hmmmmm, what color do I have on? Red? Oh yeah—bulls are color-blind. . . . Whew . . .

At this point I get on the radio and advise dispatch and the fire chief, an intermediate EMT and a farmer, of our extremely delicate situation. We hold all units at the farmhouse so as not to aggravate our foe and call for another four-wheel-drive truck for patient transport. At the farmhouse, the chief loads another EMT, the trauma bag, and backboard from the rescue into his four-wheel drive and heads for our location.

In the meantime, back at home . . .

My husband, past fire chief and an EMT, who is eating dinner with Cleaus and our boys, hears all the radio transmissions on his portable. He can tell the situation isn't cool from the start. Remember I said I took the van? Well *he* has the four-wheel-drive truck. So up gets Dad from dinner, loads the kids in the truck, (Cleaus prefers to stay home and finish eating or maybe look for the bomb shelter), and responds.

Back at the farm . . .

Our patient is conscious and alert, presenting with severe pain in the chest/abdominal area and pain to both lower legs. He says he was stomped by the aforementioned bull. My husband, another EMT, and one farmworker drive four-wheel-drive trucks to the scene and box the patient and EMS workers to provide a more secure environment for patient care.

After assessment and packaging, the patient is transferred to the bed of a four-wheel drive for the ride down the hill to the waiting ambulance. But he won't go without Jodi, his dog. To be honest, the dog, now seemingly calmer since his master is being tended to, has been as much a part of our team as any EMT.

The patient would have been in much worse condition had it not been for Jodi. She went after the bull during the attack and got its attention long enough for our patient to roll under the fence to a safer place, then stayed by him until and throughout his removal from danger.

In addition, Jodi protected us as well, watching our backs when we couldn't. Once our patient has convinced the dog to get into the four-wheel drive, we gladly allow Jodi to ride back to the farmhouse with us.

When we get to the ambulance we find three shotgun-armed state troopers waiting to rescue the rescuers if need be. All I can think of is how cute they would have been in their little gray uniforms playing round up the bull!

Our patient not only survived, he left the ER a few hours after arrival with only aches, pains, and bruises. Cleaus also survived and, as his time with us progressed, he became as blasé about Mom and Dad galloping out the front door to answer rescue calls as the rest of my sons.

We can all look back at this call and grin now about how many octaves our voices rose and how our deodorant worked overtime (or failed), but there really was clear and present danger to all of the field personnel and we were very aware of it. Fortunately, all of the rescuers were calm and levelheaded, and never lost their cool.

* * *

And one from New York City, where strange and tragic calls are the norm rather than the unusual.

I've been an EMT since I was about nineteen years old. I did some volunteer work for Central Park Medical so I thought I had seen my share of sick and trauma jobs. When I joined NYC EMS at first it was routine. . . . Routine?

Now, I laugh sometimes when I hear a rookie say that. . . .

The May day was rainy. I was working upper Manhattan with my then-partner—let's call her Wendy. She was all heart, a good EMT and a good friend. The day started with the usual rainy-day MVAs and sick jobs. The call came in for "a baby in cardiac arrest." I was driving and although not yet a parent, I was a new uncle. The look on Wendy's face said what I felt. We advised the dispatcher we were responding with an ETA of less than two minutes.

I drove as quickly as I could, with Wendy helping me look out for traffic in the very crowded streets. I steered around cars and pedestrians, none of which got out of my way without my honking the horn. Typical of New York City.

Wendy and I were also going over what we needed to bring into the building and who would be in control until ALS backup got there. Although it felt like forever, we arrived quickly since we had been very close to the scene. Somehow, it felt like we were meant to do this job.

Pulling up, I saw two cops get out of their car and run into the building. I got out of the driver's seat to get our stuff but Wendy was already in the equipment compartment. Trauma bags, oxygen equipment, and other stuff in hand, we ran up four flights behind the police and were confronted by what seemed like a mob in front of the apartment. The person at the door only spoke Spanish. He had a very strong and firm voice, but he had tears in his eyes. One of the cops translated for us.

The man was saying that the baby was dead and begged us not to take her away with us. The police, not really understanding, were insisting on entering the apartment and a mini-riot almost broke out. There was a lot of loud talk, but I finally managed to get the attention of a woman who spoke some English and finally explained the situation.

It seems that the patient, a small baby, had died about eight hours prior to the call to 911. The parents only needed someone to pronounce the baby dead so they could transfer her to the funeral home. Calming everyone down, Wendy quickly explained the situation to the police and we were finally allowed to enter the apartment.

The sight will never leave us. . . . Never . . .

We entered a room filled with baby toys. The walls were covered with brightly colored patterns that the baby could see from her crib. And on the bed, surrounded by burning candles, the infant, maybe two weeks old, was wrapped in a yellow receiving blanket and covered in flowers, toys, and rosaries.

As much as the sight disturbed us we took a few deep breaths and conducted our primary assessment. We discovered that, as we had been told, the little girl had obviously been dead for some time, so we pronounced, as we are permitted to do in a case like this.

The parents told us the baby had been born with a form of mitral valve disfunction and the family was given the choice to have her die in the hospital or at home. They took the tiny girl home, under the condition that, if they thought she had died, they would wait six to eight hours before calling 911. That way the family wouldn't suffer by seeing CPR performed on their baby.

When the young, relatively inexperienced medic arrived in the room, we realized that we had been so caught up in this call that we had forgotten to cancel the

ALS backup. We explained what had occurred to him but he started to insist that the baby had to be transported to the hospital anyway.

Wendy and I tried to share with him our understanding of Hispanic culture and the pain it would cause the family to have the baby removed from their care. Our emotions almost got the better of us as we tried to explain what was going on.

Thank heavens, as we were trying to convince the medic to leave the baby alone, our supervisor, a man with more than eighteen years of EMS service, who had worked in all sections of Manhattan and was familiar with all its cultures, arrived at the scene. He understood the situation and agreed that there was no need for additional medical help. He advised the medic that we would do the paperwork and that he could leave. After the medic left, the supervisor stayed with us. It was good to have his support since both Wendy and I were very obviously shaken. As strong as I tried to be for Wendy it just wasn't there.

We paid our tearful last respects to the baby and then to the weeping family. That was the very first time I ever cried like that with a family I had not known. But I could feel their pain as if it were my own.

In NYC EMS you don't get a real break between calls, just fifteen minutes or so for the bathroom and that's it. Our supervisor did his best to give us some extra time to finish our ambulance log, cry, and console each other. We called our families. I called my sister and listened to my nephew cry on the phone. Wendy called her children to hear them say, "I love you, Mom." We had a total of twenty-five minutes to get ourselves together and make our calls before the next call for us came in.

Business as usual . . . in NYC EMS.

This story comes from an EMT in the midwest.

* * *

I was working part-time at the local pizza restaurant to earn a few extra bucks. I was on the phone, writing down a take-out order, when one of my coworkers whispered in my ear, "When you're off the phone, there's a guy out in the parking lot. He's been shot."

Yeah, right, I thought, but, when I turned around and saw the look on the coworker's face and the blood on his shirt, I handed him the phone, yelled for him to call 911, and dashed out the door. Luckily I was wearing my waist pouch so, as I approached a tiny late-model sports car, I could pull on a pair of gloves.

The car sat in the middle of the parking lot, its driver's-side door open. In the driver's seat lay a six-foot-nine man. There was a hole in the car door caused, I figured out as the call progressed, by a bullet that had gone through the door, in and out of the man's left elbow, into his belly just above the navel, out through the side of his pelvis near his hip, and then out through the far side of the car.

Let me say that I'm a measly six-foot-five, but I somehow managed to climb into the car with the injured man. "Sir," I said, "can you hear me?"

"Yes," he said weakly.

"What happened?"

"Shot. Car."

"Your name?"

"Charles."

"What hurts, Charles?"

The patient passed out.

I pressed my fingers against first one wrist then the other, but could find no pulse. From the distended, probably blood-filled, condition of his abdomen, and the blood soaking the man's shirt and pants and spreading across the seat of the car, I assumed that he had lost so much blood that he was in serious, possibly terminal, hypovolemic shock. And I had nothing to work with.

One of the other employees ran up to the car with the store's first-aid kit. "What's inside?" I asked. He opened the kit and found three Band-Aids and a bottle of aspirin. Big help.

When the first police car arrived, the officer assured me that he had checked the scene and that it was safe. No shooter anywhere around. Now he tells me, I thought. Like a rookie, I hadn't even considered my own safety. The officer then handed me a more useful first-aid kit, one with lots of gauze and trauma dressings. "What else do you need?" the cop asked.

"I need EMS, stat!"

"I'll inform them that the scene is safe and have them expedite."

The ambulance screamed into the parking area a minute later. I filled the crew in on what I knew and they scooped and ran with the patient, speeding out of the parking lot, lights and siren, onto the interstate toward the trauma center.

Amazingly enough, and most important, the patient survived with no permanent injury. Although it had done its share of damage, the bullet had missed every major nerve, muscle, and artery.

I found out the rest of the story later. Apparently, our patient had cut off another car on the interstate. Words became gestures and gestures led to a high-powered rifle. The injured man, who was not from our area, managed to turn off the interstate and, as luck would have it, turned left at the bottom of the ramp. As he drove under the highway, he saw the lights from the pizza parlor and drove into the lot. It was sheer chance that an EMT worked at the restaurant.

He's one lucky guy. Had he turned right at the foot of the ramp, he would have driven into a large residential area and might have bled to death before anyone found him. Luck? Maybe.

Recently Ed and I got together with a group of EMTs from a corps about forty miles away from us. We spent a few enjoyable hours swapping ambulance tales. The following story was told by a longtime member.

It was about 2:00 A.M., many years ago, and we were called for an MVA, car versus tree on Hillside Road. First, you have to understand why it's called Hillside Road. The road is on a steep upgrade with many switchbacks and sharp curves. In those days it had no guardrails and, on one side, the roadway dropped off steeply into a heavy stand of trees.

We arrived at the scene to find a small pickup truck that had swerved to the right and ended up with its rear wheels on the pavement and its front end supported by heavy tree limbs about twelve feet off the ground. The middle of the car hung over nothingness. Two heavy tree trunks, one on either side, held the two doors shut. There was a man in the driver's seat, screaming for us to get him out.

"Someone will have to go up there and check him out," my partner said.

"Damn," I muttered as I zipped up my heavy jacket. "I'll go." Why? I'll never understand. I bushwacked my way down the slope to the foot of the trees, then shinnied up one trunk until I was eye level with the driver's-side window. With one foot braced on a heavy limb, I motioned for the driver to try to roll down the window. Amazingly enough, the window still worked and he rolled it down so we could communicate. "Are you hurt?"

"Nah, I'm okay." With his words came a cloud of alcohol.

"What's your name?"

"Jake," he said. In the dim light of the still-burning headlights, I could see that the man's body filled most of the tiny, two-person cab. He must have weighed over three hundred pounds. I couldn't see much else in the pitch dark so I felt around inside the cab. I felt the jagged end of the steering column, where the steering wheel had been snapped off, undoubtedly by Jake's chest. His breathing seemed regular. "Are you having any trouble breathing?"

"Nah," he said, surrounding me in another cloud of alcohol fumes. "I'm fine. Just need to get down from here."

"Take a deep breath, sir," I said, and the man did. "Feel okay?"

"Just get me down from here."

"Anything else hurt?"

"Yeah," he said. "My right foot. I think it's broken."

I couldn't reach his foot to check it and, even had I been able to, there was nothing I could have done to splint it. Since there wasn't much else I could do for the man until we figured out how to get the truck out of the tree, I climbed down to talk with my partner. "I called a tow truck," he told me.

"How about the fire department?" I asked.

"Okay," he said. "Good idea." He called, but the local fire department was all volunteer and a crew would have to gather. Since it wasn't a life-threatening emergency, it would be at least fifteen minutes before the first piece of apparatus arrived. The tow truck arrived in five.

"Holy shit," the tow-truck driver said, staring at the pickup, half on the pavement and half in the tree. "How the fuck did he get himself into that?"

"Alcohol," I muttered.

"Right," he said. "How the fuck are we going to get him out?"

"We thought you could help," I told him.

"We could cut the tree," the tow driver mused.

"But the truck would fall and the guy'd probably be hurt worse."

"Shit."

"If we could move the truck back about two feet, we could get the doors open," I suggested.

"Then what?"

"Then, at least I could get in and check the man out and maybe get him out before you move the truck any farther."

"Do you think the tree would hold?" my partner asked.

"Got a better idea?" I asked.

As the three of us stared at the truck and the tree for a few moments, the pickup driver yelled, "Hey, man. What're you standing around with your thumbs up your butts for? Get me outta here."

The tow-truck driver shrugged. "Can you help me get a line over the top of the cab and around the front axle?" I had obviously become the resident tree climber. "Then we can both lift and pull." A second tow truck arrived and we filled the second driver in on the situation. He didn't have any brilliant ideas either. Nor did the firefighters on the first engine at the scene. The lift-and-pull idea seemed the best one.

"Come on. I gotta fuckin' pee," the victim yelled.

"We're just trying to get you out of there safely," I yelled.

"Fuck that. Just get me outta here."

The two tow drivers positioned their vehicles, one slightly uphill, one slightly downhill, and they tossed the tow lines over the cab of the truck. While I attached the lines to the front axle, two firemen chocked the pickup truck's back wheels. I climbed onto the truck bed and used the window punch to break the back window. "Okay, Jake," I said. "Brace yourself."

With a lurch, each tow-truck driver started his winch. Slowly, with lots of crashing, breaking of small branches, and leaves falling all around me, the pickup moved back just enough to allow me to open the driver's-side door.

"Hold it," I yelled. Six more inches and the front end would be released from the support of the tree and crash to the ground. I used tree limbs to make my way around from the truck bed to the driver's door and I climbed in.

Trying to breathe the alcohol fumes as little as possible, I surveyed the man's body. He had several broken ribs and a probable broken foot, but otherwise seemed to have no serious injuries.

"I can jump now," the man said, alcohol slurring his speech.

"Not a chance," I said, hoping someone had a better idea. Lifting him then lowering him to the ground wasn't an option. His three-hundred-plus-pound body precluded that.

One fireman took a hand ladder and slid it out to me. I propped it on the driver's door frame and the fireman braced it against the wheel of the ambulance and tied it down.

"He can't climb," I said, thinking about his broken ribs and foot.

"Okay," one of the firemen said. "Give me a minute."

I watched as several firemen, two tow-truck drivers, and my partner discussed the situation. Finally, my partner pulled two long backboards from the side compartment and tied them to the rungs and sides of the ladder. "He'll have to slide," someone yelled.

Jake had been watching everything. "I can do that," he said. In his drunken state, I think he believed he could do almost anything. "I just gotta get outta here and pee." Broken ribs, broken foot and all, he scrambled around and got his legs on the board. With great creaking and groaning of bending wood, Jake scrambled across the makeshift slide to the waiting stretcher. When he was settled on the stretcher, I slid across to the pavement.

We did a quick survey, splinted the man's foot, and transported him to the hospital. He was treated and released two days later. I got a certificate from my squad-member friends. It simply said, "The Paul Bunyan Award."

* * *

And this story from another EMT.

A call came in for one of our regulars, a woman named Marcy, who has severe psychological problems and had occasionally attempted suicide. I had been at her house several times. Each time we had transported her to the local psych facility, where she was kept for a short while, then discharged. We had transported this woman so many times, we had all become chatting acquaintances with the admitting nurses at the psych ER.

One night, around 4:00 A.M., we were dispatched to her house for "a woman who was shot in the head." Thinking she had finally done the dirty deed, we headed out of the station, anticipating a difficult call. A police lieutenant had also responded and arrived at the house first.

When we arrived he told us we could disregard the call. Marcy had told him that she had shot herself, but that God had healed her prior to the arrival of the police. She did not need the kind of medical attention we could give her.

We all laughed about it, went back home, and got some sleep, glad that we didn't have to transport her this time. I was again on duty the following night when, around 2:00 A.M., we were called to her house for "a person who cut her throat." As we drove out of headquarters, dispatch informed us over the air, "Be advised, the victim is Marcy."

I don't know why I did it, but in a brief moment of what-the-hell-why-not attitude I asked dispatch, "Has God called en route yet?"

There was, of course, a pause while our dispatcher laughed with her hand over the mike. Then, struggling not to laugh over the air, she said, "Yes, I believe He has."

Of course Marcy was not injured and refused medical attention.

Amazingly enough, I didn't get written up for my very unprofessional radio traffic.

I think a fitting way to end this book is with this sentiment about what it means to be in the Emergency Medical Services.

Upon arriving home, someone asks an EMT, "How was your day, dear?"

How was my day?

I cooled the feverish body of a young cancer patient.

I held the ice-cold hand of a woman hit by a car.

I listened to a man's voice cry, "Please help me," as the jaws of life bit through the roof of his car.

I was called every name in the book by a self-destructive man who resented my efforts.

I was kissed by an intoxicated teenager.

I hugged a frightened child.

I pulled on my shoes when awakened from a sound sleep by the Klaxon.

I cleaned vomit off of those shoes thirty minutes later.

I gently touched the fragile hand of a ninety-eight-year-old woman.

I recoiled at the hand of a three-hundred-fifty-pound man in handcuffs.

I made a marketing list for a lonely old woman.

I found a stuffed bear for a three-year-old.

I bandaged the face of a woman who had been beaten by her husband.

I sighed as she refused to press charges.

I did CPR on a fifty-year-old heart attack victim while his wife and children looked on.

I treated the man's widow for a nervous collapse six hours later.

I delivered a baby in the back of the rig.

I watched as a sheet was pulled over the face of an eighty-three-year-old stroke victim.
I listened to the question "Why?"
I tried to think of an answer.

How was my day? I'm an EMT. It was just like many others.

The Cast

<u>**Fairfax Volunteer Ambulance Corps**</u>
Radio Call GKL-642
County prefix 45

Emergency Medical Technicians

Nick Abrams—age thirty-four—works split shifts at the local Mobil station.

Stephanie DiMartino—age twenty-one—works in the local Kmart.

Bob Fiorella—age thirty-five—sells insurance and is able to respond to day calls when he's in the area.

Heather Franks—age twenty-four—works in the lunchroom of George Washington Elementary School and goes to college part-time.

Tom Franks—age twenty-five—Heather's husband and a second-grade teacher at John Adams Elementary School in Fairfax.

Dave Hancock—age thirty-one—FVAC's Maintenance Officer—auto mechanic at a local auto-body shop.

Ed Herman—age fifty-five—publisher and biotechnology specialist who works from his home. Radio call number 45–22.

Pam Kovacs—first lieutenant—age thirty-eight—works part-time for a florist. Radio call number 45–12.

Joan Lloyd—age fifty—writer who works at home and responds to day calls. Radio call number 45–24.

Judy Lloyd—age twenty-four—rode with FVAC for four years before moving to the Southwest.

Jack McCaffrey—age forty-five—professor at Fairfax Community College.

Sam Middleton—age twenty-seven—city firefighter—rides various shifts as they fit into his schedule.

Steve Nesbitt—age fifty-one—drives a school bus for the Fairfax school system.

Phil Ortiz—age eighteen—became a first responder in the youth corps then, when he became eighteen, he advanced to the senior squad and became an EMT.

Linda Potemski—age thirty-nine—emergency room nurse at Fairfax Hospital and a longtime member of FVAC.

Fred Stevens—age forty-two—electrician with a local construction firm.

Marge Talbot—age thirty-four—CPA with a large accounting firm. Frequently works via computer modem and thus can occasionally respond to day calls.

Jill Tremonte—age twenty—dental assistant with the Fairfax Dental Group.

Pete Williamson—age twenty-five—professional paramedic with an EMS service in the city.

Probationary Members

Tim Babbett—age twenty-three—works for a local contractor—an EMT but hasn't yet become a full member of the corps.

Davida Herman—age nineteen—member of the youth group who graduated to the senior corps as a probationary member on her eighteenth birthday.

Dispatcher

Greg Horvath—age sixty-eight—retired plumber.

Fairfax Police Department

Radio Call ID GBY–639

Officers

Merve Berkowitz, car 317
Eileen Flynn, car 318
Chuck Harding, car 305
Will McAndrews, car 312
Stan Poritsky, car 308
Detective Irv Greenberg

Dispatcher

Mark Thomas

Fairfax Fire Department

Radio Call ID GCC–905

Members

Chief Paul Bradley
Lieutenant Patrick Connoly
Mike DeVito
Andy Johansen
Gerry McCarthy
Ken Stavitsky

Prescott Volunteer Fire Association Rescue Squad

Radio Call GVK–861
County prefix 21

Members

Paramedic Amy Chen
EMT Brenda Frost
EMT Ed Herman
EMT Jack Johnson
Driver Max Taylor
Paramedic Hugh Washington
EMT Sally Walsh

Dispatcher

Ted McCann

Prescott Police Department

Radio Call ID GRQ–325

Officers

Stan Garth, car 715
Mike Gold, car 706
Roy Zimmerman, car 703

At Fairfax General Hospital ER

Dr. Frank Margolis—emergency medicine specialist
Rosemary Harper, R.N.—emergency room head nurse

At Oakside Psychiatric Center

Dr. Susan Cardone—psychiatrist and crisis specialist

Glossary

ALS (advanced life support)—The crew includes at least one paramedic who can perform the life support functions detailed below. See *paramedic*.

AOB—Alcohol on breath.

ASAP—As soon as possible.

backboard—A wooden board approximately six feet long and three feet wide. It is used both as a body splint to support the patient's body and as a lifting aid. Backboards are also called longboards or long spineboards.

BLS (basic life support)—The crew members can only perform the skills of an EMT-D (emergency medical technician with added training in defibrillation).

BP (blood pressure)—BP is an indication of how strongly the heart is beating. Two numbers are usually given. (See *palp*.) The greater number, or systolic pressure, is the pressure when the heart muscle is contracting. The smaller number, or diastolic pressure, is the pressure when the heart muscle is relaxing. A typical blood pressure might be stated as 120 over 80, meaning 120 systolic and 80 diastolic.

* * *

BVM (bag valve mask)—A device that forces air or pure oxygen into a patient's lungs. It can be used during CPR or to assist inadequate respirations.

CCU—Cardiac care unit.

cervical collar—A hard-plastic specially shaped bracing device that surrounds a patient's neck to prevent additional cervical (neck area) spinal damage. Also called a c-collar.

closed fracture—One in which the skin is not broken.

contusion—Bruise.

COPD—Chronic obstructive pulmonary disease.

CPR (cardiopulmonary resuscitation)—The process of using external means to circulate the blood, fill the lungs with oxygen, or both.

crash kit—A container, often international orange, that contains emergency supplies for an EMT to use when assisting a patient. The crash kit, often called a trauma kit, crash bag, or jump bag, contains such supplies as dressings, bandages, scissors, lights, equipment to take vitals, and gloves. EMTs often carry such a kit in their cars. One crash kit carried in the ambulance is sometimes called a megaduffel; it contains oxygen supplies, such as an oxygen cylinder, bag valve mask, oral and nasal airways, and various types of masks, in addition to first-aid equipment.

defibrillator—A machine that can deliver an electrical shock to try to "jump start" a heart that is in v-fib. (See below.) The defibrillator used by Fairfax EMTs is semiautomatic. The machine assesses the rhythm and decides whether a shock is indicated. If so, it charges and requests that the EMT-D "press to shock." The manual defibrillator that the paramedics use merely shows rhythms on a screen and on a tape. From that information the medics decide which combination of shock, medications, and/or CPR is indicated.

diaphoretic—Sweaty.

EDP—Emotionally disturbed person.

EKG (electrocardiogram)—A tracing that indicates the electrical activity within the heart's muscle and nervous system.

EMT—Emergency medical technician.

EMT-D—An EMT with added training in defibrillation. (See above.) Most of the EMTs in FVAC are EMT-Ds.

ER—Emergency room.

ETA—Estimated time of arrival.

FGH—Fairfax General Hospital, the small community hospital that serves the fictional town of Fairfax. In addition to this hospital, down the parkway there is a county medical facility and trauma center.

FVAC—Abbreviation for the fictional Fairfax Volunteer Ambulance Corps. It is pronounced *eff vac.*

head blocks—Cubes of spongy material covered in heavy plastic that are placed on either side of a victim's head on a long backboard. Placed tightly against the ears and taped down, these blocks keep a patient from moving his or her head and prevent exacerbation of neck injury.

hemothorax—A condition in which blood enters the chest cavity from an internal injury. This prevents a lung from expanding to draw in air.

hypovolemic shock—A potentially life-threatening condition (see *shock* below) resulting from severe blood or plasma loss.

intubation—Inserting a tube into a patient's trachea to maintain an open airway.

IV (intravenous line)—A tube inserted into a vein that allows a paramedic, nurse, or doctor to add fluid or medication directly into a patient's bloodstream.

jaws of life—A gasoline- or electrically-powered hydraulic tool with several attachments that is used to pry metal from around an entrapped patient. The jaws, also known as the Hurst Tool, are usually used to disentangle a victim from a wrecked automobile.

KED (Kendrick Extrication Device)—A brand-name product. The KED is a plastic-covered, vertically slatted jacket used to immobilize the head, neck, and spine of a victim of an accident in order to minimize additional trauma while he is being moved.

Kling—A brand of roller gauze. Long strips of sterile gauze, prerolled and packaged, used to hold a dressing against a wound. Kling tends to adhere to itself, eliminating the necessity for ties or tape.

KVO—Keep vein open.

logroll—To turn the body as a unit to minimize the possibility of increasing any spinal injury. In order to transfer a patient lying on the ground to a backboard, we logroll the patient.

LZ (landing zone)—A helicopter needs a large open area, free of obstructions and overhead wires, in which to land to pick up a patient.

MAST (military antishock trousers)—Pants with inflatable bladders in each leg and the abdomen that can be pressurized like a blood pressure cuff. Inflation is believed to slow the deterioration of a patient in shock. PASG (pneumatic antishock garment) is another acronym for the same apparatus. There is currently a debate regarding the efficacy of this device.

MCI—Multiple casualty incident.

MVA—Motor vehicle accident.

normal sinus rhythm—The familiar lub-dub rhythm of the heart. This is the normal rhythm of a functioning heart. (See *v-fib* below.)

open fracture—One in which the skin is broken.

OR—Operating room.

oral airway—Technically called an oropharyngeal airway. This curved breathing tube is inserted into a patient's airway to hold the tongue away from the back of the throat and facilitate ventilations.

palp—Short for palpation. Obtaining a blood pressure by palp means that instead of using a stethoscope to listen to the patient's pulse at the inside of the elbow, the patient's radial pulse (see below) is felt while the BP cuff is deflated.

palpate—To touch a patient's body with light pressure.

paramedic—A member of the emergency medical

services who can provide types of patient care beyond an EMT's training. Paramedic care may include invasive procedures such as starting IVs, administering medications, and intubating.

PCR (prehospital care report)—The report that our state requires us to fill out for every call.

PDAA—Property damage auto accident.

pediatric—or pede-bag—A crash bag containing supplies and equipment in smaller sizes to treat children and infants. In addition, the bag usually contains toys and distractions for younger patients.

PFA—Psychological first aid.

PIAA—Personal injury auto accident.

pneumothorax—A condition in which air enters the chest cavity, preventing a lung from expanding during normal breathing.

point-tenderness—Pain felt when an area of injury is touched or pressed.

prone—Lying facedown.

pronounce—The process of declaring a patient dead. In most states EMTs may not pronounce, whereas paramedics may.

pulses—Places in the body where an artery runs between a bone and the surface. Pulses can be felt with the fingertips. The radial pulse is found in the wrist, the carotid pulse in the neck, the femoral in the groin, and the pedal in various locations in the feet.

Reeves—A stretcher consisting of a three-foot-wide assembly of six-foot-long plastic slats covered with plastic. A patient can be placed on the Reeves and the unit wrapped around his body. It keeps the spine supported while allowing the patient to be upended or carried at an angle through narrow hallways, over rough terrain, or down stairs. The Reeves has handles at each of the four corners and at the center of each long side, permitting a heavy patient to be lifted more easily.

RMA (refused medical attention)—A competent patient always has the right to refuse our attention. It is, of course, our job to try to convince an ill or injured person to let us help him, but sometimes all our persuasion fails.

shock—The inability of the circulatory system to provide sufficient oxygenated blood to the vital organs.

spider strap—An assembly of eight to ten connected straps used to rapidly secure a patient to a longboard for transport.

stairchair—A narrow chair with small wheels on the two rear legs and handles for easy carrying. A conscious patient can be seated in the stairchair, belted in, and carried down a flight of stairs or wheeled across a smooth floor.

stat—Immediately. From the Latin *statim.*

supine—Lying on one's back, faceup.

turnout gear—Coats, pants, hats, and boots made of heavy water- and fireproof material worn by firefighters. We in FVAC have bright yellow, heavy, lined, weatherproof rain and snow jackets that we wear in bad weather.

v-fib—Short for ventricular fibrillation. During ventricular fibrillation, the heart's electrical impulses are disorganized and do not cause the heart to beat well enough to circulate blood throughout the body. Unless v-fib is converted to a normal rhythm, possibly by using a defibrillator, the patient will die.

vitals—There are several measurable vitals, or vital signs, that indicate the stability of a sick or injured person. The vitals we measure are (1) blood pressure (see above); (2) pulse rate and quality; (3) breathing rate and quality; (4) the appearance, temperature, and moistness of the skin; and (5) the response of the pupils of the eyes to light.

water gel—Heavy gauze impregnated with a water-based bacteriacide. These sterile bandages are placed on a burned area to both cool and protect the injury.

Additional Information

Ten-codes

Ten-codes are short code phrases used during radio transmissions that relay various pieces of information. These ten-codes are supposedly easier to hear and understand over the radio than the actual words. They vary in meaning from department to department.

These are commonly used by both FVAC and Prescott Rescue:

10–1—Property damage auto accident.
10–2—Personal injury auto accident.
10–3—Illness.
10–4—I hear you and understand.

10–45—Obvious death. This is sometimes also abbreviated 10–100 or code 100.
10–99—or code 99—CPR in progress.

And these are used by the Fairfax Fire Department:
10–17—This unit is responding.
10–19—This unit is on location.

The Twenty-four-hour Clock

In order to prevent confusion when reporting times, we do not use the terms A.M. and P.M. on our reports. Instead, we use a twenty-four-hour clock. Midnight is 00:00 and the times from one minute past midnight to noon are as they are on the regular clock. 5:32 in the morning is 05:32.

From one minute past noon, 12:01, to one minute before midnight, the times are expressed as the clock time plus twelve. For example, 8:45 in the evening would be written as 20:45.

Authors' Note

We hope you enjoyed reading *Lights and Siren* as much as we enjoyed writing it. We also enjoy getting letters from people all over the country who share their stories, some of which have found their way into this book.

If you'd like to tell us your story, or just let us know how you enjoyed the book, please write to us at:

Ed Herman and Joan Lloyd
P.O. Box 255
Shrub Oak, NY 10588

DIAL 911

by Joan E. Lloyd & Edwin B. Herman

Imagine your worst fear. A loved one falls to the floor, unconscious. A car hurtles out of control at fifty miles per hour. An infant ingests poison. You dial 911, and the emergency medical technicians answer the call. Now, here are their stories, based on the authors' own experiences as members of a volunteer ambulance corps.

From the most traumatic cases to the most bizarre, every call is recounted in exact detail—and with absolute authenticity. DIAL 911 takes you inside the world of emergency medicine in a way you've never seen before.